LOW
RISK
INVESTING

How to get a good return on your money
without losing any sleep.

Gordon K. Williamson

BOB ADAMS, INC.
PUBLISHERS
Holbrook, Massachusetts

Published by Bob Adams, Inc.
260 Center Street, Holbrook, MA 02343

ISBN: 1-55850-151-7

Printed in the United States of America.

J I H G F E D C B A

This book is available at quantity discounts for bulk purchases. For information, call 1-800-872-5627.

While due care has been taken to ensure accurate and current data, the ideas, principles, conclusions, and general suggestions contained in this volume are subject to the laws and regulations of local, state, and federal authorities, as well as to court cases and any revisions of court cases. Due to the magnitude of the database and the complexity of the subject matter, occasional errors are possible; the publisher assumes no liability direct or incidental for any actions or investments made by readers of this book, and strongly suggests that readers seek consultation with legal, financial, or accounting professionals before making any investment.

This publication is designed to provide accurate and authoritative information with regard to the subject matter covered. It is sold with the understanding that the publisher is not engaged in rendering legal, accounting, or other professional advice. If legal advice or other expert assistance is required, the services of a competent professional person should be sought.
— From a *Declaration of Principles* jointly adopted by a Committee of the American Bar Association and a Committee of Publishers and Associations

Also of interest by Gordon Williamson:
  The 100 Best Mutual Funds, 1993
  All About Annuities
  The Dearborn Investment Companion
  Investment Strategies Under Clinton and Gore
  Sooner Than You Think
  Your Living Trust

Dedication

To my aunt, Kate Williamson Panzer,
and my uncle, Max L. Panzer,
my two favorite relatives.

Table of Contents

Introduction

What will your standard of living be two, five, ten, or twenty years from now? How large a financial cushion will you have to protect yourself against unforeseen expenses?

Whether you realize it or not, you make decisions about your financial future every day. If you are not setting aside any savings for long-term investments, you are making a decision about your future financial security. You are choosing not to have any.

If you decide to leave your hard-earned money in the bank, inflation will slash the real value of your savings—*even after interest.*

What about the "aggressive" investment opportunities, the kind you hear about during a rapid-fire telephone pitch from a salesperson who "all but guarantees" to double your money in nothing flat? If you're like most people, you will probably feel an initial rush of excitement when you hear about something like this—even though you may find the actual specifics of the investment hard to grasp. Well, you can rest assured that you're not alone in your bewilderment. And if you follow the salesperson's advice, odds are you won't be alone in your disappointment, either. Thousands upon thousands of investors have been left completely penniless by following hard-sell "advice" of this kind. Ask yourself: If brokers and bankers are so knowledgeable, why aren't more of them rich from following their own recommendations? And if the opportunities described are so remarkable, why is it so difficult to find anyone who has actually experienced such success?

You *can* achieve a good return on your money without losing sleep—but you must take the time to determine which investments are right for your circumstances. Many investors have a feeling of helplessness when they are presented with an opportunity by someone "in the business"—they feel that stockbrokers, bankers, and other professionals have the facts, and that everyone else doesn't. It doesn't have to be that way. When it comes to investing your hard-earned savings, *you* should be the one in control—and the way to stay in control is to understand the ins and outs of the options available to you.

You should understand, for instance, the importance of diversification. This is an important principle for all investors, especially those of modest means. Its central point is a simple one: Even if you are investing a relatively small amount of money, you should never invest all of your funds in a single instrument. Instead, you should work to build a balanced and well positioned portfolio. This book will offer you some invaluable ideas on how to do just that.

If you are used to thinking of the world of investing as complex, difficult to understand, and often boring, you are in for a pleasant surprise. This book will show that investments are not abstractions; they are interesting and worth learning more about *because they hold the key to your future and the future of your children*. My guess is that once you finish this book, you will feel quite at ease discussing investment opportunities, because you will have a clear idea of what they can and cannot do *for you*.

◆　◆　◆

The beauty of investments lies in their flexibility. In recent years, more and more Americans have had to adapt to rapid changes in the economy, severe budget cutbacks in both the private and public sectors, and prolonged uncertainty about individual careers and the stability of the job market. Well, take heart: Your employer, your industry, and your government may let you down, but there are always investments out there that fare well—even for those of us who aren't made of money.

You may be used to thinking that there are "good times" and "bad times" to invest your savings. In fact, there are wise investment choices to be made in virtually any economic climate. Consider, to use the most dramatic example possible, the period of the Great Depression in the late 1920s and early 1930s. In that span of time, U.S. government bonds appreciated almost 200 percent—not bad when you consider that Treasury bills were yielding less than 1 percent. During the inflationary years of the late 1970s and early 1980s, when long-term bonds were taking a beating, common stocks and mutual funds that invested in stocks soared in value. And while Wall Street was concentrating on stocks and bonds during the middle and late 1980s, real-estate prices in many parts of the country rose handsomely.

No matter how bad the economy looks, no matter what newspapers, magazines, and television commentators tell you, there are always sound investment opportunities to be found. When stocks and bonds seem to be going nowhere in this country, they are probably appreciating briskly in Hong Kong, Sweden, Japan, the U.K., France, or Taiwan. Since no one really knows what stocks, bonds, or real estate will do next week, much less next year or over the course of a decade, you will need to come up with a course of action that factors in these investment realities. In short, you will need a portfolio that acts rather than reacts, one that does not end up chasing last year's winners.

In this book, you will learn about many low-risk opportunities that will allow your savings to outpace inflation—and offer you secure growth over an extended period. I will explain each instrument carefully, so that even if you have never invested money before you will be able to understand all the important points of a given course of action. I will show you how much risk each investment carries, and, just as important, I will explain the nature of that risk.

Almost every instrument described in this book carries relatively little in the way of risk. For the sake of balance and to give you a full picture of the investment scene, however, I will briefly discuss investments that are, by nature, extremely risky—and worth avoiding at all costs. These unusually risky investments are covered in Part IV, "Investments You Should Avoid."

Right now, your money is *somewhere*: under the mattress, tied up in real estate, languishing in a low-interest savings account. The question is, is your money where you *want* it to be? In the early part of this book, we'll define and examine those investments that should be the foundation of any prudent portfolio—and learn how easy investing can be. Later, you'll see how those assets can work for you in attaining your goals.

Do not think for a minute that this book will show you how to get rich quick. It won't. It will, however, show you how to get rich slowly. Although that may not sound very exciting at first, I am quite confident that you will find the approach I outline to be the most helpful, objective, and valuable investment advice available today. Over time, as you use the ideas in this book to accumulate substantial wealth, you will appreciate the wisdom of a prudent approach to investing your savings—and you will also value the advantage of not having to worry constantly about whether or not your money is safe. In the final analysis, I think you'll agree that wealth and freedom from worry are exciting prospects indeed!

Gordon K. Williamson
La Jolla, California

Part I

◆ ◆ ◆

Overview

$28 a share) is not taxed until the security (or asset, such as real estate) is actually sold. Thus, the investor, you, has more control as to *when*, if ever, a tax event is triggered.

Out of fairness to debt instruments, it should be quickly pointed out that since most of the total return of such instruments is normally derived from current interest payments or yield, their total return is more predictable than equities (appreciation is always uncertain). The world of investments is a constant trade-off. No one investment offers the best predictable returns and greatest level of safety.

Current Holdings

Before making any new investments, it is important that you review your current holdings. This may stop you from "loading up" on any one investment. You may read some article or attend some seminar that tells you about how great real estate is—or stocks, or bonds, or gold, or rare coins—and that you should be buying more right now. The fact is, if real estate or stocks or whatever it is already makes up a large portion of your holdings, you would probably be making a big mistake buying more. No matter how good something looks, there is no guarantee that it will continue to appreciate.

Until the late 1980s, most people thought that real estate, particularly residential housing, would never decline. Until October 19th, 1987, a great number of investors thought the stock market would continue to climb several hundred more points before there would be any kind of correction. When silver steadily climbed to just over $50 an ounce over decade ago, a large number of financial gurus stated that it would soon be at $100 an ounce (it is at $4 an ounce as of this writing). Oil-price increases in the early 1980s made it almost a certainty, at least according to "industry experts," that a barrel of oil would soon jump from $35 to $50 (by 1988 the price of oil was in the $10-a-barrel range—today the going price is about $19 a barrel). The list of predictions goes on and on.

The point is that no matter how certain you, or anyone else, is that a commodity, security, or piece of property is going to continue to rise (or fall) in price, there is a good chance that you, the experts, or the consensus will be wrong. And one thing you do not want to be wrong about is how an investment will perform if it composes a large part of your portfolio. The more prudent course of action is to construct a portfolio that includes several different asset categories (for example, real estate, U.S. securities, foreign securities, etc.). A diversified portfolio will protect us against our own biases and any biases from the sources we rely on for information, like that stockbroker who just loves IBM, that newsletter writer who guarantees that he or she knows when to get in and out of the market, or that person on television who shows you how easy it is to make a million bucks buying and selling distressed properties.

If someone had the formula to determine which is the best investment at any given time, or if there were one or two perfect investments, that secret would not be revealed in some article, book, or course. If there were such a thing as the perfect asset or financial Nostradamus, there would be no need for banks, brokerage firms, financial planners, investment books, or financial periodicals. In fact, there would be no need for you ever to read another sentence about investing. We could simply throw everything away and tune into that magical source. As ridiculous as this sounds, there are tens of thousands of people who believe in this fantasy. The words and script may not be as transparent, but the message and the hype are.

We live in a time when a great number of people think that they can get rich quick. Yet, if you look at the real wealth in this or any other country, it did not occur overnight. This "lotto fever" is perhaps the worst financial disease that can affect people. Indeed, I have often said that the lottery is the worst thing ever to happen to poor people. Think about it. The chances of your winning the lottery are about the same as your chances of being chosen as a crew member of an Apollo mission. If a poor person spends, say, $20 a month on lottery tickets, over a year this could easily translate to the equivalent of one or two months' worth of groceries. Of course, for an upper-middle-class lottery player, $20 a month means very little.

You may not think that $20 a month ($240 a year) can make much difference in someone's life, but think again. Later in this book you will read about several safe investments that have consistently averaged 10 to 14 percent over the past years. Assuming a 12-percent rate of growth, $240 invested each year grows to $4,212 after ten years, $17,292 after twenty years, and $57,919 in thirty years. Granted, these are not *huge* amounts, but then again, we are only talking about $20 a month being invested.

Another important point about your current holdings is that you need to be conscious of any constraints. Specifically, the tax consequences of selling an existing holding in order to buy something else must be reviewed. That $40,000 worth of Ford Motor Company stock may shrink to $30,000 once capital gains taxes are paid on the profit. On the other hand, an asset that has lost value may end up giving you some tax relief (not that losses are ever something to be happy about). We all know that Uncle Sam wants to share in our profits when an investment or asset is sold, but few taxpayers know that the government will also share in any *losses* you sustain. The strategy of capital gains and losses are fully discussed in later chapters, using specific examples.

Biases or Restrictions

Finally, a portfolio needs to take into account any biases you might have. Each of us has had different life experiences. We all bring to the table different perspectives and beliefs. Sometimes these beliefs are inherited (perhaps your mother or father told you to invest only in government bonds), sometimes they are determined by a favored or respected commentator. Whatever the case may be, these restrictions or parameters need to be kept in check. If you inherited a thousand shares of a utility company stock and were told never to sell it, other investment decisions need to "work around" or be based on this core holding. This means that other utility-type investments should perhaps be avoided or minimized. Similarly, although common stocks are an excellent addition to most portfolios, you may, for one reason or another, refuse to own such securities. Other parts of your portfolio will then need to compensate for this "shortcoming," perhaps by the addition of convertible securities, preferred stocks, or a real estate investment trust, all of which are described in detail in later chapters.

Look at the table below. Notice that none of these four categories does well each and every year. Notice too that it would be impossible to predict a trend or pattern.

Annual Total Returns, 1970-1991

YEAR	U.S. STOCKS	U.S. BONDS	FOREIGN STOCKS	FOREIGN BONDS
1970	+4%	+18%	-10%	+9%
1971	+14%	+11%	+31%	+23%
1972	+19%	+7%	+37%	+5%
1973	-15%	+2%	-14%	+6%
1974	-26%	-6%	-22%	+5%
1975	+37%	+17%	+37%	+9%
1976	+24%	+19%	+4%	+11%
1977	-7%	+3%	+19%	+39%
1978	+6%	+0%	+34%	+18%
1979	+19%	-2%	+6%	-5%
1980	+32%	+0%	+24%	+14%
1981	-5%	+3%	-1%	-5%
1982	+22%	+39%	-1%	+12%
1983	+23%	+9%	+25%	+4%
1984	+6%	+17%	+8%	-2%
1985	+32%	+24%	+57%	+37%
1986	+19%	+16%	+70%	+34%
1987	+5%	+0%	+25%	+36%
1988	+17%	+8%	+27%	+3%
1989	+32%	+7%	+11%	+10%
1990	-1%	+6%	-23%	+15%
1991	+31%	+16%	+13%	+3%
number of times "best"	6	4	7	5

If you could be certain about the future rates of return on each asset class, the process of picking the perfect category would be easy: You would invest all of your capital in the asset with the highest forecasted return. However, since future returns are uncertain and since some asset classes are more uncertain than others, it is necessary to diversify.

Our goal is to hit doubles and triples. We realize that we will never hit a home run with our investments (since not all of our money will be in just one or two assets), but we will sleep better at night knowing that there will also not be any strikeouts. Such a strategy translates into returns that are better than what 98 percent of all other investors are doing. The 1 or 2 percent who will end up doing better than you will have taken substantially greater risk.

THE ORANGE JUICE ANALOGY

One of the best ways to look at any investment is through what is known as the "orange juice analogy." Imagine that you have a pitcher of orange juice and that pitcher holds exactly eight ounces. Next to that pitcher you have four glasses, and each glass holds up to four ounces. Each glass has a different label. Glass number one is called "safety," glass number two is labeled "current income," number three is titled "appreciation potential," and the last glass is described as "tax benefits." You can pour the eight ounces into as many of the four glasses you want and reap benefits from as many as you want, but keep in mind, the more ounces in each glass, the greater the benefit—and the fewer ounces you will have elsewhere. Zero ounces of liquid in a glass equals (or translates into) "poor," one ounce can be described as "fair," two ounces means "good," three ounces are "very good," and four ounces translates into "excellent." Now, before you start pouring out your eight ounces of benefits, there is one last rule you should be aware of: Every investment you can think of has eight ounces of benefits. No matter how wild or boring you think something is, it still has exactly eight ounces, no more and no less. Let us go through a couple of examples to see how this o.j. analogy works.

Let us assume that some broker or financial guru is trying to convince you to buy some investment and he tells you how great it is (it's odd that they never seem to get around to telling you how bad it could turn out to be) by proceeding to rattle off all of its benefits. Before you start to write that check, pause for a moment and remember your orange juice lesson: No investment is great in all categories. If something has excellent current income (four ounces) and excellent tax benefits (another four ounces from the pitcher), it must be "poor" in the areas of safety and appreciation potential (the remaining two glasses which must stay empty if you are looking for excellence in two other categories). This does not mean that it now becomes a terrible investment; just be aware of the tradeoffs involved. If you need something that is "good" in all four categories (safety, current income, appreciation potential, and tax benefits), that's fine too; just don't expect it also to be "very good" or "excellent" in any ("good" equals two ounces and two times four equals eight ounces and eight ounces represents all the benefits one investment can possess). Let us look at two specific investments in order to explore the limitations of benefits further.

Assume for the moment that you are trying to choose between U.S. government bonds and common stocks and you want to know what you can expect. Both categories are discussed in detail later in this book, but let us view them now in light of the o.j. analogy. As you will learn, government bonds have very good safety (three ounces), very good current income (three ounces), fair appreciation potential (one ounce) and fair tax benefits (one ounce). Common stocks, on the other hand, have fair safety (one ounce), fair current income (one ounce), excellent appreciation potential (four ounces) and good tax benefits (two ounces). As you can see, both common stocks and government bonds offer investors eight ounces of benefits; they are simply apportioned differently. Each investment appeals to a different kind of investor or pool of money.

What makes the orange juice analogy so helpful is that it is easy to remember and therefore something you can think about whenever you read or hear about an investment. Most importantly, it is a way for you to check on the validity or hype that surrounds a given investment. By remembering this simple eight-ounce story, you will not easily fall victim to some investment that alleges to be all things to all people.

After you have finished reading this book, your thinking about investing will change. Perhaps for the first time you will clearly understand how these things called "investments" work—their strengths and weaknesses. Please don't think you need any financial experience or an MBA to understand the chapters that follow—you do not. This book was written for people who want to learn, people who are tired of hearing about investments from financial writers, brokers, and seminar presenters who have hidden agendas or who simply do not present all of the facts.

2
A Call to Action

People think their money is safe. It is not. Your money is doing something right now. It is somewhere. Those who feel it is safe probably have their money invested in bank CDs, in a passbook savings account, or in T-Bills (U.S. Treasuries). What people fail to take into account is the double "taxation" this money is being subjected to: inflation and income taxes. Look at the table below. Want to know how the most popular "safe" investment, U.S. Treasury Bills, has really fared over the past twenty years? The far-right column, "Real Rate of T-Bill Return," shows how U.S. Treasury Bills have performed on an after-tax, after-inflation basis.

YEAR	T-BILL RATE	FEDERAL TAX RATE	AFTER-TAX RETURN	INFLATION RATE	REAL RATE OF T-BILL RETURN
1970	6.48%	50%	3.24%	5.6%	-2.36%
1971	4.51%	50%	2.26%	3.3%	-1.05%
1972	4.48%	50%	2.24%	3.4%	-1.16%
1973	7.20%	50%	3.60%	8.7%	-5.10%
1974	7.94%	62%	3.02%	12.3%	-9.28%
1975	6.09%	62%	2.31%	6.9%	-4.59%
1976	5.25%	62%	2.00%	4.9%	-2.91%
1977	5.53%	60%	2.21%	6.7%	-4.49%
1978	7.58%	60%	3.03%	9.0%	-5.97%
1979	10.06%	59%	4.12%	13.3%	-9.18%
1980	11.37%	59%	4.66%	12.5%	-7.84%
1981	13.80%	59%	5.66%	8.9%	-3.24%
1982	11.07%	50%	5.54%	3.8%	1.74%
1983	8.73%	48%	4.54%	3.8%	0.74%
1984	9.76%	45%	5.37%	3.9%	1.47%
1985	7.65%	45%	4.21%	3.8%	0.41%
1986	6.03%	45%	3.32%	1.1%	2.22%
1987	6.03%	38%	3.74%	4.4%	-0.66%
1988	6.91%	33%	4.63%	4.4%	0.23%
1989	8.03%	33%	5.38%	4.6%	0.78%
1990	7.46%	31%	5.15%	6.1%	-0.95%
1991	5.44%	31%	3.75%	3.1%	0.65%

How would you feel about someone who recommended an investment to you that had lost money, once adjusted for inflation and taxes, two-thirds of the time (fourteen of the last twenty-two years)? The graph below is a visual depiction of the same information.

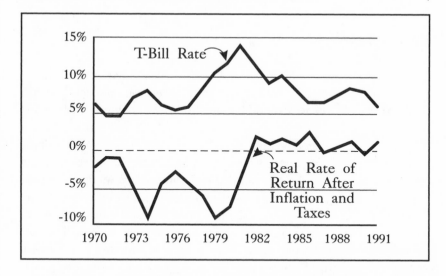

What do all of these depressing figures mean? Simple: You must begin to think differently about investing. The fact is, no investment is safe from all of the financial perils that exist. Every investment is subject to one or more kinds of risk; there is no way around this "law of nature." Investments that offer a fixed rate of return (such as bank CDs and government securities) would be fine if we lived in a country that had fixed costs, but no such country exists on earth. Fixed-rate investments may make sense in another galaxy, but they should not represent the bulk of your portfolio. Now here I somewhat contradict myself. On the one hand I have bad-mouthed this entire category of investments, a category that represents well over half of today's investments. On the other hand I have said that they should not represent the *majority* of your holdings, strongly implying that they should play a *role*.

As you read through section two of this book, which covers debt instruments, you will see that, for the most part, these investments are a poor hedge against inflation. They are still recommended for the following reasons: (1) equity instruments, such as stocks and leveraged real estate, can be very scary at times, and there must be alternatives or stabilizing parts of a portfolio; (2) *certain* kinds of debt instruments, as you will learn, have fared quite well against inflation; (3) it is tough to match the current income and overall stability that many kinds of debt instruments offer; and (4) there are periods of time, such as 1981 to 1993, when bonds fared quite well (when interest rates declined by over two-thirds). Moreover, since these instruments are clearly the most popular way to invest, they should be examined if for no other reason than to shed some real light as to their advantages and disadvantages.

FISH OR CUT BAIT

You can attend countless financial seminars, read endless magazine articles, buy dozens of investment books, and talk to several investment advisors, friends, and relatives, but there comes a time when you must act. Unfortunately, there is never an ideal time to invest. When stock prices are falling and we keep waiting for them to bottom out ("I'll go into the market when it drops another hundred points . . . ."), or when interest rates keep climbing and we plan on buying bonds when the prime rate hits X percent, or when real estate prices stop climbing (or dropping) and we are waiting for prices to level off, or whatever that certain event might be, such events never quite happen the way we were counting on—meaning that the market starts to climb sooner than expected, interest rates suddenly start to drop, or real estate prices continue ratcheting upward. By then, the tune becomes ever-so-familiar: "Gee, I wish I had bought _____ when it was at _____ [you fill in the blanks]."

The time for you to invest is now. If you don't like stocks, invest in bonds, real estate, or foreign securities. Better yet, include stocks by investing in them a little at a time, say $100 to $1,000 a month. Even if you don't like stocks and are certain that the market will crash as soon as you get into it, I am sure you will agree that stock prices go up and down. By investing a set amount each month, you can make this volatility work on your behalf. If you don't like bonds because you are certain that interest rates are headed upward (when interest rates go up, bond values drop . . . at least temporarily), then invest in a money market fund—something that benefits from rising rates. Similarly, if you think real estate prices are too depressed (or too high), start putting money into a real estate investment trust (described in a later chapter).

Believe me, I and lots of other people can give you plenty of reasons not to invest during any given year. Such reasons usually turn out to be erroneous, but if you want some justification as to why sitting on the sidelines is "smart," there will always be lots of reasons. Look at the Gulf War. Just before and during Operation Desert Storm, almost every major brokerage firm told its clients to get out of stocks. Yet during this three-week period, stocks posted a gain of over 15 percent. Just think what that would equal if you could annualize such a short-term upswing—something like a 260+ percent rate of return. There was an even more compelling reason not to invest in the stock market in 1991: the recession. Funny, but the stock market didn't seem to mind the recession that year (stocks have gone up during seven of the last eight recessions). It posted one of its biggest gains, up over 30 percent in one year. Look back to early 1981. There were plenty of reasons not to invest in bonds. The prime interest rate had passed 20 percent and was expected to hit 25 to 30 percent within a year (it peaked at 21.5 percent briefly). Within a few months of such "certainties," the bond market reversed itself, and these debt instruments went on to post their best decade ever. Finally, look at real estate. Until the mid-1960s, residential real estate was considered a poor investment. People bought a house for psychological reasons: pride of ownership, a place to call home, protection against greedy landlords. We all know what happened to home prices in many parts of the country for the next twenty years. Prices seemed to go up almost every year.

ON SALE

Is there a sad ending to all of these wonderful stories? Look at real estate prices now. Bonds aren't doing well either, and the stock market is pretty rocky. But I think it's a fallacy to look on this as a sad *ending*. I would say instead that there are certainly times when there is a sad *pause*. The trick is to view such pauses, corrections, crashes, catastrophes, or whatever you want to call them, as opportunities.

You don't have to look far to see what I mean. Do you like to buy things on sale? Sure you do, everyone likes to save money. The only thing better than buying your favorite pair of shoes at a 10-percent discount is to buy them when they are 25 percent off. People like to buy things on sale—they always have. For the life of me I can't understand why this doesn't hold true for stocks, bonds, or real estate. When the market, a stock you have been watching, or a favorite mutual fund drops by 20 to 30 percent overnight or over an extended period of time, think of it as being on sale. If you sort of liked it at $100 a unit (or share), you should *love* it at $70, assuming you are looking at something that is fundamentally strong. And when it comes to buying well-situated real estate, stocks, or bonds, you are dealing with something fundamentally strong.

It is human nature to succeed. Most people would like to make more money. Corporations that issue stocks and bonds are just groups of people. When you buy a stock or bond, you are either loaning or owning part of corporate America (or Britain or Spain or wherever). Do you think these people want to fail? Of course not. They want their company to make more money for one or more of the following reasons: to preserve their job, to get a pay raise, because they own part of the company's stock as part of their retirement plan, or they take pride in what they do.

In the case of real estate, virtually every book on the subject points out that the three most important considerations when buying a property are location, location, and location. Whether your ancestors lived in ancient Greece or currently live in Southern California, where a house or business is located has always been first in importance. To say that a choice piece of real estate is now a bad idea because prices are depressed is simply being short-sighted.

All this has been true for hundreds of years. Human nature does not really change. You would be foolish to bet against such realities. This is why I said earlier that now is the time to invest. Buy when there are opportunities, when your favorite items (financial assets) are on sale. As Sir John Templeton, the grandfather of international investing, the founder of the Templeton Mutual Funds, and the person heralded as having the best long-term track record when it comes to investing, once said, "The best place to invest is where pessimism is the highest" such as Hong Kong right after Tiennamen Square, or the U.S. during 1991.

A CHRISTMAS STORY

Did you ever hear the story about the two twin boys and what happened on Christmas morning? Well, the first boy was led to a room, the door was opened and inside the room were hundreds of toys. The child's parents told him that all of the toys were for him. Upon hearing this, the little boy began to cry. "Why are you crying?" the boy's mother asked. He replied, "With all of these toys, one or two of them must be broken." The other twin (who did not witness or hear any of this) was then taken to another room. The door was opened; the room was filled with horse manure. Upon seeing this, the second twin's eyes lit up and he jumped into the middle of the manure and began to dig. His father asked, "What are you doing?" The boy replied, "With all of this manure, there must be a pony in here somewhere!"

Perhaps a simpler analogy would have been the one about whether you see the cup as half full or half empty. But I trust the story of the two twin boys, which is more visual, will be more lasting in your memory. You must never lose sight of the fact that there will always be tremendous investment opportunities either here or elsewhere in the world.

THE POPULAR PRESS

When was the last time that you read a headline story or heard a television news story that began with "1,450 airplanes landed safely today" or "8,320 major corporations have survived so far this year"? The major concern of the news media is to sell copy or gain market share. Newspapers, magazines, radio shows, and television broadcasts all know that nothing sells better than bad news. Let us go through just a couple of the hundred examples that could be cited. Remember the stock market crash of 1987, when stocks dropped almost 21 percent in just one day? Virtually every newspaper and news program talked about the losses in the market and how terrible everything was and how much worse it was probably going to get. ABC News "Nightline With Ted Koppel" even hired two of the Muppets to explain to America how stocks worked and what caused the crash. Yet none of these magazines, newspapers, and radio or television shows (or Muppets) did a follow-up piece showing how stocks ended up for the entire year: up an average of 5.2 percent for the 1987 calendar year. Nor was there a follow-up a few years later, when the decade ended and the final figures were in for the 1980s. While much of the popular press continued to recommend ultra-safe investments only, stocks still outperformed long-term U.S. government bonds in 1987 (which were down 2.1 percent for the year) and over the entire decade in spite of the 1987 crash. Even as bonds experienced their best decade ever, stocks ignored conventional wisdom by posting their third best-performing decade ever.

The same thing is true with financial books. The best-selling investment books have generally been those that deal with some kind of doom and gloom: *The Coming Depression, The Crash of 1990, How To Prosper During The Coming Bad Years*, etc. Readers somehow think that these authors know something that the Federal Reserve, Congress, the New York Stock Exchange, and other exchanges around the world do not. Apparently none of these institutions was ever informed that there was an impending disaster, because in every case these "doomed" investments just kept appreciating.

If you have ever wondered why financial statistics such as the average national savings rate are so low, a legitimate source of blame is the popular press, which continues to reinforce the majority's concerns about risk and investing. It would be a nice and helpful change for some of these opinion-makers to write a story occasionally that begins, "Look, the economy (or national debt or interest rates) looks bad right now, but let's view this in perspective . . . ." Such stories are not likely to appear soon because good or boring news does not sell. The trick is to find out how to sell copy or attract more viewers by talking about something other than death, sex, or financial disaster.

One of the most respected newspapers in the world is *The Wall Street Journal.* More than one newscaster and journalist has called it the best paper in the country. It is an excellent publication, but even the best can make financial events seem confusing or contradictory. I often read three or four stories in the *Journal* that talk about the coming drop in stocks (or bonds). A day or two later I will see the same number of stories talk about how stocks (or bonds) are expected to perform positively because of events or announcements from the previous day. Does this mean that you or I should get out of the market one day and get back in the next? Of course not.

What all of this means is that you must learn to filter out what I call the "daily noise." These are the sounds and stories that tell us things are terrible.

Did WalMart, Apple Computer, or other corporations suddenly become poorly run because the price of their (and thousands of other) stocks dropped by 15 to 30 percent in less than three weeks? No. Did your house become a bad investment because real estate prices either leveled off or declined during the late 1980s and early 1990s? No. This, by the way, happens to real estate prices almost like clockwork every decade . . . and then prices start to go up again for several years in a row. Never lose sight of the big picture. Chances are that you did not buy a home (or stock or mutual fund or bond) with the idea of selling it in a couple of years. These assets were bought as long-term investments. It is time that you start viewing them as such, and it is also time that you learn how to pay much less attention to the "daily noise."

3
How to Use This Book

So far, you have learned that all investments can be categorized as either debt or equity, that over extended periods of time, equities almost always outperform debt instruments, that equities such as common stocks can be quite volatile, that newspaper stories and television broadcasts are almost always negative, that successful investing involves action by you, and that a proper portfolio takes into account five different factors (time horizon, risk factor, income taxes, current holdings, and biases or restrictions). The final step is to determine which investments should be part of your holdings and which ones should be avoided or minimized.

The next two sections of this book cover equity and debt instruments of all kinds. After reading these two sections, you will be ready to follow the steps described in section five, "Specific Considerations." This fifth section guides you through the maze, showing you how mistakes can be avoided when making an investment, setting up an account, and determining when something should be sold.

The twenty-six chapters that make up the next two sections detail investments that are low-risk either on their own or when coupled with one or more other investments. Each of these chapters begins with a scorecard, evaluating the investment (chapter heading) in five important areas:

Stability of principal	✔
Stability of income	✔✔
Protection against inflation	✔✔✔
Total return	✔✔✔✔
Tax benefits	✔✔✔✔✔

The possible number of checkmarks for each of these five categories ranges from zero to five; the higher the number, the better. These marks also show how the asset compares to other investments, not just those listed in the book. The number of marks can be translated as follows: ✔✔✔✔✔ means "excellent," ✔✔✔✔ means "very good," ✔✔✔ means "good," ✔✔ means "average," ✔ means "fair," and no checkmarks indicates that the investment is considered "poor" in that specific area. To make sure you understand what "stability of principal" and the other terms mean, read the descriptions that follow.

Stability of Principal
This refers to the chances of your losing some or all of your principal. Depending upon the investment being made, there is a chance that some or all of your money can be lost. Losses are a result of financial risk, market risk, and/or interest rate risk.

Financial risk has to do with a loss resulting from a company's going under. A bond may be offering an attractive yield, but if the issuer (parent company) files for bankruptcy, it may no longer be able to pay its bills or interest on your bonds. Financial risk is the most severe of all risks that you can encounter; if this risk is realized, the resulting loss may never be recoverable.

Market risk is the chance of losing money due to buying or selling pressure in the marketplace. This kind of risk is most closely associated with stocks, real estate and tangibles (gold, silver, rare coins, etc.). In short, it reflects the moves up and down in equities.

Interest-rate risk has to do with how an investment is affected by changes in interest rates and availability of credit. When the Federal Reserve (the Fed) is trying to curb inflation, it will often raise interest rates in order to deter people from borrowing money and buying more goods and services. Higher interest rates have the effect of making conservative investments look more appealing (by offering higher rates or return) and making money more difficult (or painful) to borrow. During recessionary periods, on the other hand, when the Fed is trying to stimulate peoples' buying patterns, rates are lowered, making money cheaper to obtain.

Since this book concentrates almost exclusively on low-risk investments, the marks given for stability of principal will generally be high for debt instruments, moderate for hybrid securities (balanced funds, convertible securities, etc.), and mixed-to-poor for equities. This does not mean that equities or hybrids should be avoided. It does mean that these particular investments should represent only a part of your portfolio. More conservatively rated assets can help counter the risk other investments may carry.

A rating of *"excellent"* (✔✔✔✔✔) means that your principal is guaranteed or backed by companies or governments that have the very highest credit rating. It also means that your principal will fluctuate very little, if any, as a result of adverse market or interest-rate conditions. *"Very good"* (✔✔✔✔) means that this investment is safer than about 80 percent of all of the other investments you could have chosen. Chances of a moderate or severe loss are virtually non-existent. *"Good"* (✔ ✔ ✔) means that the asset is better than normal, and although the value of the investment will go up and down, such volatility should be modest and of no great duration. *"Average"* (✔ ✔) indicates that the investment being described has normal risk and can, and will, fluctuate in value over the next several years. Sometimes the volatility will mean that your principal has increased; other times it will mean there is a paper loss, at least temporarily. *"Fair"* (✔) means that when your investment goes up and down in value, that premium or discount may last for several years. Therefore, such an investment should only be made by someone with patience. *"Poor"* (no checkmarks) means that if safety is important to you, you had better stay away from this particular investment.

Stability of Income

When you make an investment, you are looking at it as a source of income— either now or at sometime in the future. The predictability or stability of such income is an important concern, particularly for an individual or couple who relies on such monies each month. Not every investment pays income on a monthly, quarterly, semi-annual, or annual basis. This does not mean that the asset is bad and should not be considered by the income-oriented investor. It may mean that the investment is more growth-oriented and should be used as a hedge against inflation, to be tapped later when more money is needed. Or, it may be that the investment can be structured to pay income on a monthly basis through what is known as a systematic withdrawal plan (SWP). Information about how an SWP plan works, along with specific, real-life examples, can be obtained by contacting your favorite mutual fund group. An SWP can end up providing you with much more income than you might expect.

"Excellent" (✔ ✔ ✔ ✔) means that the income paid does not fluctuate. If you start off getting X dollars of interest per $1,000 invested, you will continue to get this exact amount every period (monthly, quarterly, semi-annually, or annually). The level of income will not change no matter what happens to the stock, bond, or real estate markets; nor will it change if the economy happens to be experiencing a severe recession or higher-than-expected inflation.

A rating of *"very good"* (✔ ✔ ✔ ✔) indicates that the amount of money you receive will fluctuate, but not by very much. The fluctuation will be due to the general level of interest rates. If interest rates move upward while you own this kind of investment, your level of income will also rise. Conversely, if rates fall during this period, the amount of money you will receive will also decline somewhat.

In the case of a few investments given four checkmarks for stability of income, the amount of money received may decline as a result of the return or repayment of your principal. Your yield is not fluctuating, only the principal. If part of your principal is being returned to you, you have less remaining money earning the same rate of return. When this happens, chances are that you will not be able to reinvest this return of principal and enjoy the same yield. A lower rate of return will have to be accepted, or a riskier investment substituted, to keep up the level of income that was once enjoyed. Such a return of principal may represent only a small or modest portion of your investment.

"*Good*" (✔ ✔ ✔) means that the level of income, or yield, is still quite attractive, particularly compared to other investments. However, you should expect to experience changes, for better or worse, in the amount of money paid out each period. At times your yield will be higher than what you were originally getting; at other times payments will be lower.

A rating of "*average*" (✔ ✔) for an asset shows that there are better and worse choices if your criteria is strictly current income. In short, when it comes to current income, this one ranks right in the middle. Do not immediately discount or ignore such an investment if its rating is not what you think you are looking for; by setting up a systematic withdrawal plan (SWP), income can be increased and stabilized—but the value of the underlying principal will vary.

"*Fair*" (✔) means that this investment's yield is expected to be very marginal. A single mark in this category means that some money is being generated, but only in the 1-to-2-percent annual range. A rating of "fair" here may also mean that you should investigate whether the investment can be set up for a SWP.

A "*poor*" rating (no checkmarks) clearly signals that this investment does not throw off any current income. The asset should still be considered, however, if the overall portfolio needs to be rounded out or is in need of something that should prove a good hedge against inflation later. A higher-than-normal (or sometimes safe) income-oriented investment has different kinds of risk to be aware of. Such risk can be radically reduced by diversification—and by refraining from trying to seize the very last one or two percentage points of gain or yield.

Protection Against Inflation

The focus of this book is low-risk investing. You should know that a great number of safe investments are poor or modest hedges against inflation. A 6-percent return may sound pretty good, but if you take off 2 percent for taxes (assuming a 33-percent state and federal tax bracket combined) and then subtract another 5 percent for inflation for the year, you have a real return of -1 percent.

6 percent yield
- 2 percent for income taxes
- 5 percent annual rate of inflation

_____

- 1 percent real rate of return

Since readers are in different tax brackets, the *real rate of return*, for purposes of this book, takes into account only the effects of inflation, not income taxes.

The overwhelming majority of money invested in the world is invested in things that are not good hedges against inflation. This is not necessarily bad; it just means that in return for just keeping pace with inflation, or perhaps trailing it, the investor's liquidity and safety factors increase. It probably also means that parts of the portfolio will need to be in equity instruments in order to counter the effects of inflation year in and year out.

The range ratings for this category are straightforward: The greater the number of checkmarks, the better hedge against inflation the asset is expected to provide. The more checkmarks here, the greater the likelihood that the level of current income is quite low or non-existent. As a low-risk investor, a rating of excellent, very good, or good in this category should be sufficient for at least half of your holdings. Do not expect, or want, every investment you own to get five (excellent) or four (very good) checkmarks when it comes to protection against inflation.

Total Return

This shows you what kind of return you can expect on your investment. It also factors in fluctuations of principal. For example, if a junk bond pays you 12 percent a year, but the bond (the principal) drops in value 13 percent during the same year, your total return is -1 percent. The formula for total return is: current yield plus appreciation or minus a loss of principal.

For this particular characteristic, total return, a rating of "average" (two checkmarks) is not bad. An average return means that you will be getting what most other people get on their investments, perhaps a little better. The actual investment being described may be better than what you are currently invested in, since the safety, liquidity, and/or tax consequences may be more advantageous.

Tax Benefits

This is a difficult category to rank. After all, the great majority of investments have no tax benefits; their current yield or income stream is fully taxable and cannot be controlled. If a sale occurs that results in a profit, the gain is taxed in the same year. It is for this reason that most of the investments in this book have a rating of fair or poor (only one or zero checkmarks) when it comes to tax benefits.

A handful of investments throw off income that is either tax-free, sheltered, or tax-deferred. Such assets get a rating of "excellent" (five checkmarks). A small number of the investments featured are partially or fully exempt from state or federal income taxes. In these cases a rating of "very good" or "good" is given. Unlike those investments that get five checkmarks, the *capital gains* (appreciation) is not sheltered. The same rating may apply to an investment whose gain (a sale that results in a profit greater than the purchase price) can be postponed to a later year.

To see how all of these ratings work, let us first go through a specific example that is common to us all, passbook savings accounts.

Passbook Savings Accounts

Stability of principal	✔✔✔✔✔
Stability of income	✔✔✔✔✔
Protection against inflation	✔
Total return	✔
Tax benefits	

When you deposit money with a savings bank, credit union, or savings and loan association, they take your money and, in turn, invest it in instruments such as other banks' CDs, short-term bonds, government obligations, and high-quality trust deeds. Your money is also lent out to people who need to borrow money. Thus, if a bank is paying you, say, 5 percent, it may loan out your money at 9 to 16 percent or higher. The difference between what you are paid and what the lender receives covers expenses, employee salaries and benefits, overhead, and profit. The depositor gets a set rate of return whether the borrower defaults or faithfully pays back the loan.

There are three advantages to passbook savings accounts. First, your money is insured against loss, up to a certain dollar limit, usually $100,000. Second, money can be taken out of these accounts at any time without cost, fee, or penalty; you also incur no expense when you make a deposit. This is why this investment is given five checkmarks for stability of principal. Third, savings accounts pay interest. Your investment grows by the automatic reinvestment of interest. When you receive interest on your principal and previously accumulated interest, this is known as compound interest. Thus $10,000 grows to $10,400 by the end of the first year, the entire $10,400 earns interest the second year, etc. Passbook savings accounts pay a set rate of return, and until fairly recently, this rate had not changed for many years. Because of the overall predictability of interest paid on these accounts, a rating of "excellent" is given for the second category on the scorecard, stability of income.

One of the disadvantages to passbook savings accounts is that they have never fared well against inflation over any extended period of time. Some of these periods are worse than others. There are investments out there that have actually lost money, making them an even poorer choice or hedge to combat inflation. Since there are some worse alternatives and because there are one-, two-, or three-year periods in the past when passbook savings rates have been greater than inflation, one checkmark is given for the third category, protection against inflation.

There is no appreciation potential with a savings account. The only way your deposit or principal can grow is if you reinvest the interest. The rate of return offered is usually not competitive to other investment vehicles offered by the same bank, savings and loan, or credit union. A single checkmark (fair) is given for total return. This figure is derived solely from that of current yield, a rate of return that has previously been described as "fair."

Finally, there are no tax breaks or benefits when you invest in a passbook savings account. What you see is what you get; and what you get is fully taxable at the end of each year. With some investments, such as U.S. Treasury Bills, there is a way to defer the taxable interest to the following year—by buying a T-Bill that matures next year. Since nothing positive can be said about savings accounts when it comes to income taxes, zero checkmarks are given for this final category.

You are now prepared to move on to Part II, Debt Instruments. At this point you may want to glance at the table of contents to see the different investments covered. The chapters that follow are basically in order of popularity and name recognition. However, I have made a few exceptions to group related investment vehicles together (for example, the chapter on Series HH Bonds follows the chapter on EE Bonds). The most recognizable investments are at the beginning of this section, while later chapters include assets you may have heard of but never before considered.

Try to reserve judgment on the twenty-six investments covered until the end of the book. Remember, no investment or asset will fulfill *all* of your needs. Similarly, none of the investments that follow are bad. Although the comments on certain assets may be more or less favorable than others, each does have its place, for certain investors, for a limited or extended period of time.

The final section of the book sorts out all that you have read, providing some very specific ideas and reasons as to what should go into a portfolio, depending upon your risk level, time horizon, and goals. A good number of sample, or model, portfolios will be shown and analyzed. You will find one that fits your needs. For now, let us concentrate on the different kinds of debt instruments. The chapters that follow should prove a valuable reference source in the years to come.

Part II

◆ ◆ ◆

Debt Instruments

4
Certificates of Deposit

Stability of principal	✓✓✓✓✓
Stability of income	✓✓✓✓✓
Protection against inflation	
Total return	✓
Tax benefits	

Definition

Certificates of deposit, more commonly known as "CDs," represent a kind of deposit with a bank or savings and loan association. The depositor (investor) agrees to deposit his or her money with a financial institution in exchange for a set rate of return. The return, or "yield," depends upon the amount of money being deposited, the term of the deposit, the general level of interest rates, and the competitiveness of the institution. At the end of the term, the lender (you) is free either to liquidate the entire account, principal, and accumulated interest, or to roll the maturing CD over into another CD for another term. The renewal rate may be higher, lower, or identical to the previous rate.

How It Works

When you deposit money in a bank or savings and loan association you are, in essence, lending them your money. In return for the use of your money, the financial institution loans out or invests your money at a higher rate. If they are offering you a rate of return that is X, then they are taking your money and getting X plus Y with it. The difference, or "spread," compensates the bank for any risk they may take when lending money out or investing it elsewhere, pays for overhead, and provides them with a profit.

You could certainly lend your money out to whomever you like or put it into any kind of investment, ranging from ultra-conservative to speculative. However, in most cases you would not have any assurances. By letting the bank or financial institution accept these kinds of risk instead, you also agree to a lower rate of return. It's a tradeoff.

Advantages

Whenever one thinks of bank CDs, the first things that come to mind are safety and a known rate of return. When the bank offers you a certain rate of return, you get that rate, no matter what happens to their investment portfolio, the economy, or your specific dollars. If you do not like the rate of return being offered, you are always free to shop elsewhere, getting quotes and yields from other banks or savings and loan associations.

Disadvantages

There are two possible disadvantages to investing your money in CDs. First, if you make a withdrawal before the CD matures (see "How to Buy and Sell," below), you will pay a penalty. The amount of penalty depends upon the CD's interest rate and on the financial institution. The second potential disadvantage could end up being a positive rather than a negative. That is, when you lock into a certain rate of return, you will only know after the fact whether this was a better way to go than opting for something with a floating rate, such as a money market account or an adjustable-rate mortgage fund.

You can partially or fully avoid both of these liabilities by staggering the maturity of your CDs. As an example, if you have $40,000 to invest, it may be best to divide the money equally and invest in four different CDs that have different maturity dates—say, three months, six months, one year, and two years. When the three-month CD matures, roll it over into a six-month CD if cash is not needed at that time (your existing six-month CD will only have three more months until maturity, at this point). Staggered maturities may increase your bookkeeping duties, and the rate of return could very well be different for each CD, but this approach minimizes your chances of facing a penalty, since money reaches maturity every few months.

In theory there is also a distant chance that your financial institution will run into trouble. Therefore, when you invest in a CD, make sure it is backed by the FDIC, and do not invest more than $90,000 with any one institution. In the case of an insolvency, reorganization, or FDIC takeover, your account is protected for up to $100,000, enough to cover your $90,000 of principal and any interest accumulated.

How to Buy and Sell

The best way to buy CDs is by making a few telephone calls. Find out what bank or savings and loan association near you is offering the best rates and any convenience features. These "convenience features" may include free services or the ability to add to or make a certain dollar withdrawal once or twice during the term of the CD.

Convenience is a very important consideration. If you have earmarked $10,000 for CDs and an institution near you offers, say, 5 percent, while another bank way across town guarantees 5.2 percent for the year, you have to ask yourself whether it is worth your time to spend an hour in the car to get an extra $20 for the year (perhaps only $14 on an after-tax basis).

CDs have no secondary marketplace. If you wish to sell your CD at or prior to maturity, contact your financial institution and give them liquidation instructions. You may decide that you need access to part or all of the money. Whatever the case, find out how money can be sent to you or delivered elsewhere, or whether you must make the withdrawal in person. Make sure that you find out whether there are any penalties or costs involved. Weigh such costs, if any, against the benefit of any alternate investment. If the money is being used for an important purchase, then this may be a moot point.

Tracking Performance

There are three ways to see how you are doing. First, you can contact the bank or savings and loan association to find out your current balance. Second, you can rely on monthly or quarterly statements. Third, your newspaper may include a financial section that lists CD rates from around the country.

Historical Performance

Certificates of deposit have been around for dozens of years. Until the late 1970s and early 1980s, the rates of return were not particularly competitive with other investments. With the introduction of money market accounts and the resulting mass exodus out of CDs into these more appealing accounts, banks wised up and began offering rates very similar to the more liquid money market funds.

Over the past decade, CD rates have followed the general trend and performance of other short-term instruments. Offering a somewhat lower rate in return for absolute safety and investor familiarity, they remained an extremely popular investment. Even during the early 1990s, when rates fell to the 3-to-4-percent range, hundreds of billions of dollars remained in CDs.

Tax Considerations

The interest or yield of CDs is fully taxable on a local, state, and federal basis (few localities impose a city or county income tax). At the end of each year, your financial institution will send you a 1099 form, indicating how much interest has been earned in your account. You must declare this entire dollar figure on your tax return.

Like general-purpose money market funds, the only way to avoid current taxation with CDs is to make them part of a qualified retirement plan (IRA, pension plan, etc.). For non-retirement accounts, the fact that you did not receive or ever see the accumulated interest is unimportant. Automatic re-investment plans or CDs that roll over at maturity do not escape current taxation.

Portfolio Fit
Considering that they are one of America's most popular investments, to recommend against including CDs in a portfolio might seem contrary. Yet for most people there are better alternatives. During periods when interest rates are rising, money market funds are a better choice: no penalties, and your rate of return will go up as the general level of rates also increases. When interest rates seem to be stable, or even dropping, then short-term bond funds or short-term global income funds are a better choice. Their return is often several percentage points higher than that offered by CDs, and again, there is no penalty for a "premature" withdrawal (liquidation).

Despite what has just been said, you may still find CDs appealing. First, you know upfront what you will end up with and what it will cost to take money out early. Second, since the deposit is usually local, it comes with a certain sense of safety. Third, CDs are at least familiar and easy to understand.

Risks
There is only one risk associated with bank CDs and it can be easily avoided. The risk has to do with the unlikely event of your bank or savings and loan association running into financial trouble. As already mentioned, by sticking with institutions backed by the FDIC, and by limiting deposits to well under $100,000, you will be completely protected.

It is this indirect government backing from FDIC that makes CDs so popular, particularly during uncertain financial times.

Unique Features
CDs are a straightforward investment that offers few, if any, "bells and whistles." There is really nothing unique or special about them other than their quasi-government backing. Surprisingly, this simplicity is one of the major attractions of CDs. Other than yield, there is not much you can do in the area of comparison shopping.

Comments
By the time you have finished reading this book, your need to invest in CDs will be greatly diminished. Once you have learned about all of the other alternatives, you will find it necessary to keep little, if any, money in CDs.

Taxpayers in a high bracket should instead look to tax-deferred investments such as fixed-rate and variable annuities or municipal (tax-free) bonds or bond funds. People with sheltered money or those in a low bracket should consider high-quality corporate bonds, funds, or government obligations that mature in just a couple of years.

Additional Information

Your local bank, savings and loan association, or brokerage firm can provide you with information on how CDs work. To find out where you can get the highest yields across the country, write to one of the two sources listed below.

American Bankers' Association
1120 Connecticut Avenue, NW, Washington, DC 20036. 202-663-5000.

Bauer Financial Reports
P.O. Drawer 145510, Coral Gables, FL 33114-5510. 305-441-2062.

5
Money Market Funds

Stability of principal ✔✔✔✔✔

Stability of income ✔✔✔✔

Protection against inflation ✔✔

Total return ✔

Tax benefits

Definition

Money market funds invest in short-term debt instruments, including U.S. Treasury Bills, CDs, EuroDollar CDs, and commercial paper. They are a kind of mutual fund, and in order to be called a "money market" fund, at least 95 percent of their assets must be invested in securities that are rated as extremely safe. The typical maturity of a money market fund's assets fluctuate from twenty-five to sixty-five days; each portfolio has some securities maturing within a few days, weeks, and months. As the "paper" matures, fund managers reinvest it in other short-term instruments immediately. No money market manager wants portfolio money sitting around idly, even for a day.

How It Works

When you send a check into a money market fund, your money commingles with everyone else's. Every investor, seasoned or new, gets the same yield. If the quoted yield is, say, 6.01 percent, you will get the same 6.01 percent as the investor who has been with the fund for several years and who got a much higher rate years earlier.

As an example, let us suppose you invest $4,000 in a money market fund and your check is received by the fund tomorrow. At the same time your check arrives, other checks from around the country are also being processed. The fund manager adds up the value of all of these checks and buys money market instruments, as described in the prospectus (a brochure you receive at the time of purchase). If rates are moving upward, the existing yield of 6.01 percent may go up to 6.02 percent because of the "new" money going into very short-term bonds, CDs, etc., with yields of 6.5 percent. The reason the entire portfolio would not go up very much on any given day or week is that new monies (or existing paper in the portfolio that has just matured) represent an extremely small portion of the total assets. A $2-billion money market fund with a current yield of 5.67 percent is little affected if $700,000 comes in one day and is invested at 5.74 percent. Over several days and weeks, however, if the general level of short-term interest rates are changing, all money market funds will gradually reflect those newer rates.

Advantages

Introduced in the 1970s, money market accounts have a perfect track record: no one has ever lost a dime in one of these funds. In addition to being extremely safe, they boast a rate of return that continues to be competitive with the general level of interest rates: as rates climb, so do money market yields, and vice versa. Finally, these funds are extremely liquid and marketable. Money can be added or taken out at any time.

Disadvantages

There is only one disadvantage with money market funds: the rate of return is not guaranteed but fluctuates from month to month, sometimes from day to day. This, by the way, is not a disadvantage to most investors; but the lack of certainty is to some. At first, most investors want to lock in a rate of return. However, once it is explained to them that this is not the most conservative approach, they often change their minds.

The reason a guaranteed rate of return should usually be avoided is that interest rates go up and down. When you are offered a certain rate of return, you will only know in hindsight whether your return was good in light of interim changes in interest rates and inflation. A set rate of return ends up being beneficial only if interest rates during the time of ownership end up staying the same or, better yet, decline. If instead rates go up, then a floating rate would have been better.

Since money market accounts attract investors with their dual features of easy access and safety, it is better to have a yield that adjusts to market conditions. Nevertheless, there are some people who want to know exactly what they will have at the end of six months, a year, or an even greater period of time. For these investors, short-term bonds and bank CDs are a better choice.

How to Buy and Sell

Mutual funds, banks, savings and loan associations, credit unions, and brokerage firms all offer money market accounts. All money market funds are bought and sold for $1 a share. Interest in your account is credited in the form of additional shares. You may have 4,000 shares one day (representing exactly $4,000) and 4,000.61 a day later (the .61 share represents interest for one day). Your money goes to work for you the same day it is received by the mutual fund company. Most money market funds have to be established with at least $1,000. Funds will not close down the account if your balance later falls below the initial minimum.

Most money market funds include check-writing privileges, allowing you to redeem shares at any time. Mutual funds and brokerage firms let you write as many checks as you want without cost, service fee, or monthly charge; even the checks are free. Most money market funds put a bottom limit on the dollar figure that the check can be written for; it is quite common to see a money market check imprinted with, "This check must be for at least $250." This high minimum per check cuts down on the number of checks written by shareholders. Reduced transaction costs are passed onto the investor in the form of a higher yield.

Some brokerage firms, banks, etc., have no minimum amount but charge you a nominal fee for each check written.

Tracking Performance

Since the price per share remains at a constant $1 per share, the only thing to track is current yield (return). A large number of newspapers have financial sections that list representative samples of the rates of returns of several investments, including bank CDs, T-bills, government bonds, and money market accounts.

If you want to find out what your account has been earning over some past period of time, or simply wish to find out what the current rate of return is, you can contact the person who sold you the fund or telephone the fund directly. Virtually all money market funds have toll-free telephone numbers. You can use their automated quotation system twenty-four hours a day or speak directly to an account representative during normal business hours.

Historical Performance

Since money market funds were first introduced in this country in the early-to-mid-1970s, their rate of return has consistently been higher than that of-fered by U.S. Treasury Bills and interest-bearing checking and savings accounts. Usually, but not always, money market funds have also had yields surpassing those offered by certificates of deposit.

Like interest rates in general, the return money market funds have provided has been all over the board in the past twenty years, ranging anywhere from just under 4 percent in the early 1990s to close to 20 percent during the very early 1980s.

Tax Considerations

There are three categories of money market funds: general-purpose, government-backed, and tax-free. Each category is taxed differently. The great majority of money market accounts comes under the first heading, "general-purpose." These funds are made up of instruments that are fully taxable on a federal and state level, assuming you live in a state that has an income tax.

A small number of funds are composed solely of T-bills or seasoned government obligations that mature within a year. Direct obligations of the U.S. government are exempt from state and local income taxes, and these funds enjoy the same tax-exempt status. However, even though this category of money market funds is fully loaded with government paper, it is fully taxable for *federal* income tax purposes. Such funds can be easily identified from their titles.

A fair number of money market funds are made up of municipal obligations that mature in a year or less and are therefore exempt from federal income taxes. Furthermore, no state or local income taxes are due on the interest if you invest in a money market fund composed of tax-free notes issued in your state of residency, or if you live in a state that has no income tax.

Portfolio Fit

Money market funds are the perfect place to invest a large portion of the money you want to keep liquid. This is also a good "safe haven" to park your assets during periods of economic uncertainty or disaster.

Everyone should have part of his or her portfolio in a money market fund, if for no other reason than as a means to get cash in a hurry. This investment not only provides peace of mind, it is also a good source to tap when it comes time to pay monthly bills, or in the case of emergencies.

Several financial writers suggest that you should have somewhere between six months' and a year's worth of salary or income tied up in a money market fund. These writers somehow believe that other parts of a portfolio—stocks, bonds, bank CDs, and mutual funds—are not "liquid." Your decision as to how much of your portfolio should be invested in a money market fund should depend instead upon such factors as whether: (1) you are anticipating a large purchase, such as an automobile, during the coming year; (2) the security of your job, or that of your spouse is in any way threatened; (3) major lifestyle changes are on the horizon (having a baby, remodeling the home, going back to school, going through a divorce, moving, etc.); and (4) you have a negative outlook about real estate, stocks, and/or bonds.

Risks

Just as with T-bills and bank CDs, there really is no risk associated with money market funds. True, in theory there could be moderate or massive defaults within the fund's portfolio, but this is not likely when one considers the incredible safety record of these instruments and the fact that their quality is regulated by the Securities Exchange Commission.

If you overreact to financial events over some given period of time, you can always seek out money market funds that are invested entirely in government-backed paper. Your yield will not be quite as high as a traditional, or common-purpose money fund, but you will gain that needed peace of mind.

Unique Features

Two special features are found with many money market funds: liquidity and flexibility. Liquidity in this case means you can pick up the telephone and request that a certain dollar amount be sent to you immediately. (Some funds require that this request be made in writing.) Alternatively, you may be able to structure your fund so that money can automatically be wired to or from an account. In another convenient feature, most money market accounts can be set up so that one or more of your bills are automatically paid each month. This program, known as a systematic withdrawal plan, provides you or a creditor (a home lender, for instance), with a specific dollar amount each month.

Those money market funds offered by brokerage firms and mutual fund groups also give you quite a bit of investment flexibility. With a phone call to the mutual fund family, you can instruct part or all of the ABC money market fund to be liquidated and transferred the same day into the ABC stock fund or ABC bond fund. These investment options allow you to respond quickly to market conditions without the hassle and delay of waiting for a check and filling out an application or seeing a broker in person.

Comments

Money market funds are a lot like vanilla ice cream: nice, predictable, safe, and unexciting. This category of investments is not given much attention or lip service by brokers or advisors, since it is one of the most basic, and boring, investments. Yet part of all of our holdings should be in something unexciting—something we can count on whether or not there is world tension, a stock market crash, chaos in the bond market, or a depression in real estate.

Since money market funds have higher yields than traditional checking accounts, you might want to consider having two checking accounts: one for your everyday cash needs and small bills and one to write checks for more substantial amounts, such as a credit card, car, or mortgage payment. This second account is free, costs nothing to maintain, and will give you a better rate of return.

Additional Information

Listed below are some names and addresses of money market funds in each of the three different categories. Over the past three, five, and ten years, these funds have provided superior returns within their respective categories.

All-purpose (fully taxable):
Alger Shareholder Services
30 Montgomery Street, 13th Floor, Jersey City, NJ 07302. 800-992-3863.

Federated Research
Federated Investors Tower, 1001 Liberty Avenue, Pittsburgh, PA 15222-37799. 800-245-5000.

Government-backed (exempt from state and local income taxes):
Kemper Financial Services Inc.
120 South LaSalle Street, Chicago, IL 60603. 800-621-1148.

Vanguard Financial Center
P.O. Box 2600, Valley Forge, PA 19482-2600. 800-662-7447.

Tax-free (exempt from federal, and probably state, income taxes):
Alliance Fund Services
P.O. Box 1520, Secaucus, NJ 07096. 800-221-5672.

Franklin Distributors
777 Mariners Island Boulevard, San Mateo, CA 94404. 800-342-5236.

6
U.S. Treasury Bills

Stability of principal	✔✔✔✔
Stability of income	✔✔✔✔
Protection against inflation	✔
Total return	✔
Tax benefits	✔

Definition

One way the U.S. government raises money is by borrowing it. This borrowing is done by issuing government securities consisting of the following instruments: Treasury Bills, Treasury Notes, Treasury Bonds, Series EE Bonds, and Series HH Bonds. In return for the use of your money the federal government pays you interest.

T-bills come in three *original-issue* maturities: three, six, or twelve months. You can also buy seasoned (previously issued and now available for sale again in the secondary market) Treasuries that have maturities ranging from one or two days up to almost a year. Treasury bills traded in the secondary market are simply instruments that were originally purchased by someone else and are now being sold prior to maturity.

How It Works

U.S. Treasury Bills, also referred to as T-bills, are issued by the U.S. government in increments of $5,000 with a minimum value of $10,000. Thus, you can buy a Treasury bill that has a face value of $10,000, $15,000, $20,000, etc. T-bills are always purchased at a discount, at some figure less than $10,000, $15,000, etc. If you hold them until maturity, you will receive face value. If you sell a Treasury bill before it matures, you will get less than face value. The difference between the purchase (discount) price and face value or sales price (if sold prior to maturity) is interest.

For example, a three-month Treasury bill purchased for $9,800 would be worth $10,000 if held for the entire three months. If this same T-bill were sold before it matured, the seller would receive something less than $10,000. In either case, the difference between $9,800 and the sales price or value at redemption would be interest.

When you purchase a T-bill you know exactly what you will get if you hold it until maturity: full face value. Calculating your rate of return is easy: simply take the difference between the purchase price and value at maturity and divide the resulting figure by the purchase price and then annualize this figure. Thus, if you purchase a six-month Treasury bill for $9,700, the difference between this figure and the maturity value of $10,000 is $300. Take the $300 and divide it by the purchase price of $9,700. The resulting figure is 3.1 percent. This is your rate of return for six months. To find out the annualized rate, multiply 3.1 percent by two (6 months x 2 = 1 year = the annualized rate of return). The answer is 6.2 percent.

It is important to know the rate of return so that you can compare this investment to others. The rate of return is one of the considerations used in choosing one investment over another.

Advantages

The four reasons people buy Treasury bills are safety of principal and interest, a specific rate of return, a high degree of marketability and liquidity, and modest tax benefits.

People and companies all around the world like Treasuries because they are backed by the full faith and credit of the U.S. government. Since there is no chance of default, investors feel secure in purchasing something that will be reliable in good and bad economic times. No matter what happens in the stock, bond, or real estate market, the U.S. economy, or in any other country, you can be assured that the T-bills you own will be worth their full face value at maturity.

Before you buy a Treasury, your broker will be able to tell you the rate of return you can expect. The return, or yield, depends upon market conditions; the higher the overall level of interest rates, the greater the return. When you purchase a T-bill, unlike some other investments, your return is locked in *if you hold it until maturity*. You purchase it for a specific price and redeem it for face value.

Treasury bills are the most marketable security in the world. Corporations, financial institutions, and individual investors like the fact that they can sell their T-bill at any time without penalty. This is what is referred to as a high degree of "marketability." "Marketability" is the degree to which an investment can be easily bought or sold, or in other words, the number of readily available buyers and sellers. As an example, VW bugs are highly marketable, while Rolls Royces have only a modest level of marketability;

there are not a lot of people who can afford such an expensive automobile.

Besides being marketable, T-bills are also very liquid. The term "liquidity" refers to how easily an investment or asset can be converted to cash. When investors ask whether or not an investment is "liquid," they want to know if they can get out of it quickly. More specifically, if there is an emergency (or perhaps a more attractive opportunity), they want to know how soon they can get out of the investment. Thus, when you think of investments that are liquid, assets such as T-bills, bank CDs, widely-held stocks and bonds, and mutual funds come to mind. *Illiquid* investments would include those items that are not frequently traded and have no readily available marketplace—items such as most limited partnerships, antiques, second mortgage loans, and real estate. The term "liquid" is used much more frequently in financial circles than "marketable."

"Marketability" is somewhat different than "liquidity." An investment is marketable if there is a place where it can be sold. It may take a while for the marketable asset to sell, and the "marketplace" may be difficult to get to, but it does exist. Thus, antiques can be sold to dealers, through an auction house, or by consignment. Real estate is marketable depending upon the type of parcel, its location, and general economic conditions. Obviously, given the choice, a high degree of liquidity gives the investor more peace of mind than something that is merely marketable.

What makes T-bills so liquid is that they fluctuate very little in price. And although it is possible, as we shall see, that if you sold a T-bill before it matured you might realize less than what you paid for it, such a discount would be slight. It is more likely that you would be able to sell your T-bill prematurely for more than you paid for it.

The final benefit of owning Treasuries is the tax benefit they offer, discussed under "Tax Considerations."

Disadvantages

There are four disadvantages to owning T-bills: you may end up paying a fee when you purchase them, they have no real appreciation potential, their rate of return, once adjusted for inflation and taxes, is usually minimal or even negative, and if you sell them before they mature, you could end up with less than what you began with.

If you purchase a T-bill from a source other than the Federal Reserve Bank (see "How to Buy and Sell"), you will pay a fee or commission. Such a cost may or may not be reflected on your confirmation. If it is not shown, then it is built into the purchase price.

T-bills have no chance of meaningful appreciation or depreciation, since they are *short-term* interest-bearing securities. Thus, when interest rates such as prime go up, T-bills will fall in value very little, if any, and if rates drop, the price or value of your T-bill will increase only slightly. However, if held to maturity, all T-bills are worth their face value no matter what has happened to interest rates.

During most years T-bills have outpaced inflation. Once income taxes have also been subtracted, however, the return from this investment has usually been negative. Determining an investment's *real rate of return* (yield minus income taxes minus the rate of inflation) is the best way to find out whether you are really making progress (a positive net return), treading water (net return equals zero), or losing ground (a negative net return).

Since Treasury bills are always purchased for less than face value, if you sell them before they mature you will also receive something less than face value. Most people do not realize that this figure may end up being less than the purchase price. Normally this would be the case only if short-term interest rates went up just after you bought your Treasuries.

How to Buy and Sell

You can purchase T-bills, T-notes, and T-bonds from banks, savings and loan associations, brokerage firms, financial planners, or directly from the government via the Federal Reserve Bank. Purchases from a source other than the government result in your being charged a fee or commission. This charge ranges from $30 to $60 for a T-bill with a face value of $10,000. The fee may be shown on a confirmation or statement or it may be hidden in the purchase price. Whether shown or hidden, your yield will be slightly lower if there is a cost. (For instance, a $10,000 T-bill purchased for $9,600 will have a lower yield than one bought for $9,550.) Either way, the money comes out of your pocket.

On the other hand, one of the attractive features of T-bills, T-notes, and T-bonds is that they may be purchased from a Federal Reserve Bank. This process, known as "Treasury Direct," enables you to mail your money directly to the Federal Reserve Bank in your district (see "Additional Information"). Since government securities, when originally issued, are sold by auction, as a participant in Treasury Direct you will receive the average price paid at the auction for that kind of security; such a price is ensured by the Federal Reserve. This means that your yield or rate of return will be slightly better than half the people who went to the auction and slightly worse than the other half.

Once the Federal Reserve has received your check and application, they will then send you back a confirmation showing the details of your purchase (the price you paid, the maturity date, and the value at maturity) after the auction. When you deal with Treasury Direct, you must send the full face amount; the Federal Reserve Bank you deal with will send back the difference between the face amount (value at maturity) and the check you had originally sent them.

Tracking Performance

Since T-bills fluctuate very little in value, you may not need or desire to "see how you are doing." The values of three-, six- and twelve-month Treasuries are reported each day in the newspaper. You can also telephone your investment advisor for a current quote.

Historical Performance

The rate offered by T-bills has varied widely over the past half-century. These are interest-sensitive vehicles and they reflect the general level of short-term interest rates at any given time in history. Over the past fifty years, yields on three-month T-bills have ranged from an *annualized* return of .06 percent in 1941 to 14.7 percent in 1981. It is hard to imagine that anyone would get excited about an annual return of less than 1 percent (not even adjusted for inflation or taxes) or that everyone would not want a return in the mid-teens guaranteed by the government.

Keep in mind that at the time of purchase, either through Treasury Direct or from a bank or brokerage firm, your rate of return is locked in. The only way in which your return will differ from what you are quoted is if you sell your T-bill before it matures. A premature sale may result in a yield somewhat higher or lower than what you were quoted at the time of purchase.

When viewing T-bill performance over the past half-century, keep in mind the following: (1) the best five-year return was the period 1979-1983, when T-bills had an average annual return of 11.1 percent (vs. 10.1 percent for inflation); (2) the best ten-year return was from 1978-1987, when T-bills averaged 9.2 percent (vs. 8.7 percent for inflation); and (3) the best twenty-year return was the period 1971-1990, when T-bills annualized 7.7 percent (vs. 6.4 percent for inflation).

Tax Considerations

Buying Treasury bills has two tax advantages. First, interest from these instruments is free from state and any local income taxes, a fact of particular importance if you live in a state that has high tax rates. In the case of California, with a top marginal bracket of 11 percent, a T-bill return of 5.4 percent is equal to a fully taxable return of 6 percent. If you are a resident of a state that does not have an income tax, such as Nevada, Texas, or Florida, then the income tax benefit offered by T-bills is a moot point.

The second tax benefit T-bills offer is that the interest accrued from your T-bill is not taxable until the security actually matures. This means that a six-month T-bill purchased in, say, October 1992 will not be taxed in the 1992 calendar year. This is because the T-bill in this example will not mature until 1993. The shifting of income from one year to the next may be important to someone who wants to keep his or her taxable income as low as possible for a certain year. It also means that those tax dollars you would normally be sending Uncle Sam (the tax on the interest from the T-bill) can be used by you for over a year before you have to send them to Washington, D.C.

Portfolio Fit

Since there is nothing safer than a U.S. Treasury Bill, this is an excellent candidate for consideration in any portfolio that needs a certain part of its holdings to be extremely safe and secure. Certainly there are higher-yielding investments available, but none match the day-to-day safety of a T-bill.

For those monies you want to make sure are always there at a moment's notice, this investment is for you. This is not something you can write a check against, but T-bills can be sold by your broker any Monday through Friday. Proceeds from the sale can be sent to you in one or two days after the sale.

In summary, one could say that T-bills are a good choice for your "emergency fund." They are appropriate for moderate and high risk-takers who want a stabilizing force in their portfolio. Finally, they are the investment of choice for people who want a place to park their money either because of current negative economic or financial news or because the use of such funds is anticipated within the next one or two years.

Remember, T-bills, money market funds, and bank CDs often have a *negative* real rate of return. It is for this reason that these instruments should not be considered as part of a long-term investment program. If your time horizon is five years or greater, avoid T-bills unless you are a very conservative investor, and even then, make sure they represent no more than 25 percent of a portfolio's total. For moderate and aggressive investors, there are better alternatives.

Risks

Treasury bills are often referred to as providing a "risk-free rate of return," and it is true, they do not subject you to any risk in the traditional sense. T-bills can be considered risky, however, if one were to factor in the effects of inflation and income taxes. Along the same lines, the real risk of Treasury bills is perhaps that they offer a certain false sense of security. In return for price stability and a set rate of return, investors are often not maintaining their purchasing power with these government obligations.

Unique Features

T-bills are a straightforward investment. The only thing that makes them unique is the way in which their price is quoted. Instead of saying that they are worth $9,500 or $9,650, they are traded based upon their yield. The marketplace describes them as having a certain yield, such as 5.7 percent. Without doing any math work, prospective buyers know only that whatever price they pay, their equivalent annualized yield is 5.7 percent (in this example).

Comments

T-bills are the most popular security in the world. Almost everyone likes them for one reason or another. In a world filled with a wide array of continuously changing investment choices it is nice to know that something remains reliable.

Additional Information

To find out perhaps more than you ever wanted to know about U.S. government obligations, including Treasury bills, send $5 to the following address:

Federal Reserve Bank of Richmond
P.O. Box 27622, Richmond, Virginia 23261.

Each Federal Reserve Bank specializes in specific economic reporting and publications. The Richmond bank publishes an extensive booklet detailing T-bills, T-notes, and T-bonds. Make sure you ask for the publication, *Buying Treasury Securities At Federal Reserve Banks*. It will provide you with all of the forms and instructions necessary to participate in Treasury Direct. The booklet will also include a listing of the Federal Reserve Banks throughout the country.

7
U.S. Treasury Notes and Bonds

Stability of principal	✔✔✔
Stability of income	✔✔✔✔
Protection against inflation	✔✔✔
Total return	✔✔
Tax benefits	✔

Definition

U.S. Treasury Bills, Notes, and Bonds, also referred to as T-bills, T-notes, and T-bonds, represent the entire marketable debt of the U.S. government. Unlike T-bills, T-notes and T-bonds pay interest every six months. The amount of interest you receive semiannually depends upon the coupon rate of the Treasury Note or Treasury Bond, as will be explained shortly.

T-notes have original-issue maturities ranging from two to ten years; T-bonds have original-issue maturities ranging from ten to thirty years. You can buy seasoned Treasury Notes or Bonds in the secondary market that have remaining maturities of almost any time period you are looking for. In the case of T-notes, this means a remaining life of anywhere between a few days and a period up to but not including ten years. For T-bonds, secondary issues can be bought that have a remaining life of a couple of days all the way up to but not including thirty years. Treasuries traded in the secondary market are merely instruments that were originally purchased by someone else and are now being sold prior to maturity.

How It Works

U.S. Treasury Notes and U.S. Treasury Bonds are issued in denominations of $1,000, $5,000, $10,000, $100,000, and $1,000,000. These figures are also referred to as face value. The price you pay may be higher or lower than face value, depending upon whether the T-note or T-bond is trading at a premium, discount, or par. A "premium" means that you are paying a price greater than $1,000, $5,000, $10,000, $100,000, or $1,000,000. A "discount" means that you are paying a price less than one of these figures. "Par" means that you are paying exactly face value. If you buy a T-note or T-Bond, the price you will pay depends upon the marketplace, or more specifically, upon interest rates. An example will help to clarify.

Let us suppose that you were thinking about buying a $10,000 Treasury Bond with an 8-percent coupon. This means that the bond pays $800 every year (8 percent of $10,000). Since T-bonds and T-notes pay interest semiannually, in this example the owner would receive $400 every six months. As you were pondering this purchase during the week, you read that interest rates were moving down. At the end of the week, after rates had gone down, your broker tells you that the $10,000 T-bond will now cost you $10,400. You ask, "How could this be? Why should I pay $10,400 (a premium price) for something that, if held to maturity, will only be worth $10,000? Furthermore, if I decide to pay $10,400 and will receive $800 a year, won't my interest rate be something less than 8 percent ($800/10,400 = 7.7 percent)? What may surprise you is that there is no reason you should not still go through with this purchase.

Keep in mind that the 8-percent yield in this example was something that *was* being paid. The fact that you still want 8 percent from a T-bond is not important (you and I would also like to have a 5-percent mortgage or a checking account that paid us 6-percent interest). The 8-percent figure now represents the past, not the present. The U.S. government is paying $800 a year to the owner of these $10,000 worth of T-bonds; the government does not know, or care, whether the owner paid $6,000 or $13,000 for these bonds in the secondary market. The government's only obligation is to pay what the bond certificate says which, in this example, is 8 percent of face value ($10,000).

Getting back to the example, if the T-bond now costs $10,400, which results in a current yield of 7.7 percent ($800 divided by $10,400), the marketplace is simply telling you that this yield is considered a fair deal considering the quality (backed by the U.S. government) and maturity (let us suppose this bond will mature, or come due, in twenty more years). This does not mean that you cannot get more than 7.7 percent on an investment; however, it does mean that you are not very likely to get a higher yield on an investment this safe and with this maturity.

Finishing up this example, another factor you need to consider is the $400 premium. The marketplace is saying that you are going to pay $10,400 for something that will pay you $800 a year ($400 every six months) for the next twenty years, and that at the end of twenty years, the bond will mature and you will receive $10,000. What happened to the other $400? The person you bought the bond from kept this $400; that was the extra price to be paid in order for this person to part with his or her T-bonds. This $400 "fee" was not arbitrarily made up; it simply represented what other people, the marketplace, were getting for similar bonds (Treasury Bonds with 8-percent coupons) that had a remaining life of approximately twenty years.

The $400 premium that you would have to pay in this example does not mean you are getting a "good" or a "bad" deal; it just means you are getting a fair deal. Amortizing $400 over twenty years ($20 x twenty years = $400) means that your true yield, also known as "yield to maturity" will be less than 7.7 percent ($800 minus $20 a year that is being amortized = $780; $780 divided by $10,400 equals 7.5 percent). Again, this is due to the general level of interest rates. What the market is really saying is, "Look, interest rates have gone down. The days of 8-percent returns on government bonds is over; an 8-percent return may be possible next week or next month or next decade, but for now, the rate of return you can get for such safety is a 7.5-percent yield to maturity and a current yield of 7.7 percent (which does not take into account the $400 premium that needs to be amortized over twenty years).

This example assumes that interest rates have moved down (when rates go down, the price of bonds goes up), meaning that the price of bonds has increased. However, the converse is also true. When interest rates go up, the price of bonds decline. In our example, if rates had gone from, say, 8 to 8.4 percent, anyone trying to buy 8 percent would be able to do so at a discount. This might mean that $10,000 worth (face value) of bonds are now selling for $9,650. Someone paying $9,650 for 8-percent coupon bonds would have a *current yield* of 8.3 percent ($800/$9,650 = 8.3 percent) and a *yield to maturity* (remember, we must now amortize the discount over the bond's remaining life, in our example twenty years) of approximately 8.47 percent ($800 annual interest plus $17.50 of annual amortization = $817.50; $817.50 divided by $9,650 = 8.47 percent). What is a little tricky is keeping in mind that the "bonus" of $350 (we are paying $9,650 for something that will eventually be worth $10,000) must be amortized over the T-bond's remaining life (twenty years).

Whether you pay par (face value), a discount (something less than face value) or a premium (something greater than face value) does not affect what you get when the T-note or T-bond matures; the figure is always the same: face value. A $5,000 T-note that you paid $4,500 for in the secondary market will be worth $5,000 (in addition to all the interest you received during the years you owned the bond) when it matures, whether the maturity date is three or nine years away. Similarly, a $100,000 T-bond that was purchased for $123,000 in the secondary marketplace will be worth exactly $100,000 whenever it matures. The issuer, the U.S. government in this case, pays off face value only at maturity.

A sale prior to maturity, meaning you have sold the T-note or T-bond in the secondary market, will result in your receiving a figure that may be above or below the face value (par). As a general rule, a "premature" sale, meaning one that takes place before the instrument naturally matures, will usually result in a profit if interest rates at the time of sale are lower than they were when you purchased the note or bond. Conversely, a sale in the secondary marketplace will result in a loss of principal (purchase price) if interest rates are now higher than they were than at the time you first bought the security.

If all of this talk about discounts and premiums is a little confusing, do not despair: a great number of people buy T-bonds and T-notes and hold them until they mature, relying solely on the interest payments.

It is important to compare rates of T-notes and T-bonds to other instruments of similar maturities and safety. The rate of return is one of the considerations used in selecting one investment over another. Safety of principal and volatility (price fluctuations while you own the asset) are other important concerns.

Advantages

People buy Treasury Notes and Treasury Bonds for four reasons: safety of principal and interest, a specific rate of return, a high degree of marketability, and modest tax benefits.

The biggest reason T-notes and T-bonds are so popular is that they are backed by the full faith and credit of the U.S. government. Since there is no chance of default, investors feel secure in purchasing something that will be reliable in good and bad economic times. No matter what happens in the stock, bond, or real estate market, the U.S. economy, or in any other country, you can be assured that the T-notes or T-bonds you own will be worth their full face value at maturity.

Before you buy a Treasury Note or Treasury Bond, your stockbroker will be able to tell you the rate of return you can expect (current return as well as the yield to maturity). The return, or yield, depends upon market conditions; the higher the overall level of interest rates, the greater the return you will get. When you buy a T-note or T-bond, your current yield remains constant; your *yield to maturity* is also locked in *if you hold it until maturity*.

Treasury Notes and Treasury Bonds represent some of the most marketable securities in the world. Corporations, financial institutions, and individual investors like the fact that they can sell them at any time without penalty.

Treasury Notes are usually more stable than Treasury Bonds because they are generally less susceptible to interest rate changes. Remember, we are not talking about your yield changing over the years, we are talking about the value of your underlying investment, the principal. T-notes have less volatility because they normally have shorter maturities than T-bonds. The greater the maturity—that is, the more years it takes until the bond comes to an end—the greater the price volatility.

A final benefit of owning Treasury Notes and Treasury Bonds is the tax benefit. This is discussed under "Tax Considerations."

Disadvantages

There are four disadvantages to owning T-notes and T-bonds: You may end up paying a fee when you purchase them, their value will vary during your period of ownership, their rate of return, once adjusted for inflation and taxes, is modest, and if you sell them before they mature, you could end up with less than what you began with.

If you purchase a T-note or T-bond from a source other than the Federal Reserve Bank, you will pay a fee or commission. Such a cost may or may not be reflected on your confirmation. If it is not shown, then it is built into the purchase price.

As previously mentioned, T-notes and T-bonds have appreciation and depreciation potential since they are *medium* and/or *long-term* interest-bearing securities. Thus, if the prime interest rate goes up 1 percent, T-notes will fall in value a little and T-bonds more (approximately twice as much). The converse is also true: if rates drop, the price or value of a T-note or T-bond will increase. Thus, if interest rates fall 1 percent, a thirty-year T-bond will increase approximately 7 percent in value).

During most years, T-notes and T-bonds have outpaced inflation. However, once income taxes have also been subtracted, the return figures from these investments are often only $\frac{1}{2}$ to 1 percent. During certain periods of time, such as the 1980s, the average annual returns for Treasury Notes and Treasury Bonds, even adjusted for inflation and income taxes, have been very positive. This is because inflation figures were fairly low for the decade, on average, while the dramatic decrease in interest rates (prime was as high as 21.5 percent early on in the Reagan years and less than 8 percent before he left office) helped push the value of all bonds and notes to record highs. In fact, the 1980s represent the best decade bonds have ever experienced in this country.

How to Buy and Sell

You can purchase Treasury Notes and Bonds from stockbrokers or alternatively from banks, savings and loans, or directly from the government (see "How to Buy and Sell" in the previous chapter).

Purchases through your local bank or broker are made without a commission charge; however, this does not mean there is no fee. Although a commission will not show on your confirmation or monthly statement, a commission charge is usually built into the buying or selling price. This markup can be quite reasonable, in the range of $\frac{1}{2}$ to 1 percent. Such a cost can be avoided altogether by making a purchase through *Treasury Direct* (see previous chapter). Such direct purchases do have their disadvantages: the government has use of your money for several days, interest-free, before the purchase is actually made; you do not have anyone to gain counsel or advice from when you think it might be time to buy or sell; and Treasury Direct can only be used for purchases and if the T-bill, T-note or T-bond is held to maturity—a premature sale will still require the services of a banker or broker.

If you do need money for whatever reason, Treasuries can be sold within a matter of minutes, usually seconds. Settlement only takes a couple of days, which means that you can have cash in hand quite quickly. T-bonds and T-notes sold prior to their natural maturity will receive market price plus *accrued interest*. This means that if it has been four months since your Treasury paid interest and you have now decided to sell it, you will get current market value plus four months of accrued interest. There is no loss of interest from selling a bond or note, in other words; notes and bonds accrue interest every day, and while you own them you are entitled to this interest.

Tracking Performance
T-notes and T-bonds are quoted daily in the newspaper. Financial or business radio and television reports will also indicate how the thirty-year Treasury Bond (considered to be a bellwether of long-term interest rates) fared during the trading day.

Treasuries that are held at a brokerage firm are valued each reporting period whenever a customer statement is sent out to you. If you cannot wait for these reports to arrive, contact the person who sold you the instrument at any time to get a current quotation. Remember, it is not your yield that is going to vary from month to month or year to year, it is the value of the security—the T-note or T-bond—that will change.

Historical Performance
The rate offered by T-notes and T-bonds has varied widely over the past half-century. These are interest-sensitive vehicles, and they reflect the general level of interest rates at any given time in history. Over the past fifty years, yields on T-bonds have ranged from an *annualized* return of -9.2 percent in 1967 to 40.4 percent in 1982 (both of these figures represent *total return*).

Keep in mind that at the time of purchase, either through Treasury Direct or from a bank or brokerage firm, your rate of return is locked in. The only way in which your return (yield to maturity only) will differ from what you are quoted is if you sell your T-note or T-bond before it matures. A premature sale may result in a yield that is somewhat higher or lower than what you were quoted at the time of purchase.

When viewing T-bond performance over the past half-century, keep the following figures in mind: (1) the best five-year return was the period 1982 to 1986, when T-bonds had an average annual return of 21.6 percent (vs. 3.3 percent for inflation); (2) the best ten-year return was from 1982 to 1991, when T-bonds averaged 15.6 percent (vs. 3.9 percent for inflation); and (3) the best twenty-year return was the period 1970 to 1989, when T-bonds annualized 9 percent (vs. 6.2 percent for inflation).

Tax Considerations

Buying Treasury Notes and Treasury Bonds has two tax advantages. First, interest from these instruments is free from state and any local income taxes. (For a more complete discussion, see "Tax Considerations" in the previous chapter.) Second, the interest these instruments accrue is not taxable until such interest is received or credited to your account. This means that if you own a T-note that pays interest in January and July, you are not taxed this year on the interest attributable to the months from July through December, although in the next calendar year you would then have to show such interest income on your federal tax return.

The most commonly used methods to shelter the interest that T-bills, T-notes, and T-bonds throw off is to buy them within a retirement plan, such as an IRA, Keogh, 401(k), 403(b) or pension plan, or as a portfolio within a variable annuity (see chapter 25).

Portfolio Fit

There is no chance that a U.S. government obligation such as a T-bill, T-note, or T-bond can default. As far as *financial* safety is concerned there is nothing safer in the world. People buy Treasuries because of their safety and the current yield (income) that they provide.

If there is no chance that you will sell prior to maturity, then your decision as to whether you should buy a T-note (two-to-ten-year maturity) or T-bond (ten-plus years) is simple: buy the one that has the highest yield. Usually this means Treasury Bonds. If you think there is at least a fairly good chance that you may need some of this money (your principal, so to speak) before the securities mature, and you believe that interest rates will most likely go up between the time of purchase and "premature" sale, buy T-notes; they will fall less in value. If you believe rates will drop during this period, buy T-bonds; they will increase more in value if rates do drop.

If you are honest with yourself and admit that neither you nor your favorite business journalist really knows what will happen, take a middle stance: buy new T-notes or seasoned T-notes or T-bonds that have about eight years to maturity. By taking a somewhat neutral approach, you will neither suffer nor profit much if and when rates do change. Treasuries that have maturities of five to eight years have approximately one-third to one-half the interest-rate risk (or reward) as Treasuries that have a twenty-to-thirty-year maturity.

If you do not need the current income, try to place these securities under the umbrella of a retirement plan. The "umbrella" will protect you from current taxation. (Assets in a retirement plan grow and compound tax-deferred interest until withdrawn.)

One of the nice features of T-notes and T-bonds is that they can be purchased originally (when first issued) or in the secondary market based upon your time limitations. What this means is that if you want to make absolutely certain that X amount of dollars plus interest will be there when you retire in six years or when your daughter graduates from college in fourteen years, you can buy a Treasury that has that exact maturity.

In summary, Treasury Notes and Treasury Bonds should be seriously considered by the conservative investor who is looking for something that has a better return than T-bills, money market accounts, and bank CDs. This investor must also learn that there will be fluctuations of principal and that the only guarantees are the timely payment of interest and the eventual (if held to maturity) payment of face value.

Risks

There are two somewhat hidden risks when it comes to investing in T-notes and T-bonds: purchasing power and interest-rate changes. We have already covered interest-rate risk (what happens when rates change). Purchasing power risk has to do with keeping pace with inflation—maintaining your standard of living. Both of these risks can creep up on you slowly. Over a one-, two-, or three-year period of time, the loss of purchasing power may be minimal or modest. Cumulatively, however, the effects of inflation are devastating; just ask any finance teacher or economist. As an example, suppose you just purchased a $10,000 T-bond that provides $800 per year in interest. Assuming a 5 percent rate of inflation, fourteen years from now this $800 annual interest would only be able to purchase $400 worth of goods and services.

Unique Features

Apart from the task of trying to figure out how much or how little a T-note or T-bond will be affected by a $1/2$- or-1-percent change in interest rates, both of these government securities are easy to understand. The only unique feature they possess is that their interest is free from state and local income taxes (very few cities impose a local tax).

T-notes and T-bonds are identical in virtually all categories except one: maturity. And even when it comes to maturity, or remaining life, you can buy Treasury Notes and Treasury Bonds in the secondary marketplace that have identical maturities.

Comments

Because of their modest tax benefits, high degree of reliability, and safety, T-notes and T-bonds are a fairly attractive option. By focusing on T-notes and T-bonds that have remaining maturities of five to nine years, you can get close to the same return long-term bonds enjoy with only a fraction of the interest-rate risk. By concentrating on such medium-term maturities, you can make this category of investments more appealing on a risk-adjusted return basis.

The only time you want to buy T-bonds, or any other marketable debt instruments that have maturities in the fifteen-to-thirty-year range is when you are virtually certain that the general direction of interest rates is down. And since it is very difficult to make such accurate predictions, except of course in hindsight, it is suggested that you play it safe and stick with medium-term (five-to-nine-year) maturities. Be happy with getting 80 to 90 percent of the return the long-term issues usually enjoy while accepting only 33 to 50 percent of the interest-rate risk.

Additional Information

If you are interested in learning more about Treasury Direct (the method of buying Treasuries without having to go through a banker or broker), contact the Federal Reserve Bank in your area. If you have an interest in the auction process, which determines the rate new Treasuries are yielding, contact:

Department of the Treasury
c/o Bureau of Public Debt Information Center, 13th and C Streets, SW, Washington, DC 20228. 800-287-4088.

Federal Reserve Bank of New York
Public Information Department, 33 Liberty Street, New York, NY 10045. 212-791-7773.

8
Series EE Bonds

Stability of principal	✔✔✔✔✔
Stability of income	✔✔✔✔✔
Protection against inflation	✔✔✔
Total return	✔✔
Tax benefits	✔✔

Definition

Series EE Bonds, formerly known as E Bonds, are issued and backed by the U.S. government. They are a direct obligation of the government and have a maturity of twelve years. These bonds are purchased at one-half of face value and, if held to maturity, are redeemed for full face value. The difference between purchase price and sales price is interest. Series EE Bonds do not pay interest every six months, like other bonds.

How It Works

Also known as "defense bonds," Series EE Bonds were the first zero coupon bonds. They do not pay interest; instead they *accrete* interest (see chapter 17, Zero Coupon Bonds). People buy these bonds as a way of saving or accumulating wealth. They are not purchased as a means of obtaining current income.

Advantages

EE Bonds have three advantages: complete safety of principal, an interest rate that can increase if other rates go up, and tax deferral. Although they are purchased for half of face value, these securities are always sold for more than their purchase price. An investor cannot lose any money. The second advantage has to do with the fact that although a minimum rate of return is known and guaranteed, that rate can increase if the rate of return offered by five-year Treasury Bonds also increases. Here is how it works. Let us suppose that the quoted rate is 6 percent but that sometime during the life of the EE Bond, five-year Treasuries are paying 10 percent. The owner of the EE Bond would get 85 percent of 10 percent (8.5 percent in this example). Therefore, when you buy an EE Bond, you are guaranteed to get *the greater of:* (a) the original rate quoted or (b) 85 percent of what T-bonds are paying. Thus, you may receive one rate of return during one six-month period and a higher rate during the next six months. The third advantage is that the accreted interest is not taxed until the bonds are sold.

Disadvantages

There are two disadvantages to EE Bonds: a reduced rate of interest if the bonds are sold within the first five years of ownership and no current income. The 6 percent interest rate you thought you were going to get drops down to 4.16 percent if the securities are sold during the first year. This rate increases by .5 percent for each half-year the bonds are held. This rate tops out at 6 percent (unless five-year T-bonds end up yielding more).

The second disadvantage, no current interest payments, means that you do not want to own these things if you need income on a regular basis. It is for this reason that more people do not own Series EE Bonds.

Neither of these points is necessarily a disadvantage. First, if the investor needs cash, he or she could sell other assets before having to liquidate part or all of any EE Bonds. Furthermore, the "penalty interest" period only lasts for the first couple of years of ownership. Second, income-oriented investors could possibly dip into some of their principal to supplement their cash needs until the bonds matured or until the full rate of interest was being credited to the EE Bonds.

How to Buy and Sell

These securities are purchased and sold through banks, savings and loan associations, and directly through the Federal Reserve. You cannot buy more than $30,000 (face value) of these bonds in any one calendar year. Series EE Bonds have the following denominations: $50, $100, $500, and $1,000. They are bought for exactly one-half of these face value figures. After the purchase has been made, EE Bonds cannot be sold for at least a month. The sale or redemption can be made through any of the institutions listed above; you do not have to go through the original source.

Series EE Bonds can be readily sold any time after the first month of ownership. They have no marketability, meaning that they are not sold in the secondary market like other securities and government obligations. It is for this reason that they are not, and cannot, ever be sold for a loss or a gain. (The excess above the purchase price is always considered to be interest.)

If you sell these bonds within the first five years of ownership, the interest rate you were being credited with (the accreted interest) is reduced. The base rate paid by EE Bonds is 4.16 percent. For every six months of ownership, the owner is credited an additional .5-percent rate of interest. This "credit" continues for the first two years until a 6-percent rate is reached. If you hold them for at least five years, you receive the full interest rate.

There is no fee, commission, or charge when you buy or sell Series EE Bonds. This is one of the few financial instruments or securities you can purchase (or liquidate) without having to pay someone a fee or commission.

Tracking Performance

Since EE Bonds are not traded in the secondary marketplace, there is really no need to track their performance. In fact, since they have no appreciation or loss potential, there is no performance to track. The only thing that can change while you own one of these bonds is the rate of interest being credited to the account.

To find out how much your EE Bonds are worth or what the current yield is, simply contact a bank or savings and loan association. The value of these bonds is not quoted in any newspaper or on any exchange.

Historical Performance

The government has been offering these instruments for dozens of years. They are particularly popular during periods of war and with firms that have contracts with the U.S. government. Their rate of return was always lower than rates offered by similar securities until the early 1980s. At this time these bonds were given the extra boost of providing a somewhat floating rate, which could increase if the general level of interest rates also went up.

Tax Considerations

A major attraction of Series EE Bonds is the fact that you do not pay taxes on the interest (deferred "growth") until the bonds are sold, either prematurely or at maturity. The difference between the selling and purchase price represents interest and must be included as taxable interest for the calendar year in which the bonds are sold. However, there is a way to postpone taxes for an additional twelve years.

If the bonds are held until their natural maturity, the owner can either redeem them or exchange them for Series HH Bonds. Unlike Series EE Bonds, HH Bonds pay interest every six months. The interest from HH Bonds is fully taxable on the federal level but is exempt from any state and local income taxes. Once the HH Bonds mature, or are sold prematurely, the interest accreted by the EE Bonds must now be reported and taxes paid.

Like other direct obligations of the U.S. government, the interest on EE Bonds, whenever it is paid, is subject only to federal income taxes, not state or local taxes. To understand how this works, an example may be useful.

Let us suppose you bought a $10,000 EE Bond, which means you paid exactly $5,000 for it. When the bond matured twelve years later for $10,000, you decided to roll it over into an HH Bond, thereby postponing taxes on the $5,000 of interest that had been accruing. The HH Bond you exchanged into pays interest every six months. The HH interest is taxable on a federal level. Twenty years after you get the HH security, it matures. At this point, time has run out. Taxes cannot be postponed any longer. You now have to declare the $5,000 of interest from the old EE Bond. Again, this interest is only taxable on a federal level.

As you may have gathered, the investor gets to decide, within a several-year corridor, when he or she will pay taxes on the EE Bond interest. Interest can be declared and paid at any time during the life of the EE or HH Bond. This means that you can wait until you are in a lower tax bracket and then sell off some or all of your EE (or HH) Bonds.

Portfolio Fit

Series EE Bonds are best suited for someone who is looking for a way to accumulate money or who wants to provide for retirement or help out loved ones (a college fund, a way of saving for a house, etc.).

This is not an investment for people who need to maximize their current income. It is also not for someone who wants to take a little risk. EE Bonds, in many respects, are one of the very safest investments described in this book.

Risks

There is really no risk in owning EE Bonds. They are fully backed by the U.S. government, which means that they are not subject to any financial risk. They are not traded anywhere (no secondary market) so there is no interest-rate risk. Their interest rate cannot fall below the 6-percent guarantee rate and can climb up from there. This means that if Treasury Bonds with a remaining maturity of five years are, for some reason, yielding 17 percent, EE bondholders will get 85 percent of that figure (85% of 17% = 14.45%).

Unique Features

What is special about these securities is that, unlike almost every other debt instrument, they have a return that can fluctuate upward. This is also one of the few investments whose interest is tax-deferred. In fact, EE Bonds are the only security issued by the U.S. government that has good tax benefits.

Comments

EE Bonds are a good choice for an ultra-conservative investor who wants the backing of the U.S. government and would like to help out a child or grandchild. Since the accreted interest is not currently being taxed, parents do not have to be concerned about the "kiddie tax" with these bonds. Under the current tax law, for the tax years ending in 1992 and 1993, the first $600 of interest, dividends, or capital gains generated under a child's social security number is free of federal taxes, regardless of the parents' tax status. For the tax years 1992 and 1993, the second $600 of this income is subject to a tax of 15 percent. These brackets, which are currently $600, are subject to change depending on the inflation rate, but the current rule is that the brackets only adjust in $50 increments; over $1,200 the parents' tax rate applies. Once the child reaches age fourteen or older, the first $600 is still tax-free, but then the rest of the child's income is taxed at the rate of a single individual. For example, for 1992, if the child had no earned income (e.g., salary), then after the first tax-free $600 of income, the next $21,450 would be taxed at the 15 percent rate—which for many children would be significantly lower than their parents' rate.

Additional Information

Since brokerage firms and insurance companies do not deal in EE Bonds, you will need either to contact your local bank or savings and loan association or write to the federal government by writing to:

U.S. Savings Bonds
Washington, DC 20226. 800-872-6637.

9
Series HH Bonds

Stability of principal	✔✔✔✔✔
Stability of income	✔✔✔✔✔
Protection against inflation	✔✔
Total return	✔
Tax benefits	✔

Definition

These interest-bearing instruments are issued by the U.S. government only to people who have Series EE Bonds they want to exchange. When a Series EE Bond matures, the investor can either redeem it or exchange it for an HH Bond. The choice is up to the investor. Unlike EE Bonds, HH Bonds pay interest every six months. All HH Bonds have a maturity of twenty years.

How It Works

If you own one or more EE Bonds that are about to mature, you can exchange some or all of them for one or more HH Bonds. You cannot go out and buy HH Bonds; they can only be acquired by EE bondholders through an exchange.

Every six months HH Bonds pay interest to the owner of record. These interest checks are sent directly to the investor. The interest from HH Bonds is fully taxable for federal income tax purposes.

Advantages

Owning HH Bonds has four benefits. First, the semiannual interest payments are exempt from state and local income taxes. Second, their ownership is the only way to *postpone* taxation from the redemption of Series EE Bonds. Third, they are backed by the full faith and credit of the U.S. government. Fourth, they can be sold back to a bank or savings and loan association or through the Federal Reserve at any time after the first six months of ownership. Fifth, they do not fluctuate in value. If you own, say, $50,000 worth of HH Bonds, you will always be able to sell them for exactly $50,000—no more, no less.

Disadvantages

There are two disadvantages to owning Series HH Bonds. First, an investor can get a somewhat higher return by buying T-bonds with a similar maturity. Second, since these are not traded in the secondary market, HH Bonds do not have any appreciation potential.

Like other "disadvantages" described throughout the book, there is also a positive side to each of these points. True, you can get a higher return from some other kinds of government obligations, but there are also government obligations that have a lower yield. Second, although there is no appreciation potential (when interest rates fall, most other government securities go up in value), there is also no loss potential. Therefore, alternate investments can end up giving you a higher total return (current yield plus appreciation of principal) or you can end up with a lower total return (current yield minus loss in principal value).

How to Buy and Sell

Once again, you cannot go out and buy HH Bonds. The only way they can be "purchased" is if you have EE Bonds that are maturing. Even then you cannot sell EE Bonds and then use the proceeds to acquire HH Bonds. The acquisition must be made by an exchange.

Once you own Series HH Bonds, you can sell them at any time; you do not have to wait for an anniversary or maturity date. Speaking of maturity, once an HH Bond matures, it must be cashed in. If you hold the bond after maturity, it will cease earning interest. Thus, it is important to keep track of redemption dates.

As with Series EE Bonds, there is no fee, cost, or commission when you buy or sell Series HH Bonds. You can get in and out of this investment at any time without jeopardizing your principal. Only a handful of investments can make such a claim.

Tracking Performance

There is no way or need to track performance. These government obligations do not fluctuate in value no matter how high up or down interest rates go and no matter what state the economy is in. They are what is known as "fixed-rate" instruments, paying a set rate of return.

Historical Performance

Previously known as Series H Bonds, these securities have been around for several dozen years. In the early 1980s, when the interest paid on Series EE Bonds was increased, Series H Bonds were renamed Series HH Bonds. At this same time the yield on HH Bonds also went up.

Tax Considerations

As described, interest from HH Bonds is exempt from state income taxes. If you happen to live in an area with a local income tax, you will be happy to know that it is exempt from these income taxes as well. People who live in states that do not impose an income tax will not benefit from this feature.

HH issues, like Series EE Bonds, are also not subject to capital gains taxes since there is no chance of a capital gain or capital loss.

Portfolio Fit

HH Bonds have a limited appeal. They are really only designed for someone who has Series EE Bonds that are about to mature and who does not want to pay taxes on their accreted interest. EE bondholders would not want to exchange into HH Bonds if they were in a low tax bracket at the time of EE Bond redemption. A low-tax-bracket investor may be better off paying any tax liability and then using the proceeds to go into one or another different investments.

Series HH Bonds, if you can acquire them, would be something worth considering as an alternative to a savings account that you did not use on a regular basis. The interest payments are often higher than the yield you can get with a traditional savings account. You will also discover that the rate of return provided by HH Bonds is higher than what you can get when CD rates are low.

Risks

There are no risks with Series HH Bonds. Like Series EE Bonds, there is no chance that they will not pay interest or principal upon sale or redemption, since they are fully backed by the federal government. Since they are not traded anywhere, there is also no interest-rate or market risk. Principal is stable at all times.

Unique Features

All that is special about these bonds is that they are about the only investment you cannot go out and buy. They are the only government issue that must be acquired by an exchange.

Comments

This investment would be a sound choice for the investor who cannot bear to see his or her bonds go up and down in value. Series EE and Series HH Bonds are the perfect choice for the individual or couple who likes the safety of CDs but does not want to be subject to a possible penalty, who likes the state and local income tax advantage that CDs do not offer, and who, during certain periods of time, wants to get a higher rate of return than that offered by CDs and money market accounts.

Additional Information

World Information Services—Department 3015
Bank of America, Box 37000, San Francisco, CA 94137. 800-645-6667.

Chase Manhattan Bank
One Chase Manhattan Plaza, New York, NY 10081. 212-552-2222.

Federal Reserve Bank of Dallas
Public Affairs Department, Station K, Dallas, TX 75222. 214-922-6000.

10
Municipal Bonds

Stability of principal	✔✔✔
Stability of income	✔✔✔✔✔
Protection against inflation	✔✔✔
Total return	✔✔
Tax benefits	✔✔✔

Definition

Municipal bonds are issued by states, counties, and municipalities as a means of financing public works such as street lights, libraries, roads, airports, etc. The municipality issues you a bond that represents its promise to pay the face amount of the bond when it matures, along with interest payments every six months. Apart from levying taxes and receiving funds from the federal government, this is the only way a municipality is able to raise money. One could say that municipalities are just like the U.S. government: they spend more than they take in and therefore have to issue bonds in order to help pay for some of these "excesses." (Almost all states have constitutions that require them to balance their budgets.)

Since you cannot own equity in a municipality, which means you cannot buy stock in a county or state, the municipality has no choice but to issue bonds or notes (these are like short-term bonds and mature in a year or less) if it wants to raise money other than through taxes and fees. Municipal bonds share many of the same characteristics of government and corporate bonds, but there are differences. These differences are described below.

How It Works

When you buy a municipal bond, the municipality (state, county, city, or political subdivision) makes an agreement with you. As long as you own the bond, the agreement is valid. If the issuer decides it cannot or will not pay you interest (every six months) or principal (when the bond matures), you have legal recourse. If the municipality lives up to its promises, that is, it agrees to pay you interest every six months and also pays you the face amount of your bond when it matures, then you cannot expect anything more or less.

For the privilege of using your money, the issuer (the municipality) will pay you a fee twice a year. This fee is called interest. (Stocks pay dividends, bonds pay interest.) You are entitled to receive interest for as long as you own the bond. Eventually, the bond comes due—the agreement ends. When the bond matures, the municipality will pay you the *face amount* of the bond.

The face amount paid may be more or less than what you paid for the security. If you end up receiving less than what you paid for the bond, this means that you originally paid a premium for it (you paid more than face value). If the value at maturity is more than what you bought the bond for, you got it at a discount (you paid less than face value). As odd as it might sound, discounts and premiums are not necessarily good or bad. Determining whether a purchase price was, in hindsight, a good or bad deal depends upon how much interest you received and how much you got at the end, when the bond came due. In other words, you want to look at the "whole enchilada"—the *total return*.

Advantages

There are five advantages to owning municipal bonds: safety, tax-free interest, comparative price stability, flexibility, and marketability. Next to obligations guaranteed or backed by the U.S. government and certain insurance policies and fixed-rate annuities, nothing is safer than municipal bonds. The default rate of municipal bonds has been extremely small since their introduction almost a half-century ago. Like other bonds, municipal securities pay interest twice a year; unlike other bonds, this interest is tax-free. There is also the benefit of relative price stability. When interest rates go up and down, so do the value of bonds; there is an inverse relationship between the value of a bond and interest rates. Municipal bonds, however, are less volatile, or susceptible, to interest-rate movements than corporate or U.S. government bonds with a similar maturity.

The fourth benefit of municipal bonds is flexibility. This feature is found with other bonds also. You can buy a municipal bond that matures in whatever number of years you desire. Thus, if you anticipate an event in fourteen years and you want the face value of the bonds to be available (to buy a retirement home or vehicle, to have vacation money, pay tuition bills, etc.), you can find tax-free bonds that mature in fourteen years. The final benefit of municipals is marketability. This means that if you ever want to sell your bond(s) before their natural maturity date, there is a large marketplace ready to buy them from you at a fair price. It takes less than five minutes to buy or sell a municipal bond, whether you are dealing with $5,000 worth of bonds or $5,000,000.

Disadvantages

Municipal bonds have only three disadvantages: price fluctuation, potential for default, and a chance of being "called away" from you. Municipal bonds go up and down in value. This does not mean that your interest rate or yield varies—it does not. In fact, if you do not plan on selling your municipal, or tax-free, bonds before they mature, then you probably need not be concerned with changing values. However, if an emergency arises, or you see a better investment opportunity, keep in mind that your purchase price may be higher or lower than your selling, or redemption, price.

When interest rates go up, the value of bonds go down; when rates fall, bond values (your principal, *not* your interest payment) increase. The amount of price variance depends upon how much rates increase and upon the *remaining* maturity of the bond. The greater the change in rates and maturity, the greater the price movement, for better or for worse. Fortunately, municipal bonds experience only one-half to one-third the fluctuations that similar corporate or government bonds experience. It may seem strange that municipals move up and down less than governments, but the reason for this is quite logical: demand versus supply. The high demand for tax-free bonds, compared to the outstanding supply, forces prices to change only modestly during any given year.

The second issue is that of default. Like all other investments, except those backed by or insured by the U.S. government or one of its agencies, there is always a chance that your municipal bond issuer may become a victim of troubled times. This risk can be avoided or minimized in one of two ways. First, you can buy municipal bonds that are insured, both as to the semiannual interest payments and face value at maturity. Insured municipal bonds are quite common. Second, you can limit your purchases to muni bonds that are highly rated (AAA, AA, A or BAA). If your comfort level necessitates your owning only AA-rated bonds and your tax-free issue has a rating change from AA to A, you can quickly sell the bond and buy a new security that is AA- or AAA-rated.

The issue of default is often blown out of proportion. Only a small fraction of 1 percent of all quality municipal bonds ever become troubled. Even then, this does not spell complete disaster. Studies indicate that defaulting bonds usually means that the investors lose about 25 percent of their principal, on average. No loss is "good," but these figures should at least make you feel quite a bit better.

The final potential disadvantage of municipal bonds has to do with what is known as a "call feature." Most municipal and many corporate bonds have this feature. If a bond has a call provision, it can be "called away" by the issuer (the municipality or corporation) before the bond's natural maturity date. Thus, you might buy a bond that matures in, say, 2015, and have it called away by the municipality in 2010, or 2005. A bond being called away is equivalent to a forced sale. Interest payments cease after the call date and you must turn your bond in at which time the issuer will pay you face value or a slight premium.

In order to protect yourself, ask your broker, at the time of purchase, if the bond you are buying has a call feature, and if so, what its provisions are (most bonds that have a call feature can't be called away during the first ten years of the bonds' life). A call feature is not a terrible thing, but it is something you should be aware of.

As you can see, the disadvantages to owning municipal bonds are slight and can be countered or minimized. The reasons why these bonds are not more popular are, first, ignorance (many people just don't know that they exist) and second, because they are less desirable for those in low tax brackets. Though munis sound appealing, not everyone should own them. The decision really depends upon your tax bracket and goals (see "Portfolio Fit").

How to Buy and Sell

You buy and sell municipal bonds just like you buy and sell corporate or government bonds: by seeing or telephoning your broker. Tax-free bonds are sold by brokerage firms, financial planners and advisors, municipal bond speciality houses, and even banks and savings and loan associations. Your counselor can show you a wide range of maturities (ranging anywhere from less than a year up to thirty years), yields (different returns on your investment), quality (from AAA all the way down to different grades of "junk bonds"), and prices (face value, also referred to as "par," "premiums," and "discounts").

The type, quality, maturity, price, and yield that are best for you can be determined by your financial expert. You may find that you know exactly what you want and do not need any outside counseling. One of the nice features of municipal bonds is that you do not pay a commission when you buy or sell them. The brokerage firm you deal with, whether it is a discount or full-service firm, will mark up the bonds (this is how they are compensated), but such a fee can be less than one-fourth of a point (less than a fourth of a percent). This fee, or charge, is very reasonable and will probably have very little, if any, effect on your return.

You can also own municipal bonds indirectly by buying a "packaged product" such as a municipal bond fund or unit trust. A bond fund allows you to move your money around within the fund family. Thus, if you later decide that munis are not for you, you can switch, for only $5, from the XYZ

Tax-Free Fund into the XYZ Growth Fund. A unit trust, also referred to as a unit investment trust (UIT), is a fixed portfolio of bonds that is not part of a "family." If you wish to get out of a UIT, you can do so without cost or fee, but your money would then have to be invested with another company or product. This is not a big concern, but it may be important to those investors who like the convenience of being able to move easily from one investment into another.

The decision as to whether you should own individual bonds, a unit trust, or fund will depend upon your particular circumstances. If you think that your tax bracket may be lower in the future, you should probably lean toward a fund. (You could switch into a government or corporate bond fund later by making one telephone call.) If professional, ongoing management is important, then funds and unit trusts should both be looked at. (Funds do have more active management, but problems with unit trusts are miniscule.) If you think interest rates are going to go down and you want to sell your bonds at a profit, than you will see your greatest appreciation with individual issues.

Tracking Performance
The value of a unit trust or fund can be quickly determined by telephoning the company's toll-free number. During business hours on any given day, the fund or unit trust group will be happy to tell you the buying and selling price of your units or shares. (When you buy a fund you own shares; when you purchase a UIT you own units.)

Finding out the value of your individual bonds is a little more difficult. Your broker or advisor can certainly do the legwork for you, or you can look in the newspaper. Many newspapers cover a very small number of municipal issues. By seeing how these bonds are doing, you will have a good idea as to how you are doing. If the muni bonds listed are up one point for the day, your bonds are probably up (increased in value) about $10 per bond (one point equals $10; one half-point equals $5). Again, this is only important if you decide to sell your bonds before they mature.

Historical Performance
Municipal bonds have been in existence for dozens of years. Yields on tax-free issues have moved up and down in a fashion similar to other government or corporate bonds.

The 1980s was an extremely good decade for municipal bonds. The combination of high current yields and falling interest rates (appreciation of principal) provided munis with total returns that have not been seen before or since.

Tax Considerations
When you own a bond, there are two tax considerations: taxation of interest

and gains or losses resulting from the sale of the security. Like other bonds, municipals pay interest every six months. Interest received from munis is exempt from federal income taxes. If you own a bond that was issued in your state of residence, it is also exempt from any state and local taxes. The only exceptions to this exemption are "private issue" bonds (securities issued by the private sector, a corporation) and a few states that tax certain municipal bonds issued within their state. Private-issue bonds are rare, and instances of a state not recognizing the tax-exempt status of some of its issues are even rarer. Still, to be on the safe side, always ask your broker whether the interest from the bond you are thinking of buying is free from state and federal income taxes.

The second tax consideration is what happens when you sell or redeem a bond for a price different from what you paid for it. After all, you may buy a bond for $930 and sell it later for $1,000. Conversely, if you paid $1,300 for a bond and it is sold for $850, there is a capital loss. A sales price different from the purchase price means that a taxable event has been triggered. The interest income remains tax-free; it is the proceeds from the sale that cause a tax event. If you sell or redeem a bond for more than you paid for it, this translates into a capital gain. If the proceeds are less than the original purchase price, it is a capital loss. Gains or losses must be reported on your tax return for the calendar year in which the bond(s) were sold. Appreciation or depreciation is not taxable until the bonds are actually sold.

Many people are under the mistaken belief that everything about municipal bonds is tax-free. As you now know, nothing is free but the interest payments. Still, ever since 1986, munis remain one of the few "tax-shelters" and, in some respects, the only true form of tax-free income.

Portfolio Fit

Municipal bonds are an attractive addition to a wide range of portfolios. For the aggressive investor, they are a way to tone down the overall volatility of a portfolio. For the moderate investor they are a way of seeing growth through the reinvestment of tax-free interest payments. For the conservative investor, munis provide a reliable source of income that does not go up or down.

Speaking of stability of principal, you should know that the income stream from a tax-free bond fund or unit trust will fluctuate; sometimes for the better, sometimes for the worse. The variations are due to a changing portfolio. In the case of a bond fund, new issues are being added all the time as investors add or redeem shares. When new money is added to a fund or a bond in the fund's portfolio is redeemed or is "called away" (that is, sold back to the municipality whether the holder likes it or not), it is replaced by another bond. This new bond may have a yield a little higher or lower than what it is replacing. The "replacements" are added to the existing portfolio, slightly altering the current yield. As interest rates move upward, so will your return in a bond fund. When rates drop, so do yields on muni funds.

A unit trust is different than a fund. A unit trust is a fixed portfolio of bonds. The yield on unit trusts change when a bond is either *called away* by the issuer or redeemed. In the case of a unit trust, the bond is not replaced. Proceeds from the bond(s) no longer in the portfolio are distributed to the unit holders, you and everyone else who owns this particular unit trust. As you might suspect, when a bond, or series of bonds, are removed from the trust, the yield goes down by a very small amount. This is because bonds are not called away by the issuer unless the municipality can issue a new security at a lower rate. This fact does not make unit trusts better or worse than individual bonds or funds, it just makes them different.

Getting back to the issue of portfolio fit, if you are not an active investor, you will be better off with a unit trust or fund. These portfolios are professionally managed. When you own an individual bond, there is always the chance that it will be called away, increase or decrease in value, or have its rating changed without your immediate knowledge. Individual bonds are probably best for the investor who wants a known maturity date.

Whatever you decide, never make municipal bonds part of a qualified retirement plan. Everything in a Keogh, pension, profit-sharing, or IRA is fully taxable when it is withdrawn (taken out by you). The IRS does not, and will not, make a distinction just because you did not know any better. In fact, the only thing not taxed when it is withdrawn from a retirement account by you or your beneficiaries is the portion considered a "return of after-tax dollars" (contributions that were not deductible when they went in). Only a small percentage of retirees are affected by this exemption, and so we will not go into any greater detail as to how it works.

Risks
For practical purposes, if you choose a good-quality muni, unit trust, or fund, your only real risk is potential loss of purchasing power; 6-, 7-, or 8-percent tax-free may sound wonderful, but if inflation is 10, 11, or 12 percent, you are losing purchasing power. It can be difficult even to *imagine* that inflation will ever reach these levels in the U.S. And yet unlikely as this situation is, it is still something that you should at least be conscious of, since we saw such inflation levels in the early 1980s.

Unique Features
The tax-free interest is the unique feature of municipal bonds. That munis are less volatile than government or corporate bonds of similar maturity is also somewhat special. When all is said and done, it is the *real return* of this investment that makes it different from other debt instruments. Once you

subtract the effects of taxes and inflation from most bond investments, the return is often negative or only slightly positive. When you own municipal bonds, the real return is often positive by two or three percentage points.

Comments

Municipal bonds make sense for moderate and conservative investors alike. The tax-free interest coupled with reduced volatility makes this a solid choice. Many investors at or near retirement find munis to be a worry-free investment. As you can now see, their belief is well-founded.

One of the most overlooked areas of municipal bonds is the "high-yield," also known as the "junk bond," sector. When most investors think of junk or high-yield bonds, the first thing that comes to their minds is "high risk." Although this can certainly be the case when you are talking about low-rated corporate bonds, the same thing cannot really be said for municipals rated below investment grade or simply NR (not rated).

High-yield tax-free issues, like their corporate peers, have different ratings, and, as with junk corporate bonds, there are certainly categories that should be avoided. Nevertheless, if you stick to the top two or three grades of junk, you should be amply rewarded for the additional risk. High-yield munis have a current yield about $1\frac{1}{2}$ points higher than an A, AA, or AAA tax-free issue. This enhanced yield, an increase in return of over 20 percent ($6.5\% \times 1.20 = 7.8\%$, which is what high-yield tax-frees were yielding at the time this book was written), also provides a second advantage to the investor: less volatility during normal economic conditions. The higher the yield of a bond, the less it will fluctuate when interest rates go up or down.

The percentage of defaults seen in the junk sector of tax-frees is much smaller than what high-yield corporate bonds have experienced. What makes high-yield tax-frees somewhat of a hidden treasure is that they have been painted with the same brush that has tainted certain corporate bonds. It is for this reason that investors who are in a moderate or high tax bracket should consider diversifying their tax-free portfolios with some bonds that offer a higher yield. Because of the increased financial risk, it is recommended that these bonds be purchased within a unit trust or fund where experts can constantly evaluate the economic environment and the financial well-being of the issuers.

Additional Information

One of the best ways to learn about municipal bonds is to contact specialists in the area of individual issues, funds, and unit trusts. You may also wish to contact one or more of the following:

John Nuveen & Company, Inc.
333 W. Wacker Drive, Chicago, IL 60606. 800-351-4100.

SteinRoe & Farnham
P.O. Box 1143, Chicago, IL 60690. 800-338-2550.

USAA Investment Management Co.
USAA Building, San Antonio, TX 78284. 800-531-8181.

Van Kampen Merritt Investment Advisory
1 Parkview Road, Oakbrook Terrace, IL 60181. 800-225-2222.

11
GNMAs

Stability of principal	✔✔✔
Stability of income	✔✔✔✔
Protection against inflation	✔✔✔
Total return	✔✔
Tax benefits	✔

Definition

GNMA stands for Government National Mortgage Association. These securities are a kind of bond backed by the U.S. government. They are considered an *indirect* obligation of the federal government. GNMAs are issued by a corporation created by Congress. Interest on these obligations is paid monthly. They have an average maturity of fourteen to sixteen years. Interest and principal is guaranteed by the government. Each monthly payment represents interest and principal.

How It Works

When you purchase a GNMA, you are buying a small interest in a pool of mortgages. These mortgages originate at banks and savings and loan associations. Home mortgages that fulfill stringent GNMA requirements can be packaged in $1,000,000 pools and sold to GNMA. The GNMA corporation then reviews this pool of mortgages and, if everything looks fine, sends the original lender a check. The lender now has a new source of money that can be lent out to other borrowers. This lender, the bank or savings and loan association, continues to service the loans, receiving a servicing fee from GNMA.

GNMA packages these home loans into what are known as "pools." A pool represents $1,000,000 worth of high-quality loans. GNMA then sells these pools to financial institutions and their clients. Investors buy an interest in a GNMA pool and, in return, receive income on a regular basis. As the mortgages in the pool are paid down, either very slowly by amortization or rapidly by a refinance or sale, investors receive back their principal.

GNMAs are a good deal for lenders, the GNMA people, and the investing public for several reasons. First, this full-circle process (packaging loans, sending them off to Washington, DC, getting a check back, and then lending out new money) allows lenders to process and service more loans. The lender makes money by charging the mortgager (the person who wants to buy a house) fees and points for the loan. The lender receives a fee for servicing the loan once GNMA purchases it. Finally, the lender has up to ninety days to send the mortgage payments into GNMA. (Borrowers do not know that their loan has been sold to GNMA and therefore continue to make payments to the original lender; this does not represent an advantage or disadvantage for the borrower.)

GNMAs are also a good deal for the country and the federal government. First, the GNMA corporation is a kind of broker. The money it sends back to the original lenders is obtained by selling the GNMA securities in the secondary marketplace (via brokerage firms to people like you and me). Second, the loans are quite safe, since GNMA has stringent requirements; it will not accept a bank's or savings and loan association's mortgages unless certain criteria are met. Third, GNMAs allow Americans a way of obtaining financing that is less expensive than other sources of funding. When mortgage money is cheap, home ownership becomes more attractive. People buy more houses, communities become more stable (pride of ownership), the tax base increases (property taxes) and employment goes up (it takes labor and resources to build and maintain a home).

Finally, GNMAs are a good deal for investors. They provide an investment different from others offered by the U.S. government and its agencies (see "Advantages" below).

Advantages

There are numerous advantages to owning GNMAs. First, unlike traditional bonds, which pay interest semiannually, GNMAs pay interest every month. Second, the interest payments are backed by their underlying mortgages and the U.S. government. Third, monthly payments are enhanced, since each check includes a portion that represents principal. This, by the way, is exactly what happens if you have ever owned a piece of indebted property. You make monthly payments to a local lender. In the early years of the loan, the great majority of each one of your checks represents interest and only a small part is the repayment of principal. In the later years, an increasing portion of each payment represents principal. Now just imagine that you are on the other side of the table—becoming the lender instead of the borrower. As homeowners are paying you off (in an indirect manner, since they pay their local bank first, which in turn pays GNMA), the early checks that you receive represent mostly interest and only a small amount goes to repaying the actual loan. As the loan matures, the exact opposite happens. This distinction is important for tax purposes (see below).

Even though you are acting as sort of a lender, you do not need to worry about late payments or defaults. GNMA makes payments directly to you each month. If there is a problem with one or more mortgages in your particular pool, you will never know—nor need to know. Investors are not rewarded or punished for delinquent borrowers. This represents an advantage mentioned at the beginning of the previous paragraph—government backing. Not only does GNMA itself have a great deal of money, it also has the authority to borrow several billion dollars from the Treasury if necessary.

Another advantage of GNMAs is their marketability. There are many billions of dollars worth of GNMAs outstanding. A number of investors are already familiar with these securities, and so are all financial institutions. Their popularity makes them very easy to buy and sell.

The yield offered by GNMAs is also appealing. When you buy a GNMA, chances are that you will get a return that is $^1/_2$ to 1 percent higher than that offered by Treasury Bonds with a similar maturity. The final advantage of GNMAs is that they have the potential to appreciate in value. You can buy a GNMA for, say, $25,000 (which is considered a normal trading block among individual investors), and possibly sell it for a profit of a few hundred or thousand dollars. Like other debt instruments, GNMAs increase in value when interest rates fall. This gain becomes a profit only if the GNMAs are sold before their maturity and when interest rates are lower than at the time of purchase.

Disadvantages

The disadvantages to owning GNMAs are as numerous as the advantages. First, unlike other instruments backed by the federal government, GNMAs are fully taxable on a local, state, and national basis. Second, their appreciation potential is somewhat limited. When interest rates fall a couple of percentage points, people refinance their mortgages. When a refinancing or sale (the typical family moves every five to seven years) occurs, the mortgage is removed from the pool. (Investors do not lose any principal when this happens because GNMA distributes principal back to the owners of any affected pool.) At first this may not sound like a disadvantage, but it is. When interest rates fall, you do not want to have to reinvest part or all of your money in new securities that provide a lower yield. If you own $25,000 of a GNMA pool that has just had a paydown of principal representing $2,000, in your particular case, you do not want to go out and reinvest that $2,000 for, say 8 percent instead of the 10 percent you were getting (and are still getting on the remaining $23,000). Unfortunately, you have no choice. If GNMA sends you a check, you cannot send it back and ask them to reinvest it.

You can now begin to see why the "upside potential" of GNMAs is limited. When interest rates drop enough, people will refinance their mortgages, stripping them out of different GNMA pools. Yet the reverse is not true—GNMAs do not have limited downside risk. When interest rates go up, and bond prices, as well as GNMA prices, drop, people do not refinance their loan. No one wants to pay more on his or her mortgage. If rates go up several points, the price of existing GNMAs and bonds can drop by quite a bit. True, these are only paper losses, and such losses are said to be "real" only if one were to sell at that time, but don't you believe it. If I buy a stock for $14 a share and it goes down $2 a share, my net worth has decreased by that amount, whether I sell it or not. The same analogy holds true with bonds, real estate, and GNMAs that are now worth more or less than what was paid for them.

A further disadvantage of GNMAs has to do with disciplined investing. As you recall, each check you receive from GNMA represents interest and principal. The principal portions are small every month for the first several years. Many investors have a tendency to spend the entire check. They either forget or regard the amounts as negligible; don't let this happen to you. Remember, when you get back principal, you are getting back part of your original investment. Ideally, that money, small as it may seem at first, should be reinvested somewhere else. Most people who buy bonds or other investments are used to getting back all of their principal upon maturity or sale; this is not true in the case of GNMAs.

How to Buy and Sell

GNMAs are bought and sold through brokerage firms and financial planning firms. It takes less than five minutes to buy or sell a GNMA, no matter how large or small the order is; in order to get the best prices, make sure your broker gets competitive bids from several dealers.

GNMAs are sold at market prices. This means that they can fluctuate in value during any given day. The price you pay includes the purchase price and any accumulated interest. GNMAs accumulate interest for up to thirty days and no longer, since payments are made monthly. If you sell a GNMA, you will receive the going market price for that day plus any accrued interest you are entitled to.

GNMAs are originally sold in $25,000 increments. These increments, or "blocks," are part of a $1,000,000 pool. You are free to buy as much of any one or more pools as is available. GNMAs can also be purchased in the secondary market. This means that your broker can buy you a "seasoned" GNMA (one previously issued and now available for sale again in the secondary market). If you buy a seasoned GNMA, always ask what the purchase price will be and what the remaining value of your share in the pool represents. An example will clarify this very important point.

Let us suppose that new GNMAs are paying 9 percent and your broker phones you up and says that she has some GNMAs that are paying 11 percent and that the purchase price is only $19,000. This, at first, sounds great. You are thinking that you will be getting a top yield and a discount price to boot. Unfortunately, you are wrong on both counts. You are actually paying a *premium* for these GNMAs, and your true yield is probably only in the 9-percent range. This is because the share of the pool you are buying into is worth about $16,500; over the remaining life of the pool, you will be receiving principal payments that total $16,500, not $19,000. The reason some people are willing to pay $19,000 in order to end up with $16,500 eventually is that their current interest payments, or checks, are higher. The current yield may indeed be 11 percent, but the yield to maturity (yield to maturity amortizes any discount, or in this case, premium, over the remaining life of the security) is right around 9 percent (the premium purchase price pulls down the current yield).

The example described above is not necessarily bad. It is a wise strategy if your biggest concern is immediate income or if you have a good alternate investment for the monthly payments. It is a poor idea if you thought you were going to make some kind of "killing."

GNMAs can also be purchased indirectly by buying shares of a mutual fund or units of a unit trust that contains these securities. Unit trusts can be purchased with as little as $1,000; several mutual funds have a minimum purchase of only $250. In order to determine what percentage of a mutual fund or unit trust's holdings are made up of GNMAs, review the prospectus, ask your broker, or contact the fund or unit trust's marketing division. Often the name of the fund or unit trust will give you a good indication as to whether it contains GNMAs (for example, The XYZ Government Securities Fund or the ABC Mortgage-Backed Unit Trust).

Tracking Performance

Hundreds of millions of dollars of GNMAs are traded each day; sometimes the figures are in the billions. You can find out how your GNMA is doing by looking in the newspaper or telephoning your broker. He or she can get you a bid (selling price) or ask (purchase price) at any time during the trading day.

If your GNMA certificates are held at a brokerage firm, your monthly or quarterly statement will also reflect an *approximate* market price. You should be careful about brokerage firm statements when it comes to GNMAs or bonds of any kind. These statement figures are often exaggerated by several percentage points, not because the firm is trying to mislead you but because the pricing, or value, is based on the entire $1,000,000 pool. Smaller amounts, which is what almost every individual investor owns, are not worth as much. Perhaps the brokerage industry will someday correct this frustrating situation.

Historical Performance

GNMAs have been around since the 1930s. The yield, or return, on GNMAs has generally gone up and down with the returns on other government and high-quality corporate bonds with similar maturities. During a given year, when the level of interest rates falls several points, GNMAs can appreciate nicely. Conversely, when rates go up a couple of points, the value of a GNMA will drop. These rises and drops are only paper profits or losses, but we would all prefer to see gains on our statements instead of losses.

Tax Considerations

The interest portion of each check you receive is fully taxable. It is considered interest income and should be included on your state and federal tax returns. Though GNMAs are issued by an agency of the U.S. government, they are not exempt from any state or local income taxes.

GNMAs are also subject to capital gains or losses. If you sell a GNMA for more than you paid for it, there is a capital gain. If the GNMA is sold for less than the purchase price, once adjusted for any return of principal, then there is a capital loss.

The issue of interest and capital gains taxation can be avoided, or at least postponed, if the GNMA is part of a qualified retirement plan or within a variable annuity. This is something you should discuss with your tax or financial planning advisor. For most investors, the current taxation of the monthly payments is the concern. This liability can be minimized by owning GNMAs issued ten or more years ago. A seasoned GNMA will often throw off more principal than interest each month. And as you may recall, the principal portion is not taxable.

Portfolio Fit

Since GNMAs throw off a rather large amount of fully taxable interest each month, they are best used as part of a qualified retirement plan. The IRA, Keogh, pension plan, etc. will shelter the interest income.

Individuals and couples who are in a low tax bracket will find GNMAs very appealing as a source of monthly income that is both safe and reliable. If you are in a high tax bracket and are not able, or willing, to shelter your GNMA income, look into seasoned issues that provide high levels of principal and competitive levels of interest. Seasoned GNMAs can provide you with yields similar to new issues and are less volatile than new issues. This is because they have shorter remaining maturities and are not as susceptible to interest-rate movements in the bond market. Thus, seasoned GNMAs are a good portfolio fit for the ultra-conservative investor. New issues are best for someone who will not get excited or depressed about increases and decreases in principal as interest rates fall and climb—in short, the investor who does not plan on trading.

Risks

The only real risk of GNMAs is interest-rate risk. This is the risk associated with medium (five-to-fifteen-year maturity) and long-term (fifteen or more years) debt instruments such as government securities, corporate bonds, municipal issues, and GNMAs. In these cases, again, the interest-rate risk (when the general level of interest rates goes up, GNMA prices fall, and vice versa) can be greatly reduced by having your stockbroker seek out seasoned issues that are expected to have a remaining life of less than eight years.

There is no risk of default or late payments, since GNMA is backed by the full faith and credit of the U.S. government, not to mention the diversified, high-quality portfolio of mortgages that provides the first level of default defense.

Unique Features

GNMAs are the only investment backed by the federal government that pays monthly income. The fact that the investor is receiving payments made up of interest and principal is somewhat special but certainly not unique.

Comments

For *disciplined* investors in a low tax bracket, this is a very good investment. I say "disciplined investors" because people frequently spend the entire monthly check, giving little or no thought to the fact that they are also spending part of their principal—albeit very slowly. High-bracket tax payers who want federal backing may be better off with government bonds and notes, two instruments that are free from state and local income taxes.

Additional Information

Federated Investors
Federated Investors Tower, 1001 Liberty Ave, Pittsburgh, PA 15222.
800-245-5000.

Putnam Financial Services
P.O. Box 41203, Providence, RI 02904. 800-225-1581.

Shearson Lehman Advisors
388 Greenwich Street, 37th Floor, New York, NY 10013. 212-298-2000.

GNMA
451 7th Street SW, Room 6100, Washington, DC 20410. 202-708-0926.

12
FNMAs

Stability of principal	✓✓✓
Stability of income	✓✓✓✓
Protection against inflation	✓✓✓
Total return	✓✓
Tax benefits	✓

Definition

The Federal National Mortgage Association (FNMA) was created in 1938 as an offshoot of GNMA (Government National Mortgage Association). Both entities exist in order to help homeowners obtain mortgage money more readily. FNMA is not directly backed by the U.S. government. Instead, this quasi-government entity (actually it is a private corporation) is funded by issuing FNMA bonds. Additionally, FNMA has the ability to borrow up to $5 billion from the U.S. Treasury if the need ever arises.

Like GNMA, FNMA was created as a source of funds for people who wish to buy a home and qualify for a FNMA or GNMA loan (good credit standing, a loan amount up to $202,300, etc.). A greater supply of money makes borrowing easier and more likely. This, in turn, creates greater demand for homes, which helps the housing industry.

How It Works

When FNMA decides it needs additional monies, it goes to the public and floats (sells) new bonds (IOUs). People and institutions lend FNMA money by purchasing these IOUs, receiving interest every month. FNMA pays investors interest on these borrowed funds from the interest it collects from FNMA borrowers (homeowners who have opted for a FNMA loan). Monthly mortgage payments are actually collected by participating banks (where the loan originated) and passed onto FNMA. In return for originating and servicing the loan, the bank or other lender collects a small fee from each

79

homeowner's monthly payment before it is sent onto FNMA.

FNMA, a private corporation created by Congress, is like any other corporation in that it has the power and the ability to issue corporate debt (bonds). The bonds have an *original issue* maturity that ranges anywhere from one to thirty years. The investor (you, an institution, brokerage firm, etc.) can choose to buy these securities if the price appears fair, the yield seems good, and/or the remaining maturity is acceptable. Like any other kind of bond, FNMAs can be bought or sold at any time prior to their natural maturity in the secondary marketplace.

When you buy a FNMA, your security is identified by a pool number. This "pool number" represents a specific pool of mortgages in a certain part of the country. The location of these home loans is unimportant, since all loans in the pool had to meet stringent FNMA requirements before money was ever lent. FNMA reviews all loans submitted to it by lenders such as banks. A loan is not packaged within a pool unless it is approved by FNMA.

Advantages

FNMAs have three advantages: a high degree of marketability, tremendous safety, and monthly income. The difference in safety between a FNMA and a GNMA security is negligible. Neither entity has ever defaulted or delayed a payment to an investor. Furthermore, the marketplace, the ultimate determiner of safety and similarity, usually prices FNMAs such that their yield advantage over a GNMA is 0.25 percent *or less*. Although FNMAs can offer a return that is only up to a fourth of a percentage point higher than GNMAs, the public is still attracted to this private corporation. There are tens of billions of dollars of outstanding FNMAs.

Like GNMAs, FNMAs are pass-through, mortgage-backed securities. Each month the owner of a FNMA bond receives a check representing interest and principal. During the early years of the loan (or bond), almost the entire payment is interest and only a very small portion represents capital. As the loan begins to mature, a greater and greater portion of each check is principal. This is why they are called "pass through"; the borrower's mortgage payment passes through to the investor (you or whoever owns the FNMA bond). These are "mortgage backed," since the loans are secured (collateralized) by the underlying mortgages.

Disadvantages

FNMAs have two disadvantages: uncertainty as to when the security will be fully paid off and marketplace changes in value. As you will see, these two points are not always disadvantages.

As you recall, FNMAs, like GNMAs, are made up of thirty-year mortgages, and like any other kind of mortgage, these can be paid off early. People pay off mortgages early because they have either sold their home or decided to refinance it. Either event will remove the mortgage from the pool. When a mortgage is removed, it is not replaced. Instead, the owners (investors) of that pool receive an additional amount of principal in their next monthly check. This "one-time" addition represents the investor's pro-rata share of the pool. I say "one-time" because other homeowners in the pool may also decide to refinance or sell their homes, causing another partial "return of principal."

The history of FNMA and GNMA pools has shown that these securities have an average, original-issue life of fifteen years. Even though the underlying mortgages are all thirty years, the selling and refinancing of homes is such that these pools do not last thirty years. For better or worse, the investor cannot control the duration of the pool. In short, you cannot tell a homeowner when he or she can sell or refinance.

The reason this "prepayment potential" is usually considered a disadvantage is that it is almost always done when interest rates are falling. After all, who wants to refinance at a higher rate? I say "almost always" because people buy and sell homes whether rates are going up or down. However, it is also true that the housing market likes low rates, which, in turn, increases the likelihood of a sale or purchase. Thus, when rates are falling and you, the FNMA investor, want as much of your principal to continue earning a high rate of interest as long as possible, little can be done if several homeowners in your pool decide to sell or refinance. True, such an event means that you will be getting back principal, but you will not be able to get the same rate of return. If rates are falling, so are returns on securities such as FNMAs and GNMAs.

The second potential disadvantage of FNMAs (and GNMAs) is also related to interest-rate changes. As you now know, when interest rates go up, the value of bonds and mortgage-backed securities falls. The converse is also true: when rates fall, investors' principal increases. Interest rates are a double-edged sword, in that when they are falling, people like to see the value of their bonds and other fixed-rate instruments increase. The drop in yields is a negative because people who own short-term debt instruments (bank CDs, money market accounts, and bonds that are maturing within several months) will get a smaller return on their money when principal is reinvested.

How to Buy and Sell
FNMAs, like GNMAs, can be bought and sold through brokerage firms, certain banks, financial planners, investment advisors, or anyone who has a securities license. These mortgage-backed securities are originally sold for $25,000. Seasoned FNMAs and GNMAs can be purchased or sold in the secondary marketplace for more or less than $25,000 (more if the pool is still relatively new and interest rates have fallen; less if rates have fallen and/or a certain amount of principal has already been returned to the current investor).

As a general rule, if you own a FNMA and interest rates are lower now than when you purchased the instrument, there will be some appreciation. Some of this appreciation may be offset by the amount of principal that has been returned to you over the previous months. As an example, if you bought a new GNMA for $25,000 and decided to sell it a few years later, after you had been receiving monthly interest and principal that totaled a few thousand dollars, you should not expect to get $25,000 for the investment. After all, you have already received a competitive rate of interest along with some of your principal. Thus, you might get something in the neighborhood of $23,000. The exact figure is difficult to pin down unless the current level of interest rates is known and the exact amount of the paydown in the pool is determined.

Because of their tremendous popularity, it takes less than five minutes to buy or sell these securities. The value of a FNMA or GNMA depends upon three things: the general level of interest rates, the remaining maturity of the security (how much life is left in the underlying pool of mortgages), and the coupon rate (yield) of the mortgages in the pool.

If you do not have $25,000, you can buy a seasoned FNMA or GNMA. This means that you will be buying a mortgage-backed security that was issued several years ago. There is nothing wrong with this kind of purchase. Your broker may phone you and say, "I have a FNMA you can buy for $5,000. It has a current yield of 8 percent and a remaining life of six years. The remaining face value is $5,200. This means that you can buy it at a discount" (pay $5,000 and eventually get back a total of $5,200 in principal plus 8 percent worth of interest along the way). Whenever you buy a FNMA or GNMA, make sure that you find out what the remaining face value is; sometimes people *unknowingly* buy one of these securities at a premium, paying, say, $12,000 for something that has a remaining value of $10,600.

Investors are sometimes attracted to FNMAs and GNMAs selling at a premium because they will be getting a higher current yield. If you want to maximize your current income, such a strategy may appeal to you. Just keep in mind that higher-than-normal returns come at a price: your cumulative returns of principal will be less than your purchase price.

Tracking Performance

You can get a good idea as to how your FNMA is doing by seeing how long-term U.S. government bonds are performing. If you hear that rates on government bonds are down, this means that your FNMA has gone up in value. Conversely, if yields on the bellwether, thirty-year government bond are up, this means that prices (or values) are down for the day. Remember that there is an inverse relationship between bond (and mortgage-backed securities) prices and interest rates: when one goes up, the other always goes down.

To get a more exact value of your FNMA, you can look up its value in the newspaper each morning. An easier way is to telephone the brokerage firm where you bought the security and find out its current value. Monthly or quarterly brokerage firm statements will show you the approximate value. Be careful of your monthly statements, however. When it comes to pricing bonds or mortgage-backed securities, the prices shown on statements are notoriously optimistic. The actual value of the FNMA, GNMA, or bond is usually 1 to 10 percent less than what is quoted. I did even see one case where the value was overstated by close to 25 percent, but 5 percent is more the norm.

Historical Performance

The track record of FNMAs has been pretty much the same as long-term bonds. They declined in value by almost 50 percent between 1975 and 1981 before appreciating substantially during the balance of the 1980s and early 1990s. FNMAs went up in value more in the 1980s than any other decade. Their performance for the rest of the 1990s will depend upon how much interest rates increase or decrease.

Tax Considerations

The interest portion of each FNMA payment is fully taxable on a state and federal level, but any return of principal is not taxed. GNMA and FNMA bondholders are given annual summaries for income tax purposes. (The portion of each check that represents a return of capital is not taxable.)

If you sell a FNMA for a premium, the amount that represents the premium is taxed as a capital gain. If a FNMA is sold for a loss (once an adjustment has been made for all principal repayments), a capital loss will result.

Portfolio Fit

FNMAs, like GNMAs, are a good choice for someone who wants monthly income that will fluctuate. (When principal is paid down, the check will be larger than normal, but there will then be less remaining balance, so the remaining monthly checks will be lower.) Since FNMAs can be bought in the secondary marketplace, investors can purchase these instruments with a remaining maturity that coincides with a specific event, such as retirement, college education, etc.

If you think interest rates are going to increase, then only FNMAs with a remaining life of five years or less should be considered. A short-term maturity means that your investment will drop little in value if rates do decline. Equally important, any such paper loss will only be temporary, since the FNMA will be maturing within a few years. (The last few years of a FNMA's life are made up mostly of principal, so repayment is much quicker than expected.)

Risks

There are two risks to owning FNMAs and GNMAs. First, as mentioned in the chapter on GNMAs, there is the risk that the investor will spend each monthly check, thereby slowly spending his or her capital. It is important to remember that these mortgage-backed securities, unlike traditional bonds, pay back principal, not just interest, on a regular basis. The second risk has also been discussed—interest-rate risk. (When rates go up, the value of a FNMA and GNMA will drop.) This risk can be minimized by sticking to pass-through securities that are seasoned (purchased in the secondary market) and have only about five to seven years left before they fully mature. Short-term debt instruments do not move up and down in value very much; they are largely insulated from changes in interest rates.

Unique Features

FNMAs are very similar to GNMAs. Like GNMAs, they pay interest (and some principal) monthly. Apart from mutual funds, an investment that makes monthly payments is not very common. The modest degree of unpredictability (resulting from mortgages being removed from the pool) is also unique to this and other mortgage-backed securities.

Comments

FNMAs are a good choice for the current-income-oriented investor. They are particularly appropriate for someone who does not mind spending (or reinvesting) part of his or her principal each month. This "principal kicker" gives an extra boost of money to someone who wants to maximize his or her income.

If you do not know which way interest rates are going, and you are concerned with daily or monthly fluctuations of your underlying principal, stick to short-term (remaining maturity of five years or less) or intermediate-term (remaining life of six to fifteen years) FNMAs. By sacrificing a little bit of your income (FNMAs that mature in twenty to thirty years pay more interest than their shorter-term brethren), you will see more stability of income and perhaps sleep a little better at night.

Additional Information

Oppenheimer Shareholders Services
P.O. Box 300, Denver, CO 80201. 800-525-7048.

IDS Financial Services, Inc.
P.O. Box 534, Minneapolis, MN 55440. 800-328-8300.

FNMA
Public Information Office, 3900 Wisconsin Avenue NW, Washington, DC 20016. 202-752-7000.

13
Adjustable-Rate GNMAs and FNMAs

Stability of principal	✔✔✔✔
Stability of income	✔✔✔
Protection against inflation	✔✔✔
Total return	✔✔
Tax benefits	

Definition

GNMAs and FNMAs are mortgage-participation certificates wherein the investor is entitled to interest and amortized principal repayments each month. Commonly referred to as "pass-through" securities (the interest and principal payment pass directly to the investor), these instruments are issued by government or "quasi-government" agencies. GNMAs, the Government National Mortgage Association, are backed by the full faith and credit of the U.S. government. FNMAs, Federal National Mortgage Association, is a private corporation that works closely with the federal government and has the ability to borrow billions of dollars from the Treasury if an emergency were to arise.

Adjustable-rate means that investors' yield will go up or down with the general level of interest rates. The adjustments are made on a semiannual basis and reflect a return slightly lower than that offered by standard GNMAs and FNMAs at the time.

How It Works

When you buy a home and obtain a mortgage, you then start making monthly mortgage payments to the lender. What you may not know is that the lender may have taken your loan, packaged it with a number of other mortgages, and sent that "package" on to GNMA or FNMA. If FNMA or GNMA determines that this $1,000,000 package of loans fulfills their criteria for safety and suitability, they will send the lender a check for $1,000,000. The lender continues to process your loan each month, sending your check either to GNMA or FNMA. Your original lender keeps any points collected and receives a servicing fee from GNMA or FNMA each month. Once a lender gets back the $1,000,000 check, it now has more money to lend out to other borrowers. The homeowner has no knowledge, nor does he or she care, what has transpired; the terms and conditions of the loan have not changed.

When you buy a GNMA or FNMA, you are investing in a pool of high-quality mortgages in a certain region of the country. These pools are $1,000,000 in size, and you can buy as much of the pool as is available. Each pool is assigned a number for processing and marketability purposes. It is your investment money that allows these two institutions to stay in business; you are their banker. Once the loans are up and running, the monthly payments, which are largely passed onto the investors, keep things afloat.

Since traditional home loans have original durations of thirty years, GNMA and FNMA loans do too. One would then think that the length of this investment would also be thirty years. In theory, the GNMA or FNMA could end up lasting that long. However, extensive experience has shown that the typical GNMA or FNMA has a life of approximately fifteen years. This is because people refinance or sell homes on a fairly regular basis. A sale or refinance removes the mortgage from the pool. The GNMA or FNMA investor then receives a monthly check that reflects interest, principal, and any paid-off mortgages. An example may be helpful at this point.

Let us suppose that you bought $100,000 of GNMA pool #200673; this purchase would represent 10 percent of the entire pool ($1,000,000 x 10% = $100,000). Let us further assume that the pool had a current yield of 9 percent. This means that each month you would receive a check for $750 (interest) plus a nominal amount of principal ($100,000 amortized over thirty years translates into only a few dollars each month during the early years of the pool or loan). Finally, let us assume that three homeowners in pool #200673 sell their homes; the total amount of the three mortgages being paid off equals $200,000. If this were the case, the pool would now only have a remaining balance of $800,000. As a part-owner in this pool, two things will happen to you. First, your monthly payments will drop by 20 percent, since the pool is now 20 percent smaller. Second, your next check will also include a one-time additional payment of $20,000 (the $200,000 being paid off multiplied by your 10-percent interest in the pool).

Adjustable GNMAs and FNMAs are just like traditional GNMAs and FNMAs as described in the paragraph above with one important difference: the rate of return may fluctuate every six months, excluding amortized principal payments and any pool size reduction. A homeowner who opts for an adjustable-rate mortgage may end up paying more or less each month than someone else who chose a fixed-rate mortgage. As the indirect "lender," this means that your rate of return will also fluctuate. Unlike the homeowner, you hope that rates go up so that the monthly checks you receive will also go up.

Advantages

There are four advantages to adjustable-rate mortgages: safety, avoiding any interest-rate risk, regularity, and marketability. Let us look at each of these points individually.

First, all of the mortgages in a GNMA or FNMA pool must meet stringent criteria before they can become part of the pool. Second, as a partial owner of one or more of these pools, your investment is diversified, since you now own a certain percentage of perhaps a dozen different mortgages. Finally, GNMAs are backed by the full faith and credit of the U.S. government, while FNMAs are considered by the marketplace to be virtually identical in safety. (The yield difference between a GNMA and FNMA is less than one-quarter of a percentage point.)

Since we are talking about adjustable-rate mortgages, the investor does not have to worry about being stuck with something in the future that does not then offer a competitive rate of return. Again, the mortgages in these pools are adjusted every six months if interest rates in general have gone up or down. As an owner of a GNMA or FNMA certificate, you do not have to wait more than six months to get the new higher (or lower) rate of return. This constant adjusting means that you, the investor, are not faced with any real interest-rate risk.

GNMAs and FNMAs of all varieties have excellent track records. Investors have never had their monthly checks delayed. If a homeowner in your pool happens to default or is tardy in making a payment, you will never know—or care. The *timely* interest and principal payments are guaranteed by either FNMA or GNMA.

Regular GNMAs and FNMAs are very popular; hundreds of millions of dollars of these securities trade daily. Adjustable-rate GNMAs and FNMAs are also quite popular, but the supply is quite limited, which makes these securities easy to sell at a moment's notice.

Disadvantages

There are two potential pitfalls when it comes to adjustable securities. First, there is a limit to the amount of upward adjustments. For example, if you buy a 7-percent adjustable-rate mortgage security, the lifetime cap on the underlying mortgage will probably be in the 11-to-12-percent range. If, for some unlikely reason, interest rates eclipse this cap rate, you, the investor, are out of luck. Your rate of return will cap out at that 11-to-12-percent figure. The second disadvantage has to do with discipline. Like any other pass-through or mortgage security, each monthly payment represents interest and a partial return of principal. It is important that you do not spend the principal portion of your check but instead reinvest it elsewhere so your *principal* remains intact overall. There are ways to deal with both of these possible negative aspects of adjustable-rate GNMAs and FNMAs.

By purchasing seasoned securities, you greatly lessen the chances that interest rates will move up above the cap rate. A seasoned GNMA or FNMA is one that has been in existence for a number of years already and has a remaining life of only eight years or less. An adjustable mortgage that has five, six, seven, or eight years to mature does not have the same interest-rate risk as a new pass-through security that could last fifteen years or more.

The way to discipline yourself is to make sure that you make a note of each monthly statement, carefully writing down how much represents interest and what dollar figure is principal. In the early years of the security's life, the great majority of each payment will be interest. Investors are often tempted to spend the principal portion also, since it may only represent $20 or $30. If you decide to spend the entire check, make sure that you are replacing this "return of principal" by investing a similar amount of money somewhere else. Such supplemental investments do not have to be made each month; an annual contribution is sufficient.

This second potential negative, the tendency to spend the entire monthly payment, cannot be overstated. For some reason a large number of people who own regular or adjustable-rate GNMAs or FNMAs somehow think that when the pool matures, there will be a final distribution representing all of the original principal. This is simply not true. You were getting your principal back all along the way, in "dribs and drabs" each month. Mortgage-backed securities are not like corporate bonds, government obligations, or municipal bonds, paying off face value at maturity.

How to Buy and Sell

Individual adjustable-rate GNMAs and FNMAs sell in increments of $25,000 face value, $25,000 being the minimum investment for a new issue. Purchases can be made for less than $25,000 in the secondary marketplace; seasoned GNMAs and FNMAs in the secondary market are not as expensive because their remaining face value is less than the original amount, due to monthly pay-downs of principal. Since the supply of adjustable-rate mortgage-backed securities is quite limited compared to the supply of "regular" GNMAs and FNMAs, you may find it difficult to buy these securities. Fortunately, there are different ways to participate in these debt instruments.

You can invest in adjustable-rate securities by buying shares of a mutual fund or unit investment trust (UIT) that specializes in this area. In fact, UITs and funds own a large percentage of these pass-through investments. You can buy into a mutual fund with as little as $250 ($1,000 with some funds); unit investment trusts require minimum investments of at least $1,000. Additional money can be added to a mutual fund at any time. The usual minimum addition is in the $25-to-$100 range. These modest amounts make such accounts attractive gifts for children and grandchildren.

Individual securities, shares of mutual funds, and unit trusts can be sold at any time. You do not have to wait until the underlying mortgage-backed instrument matures. Investors sometimes think that if they buy a twenty-year bond or an adjustable-rate GNMA or FNMA with a life expectancy of fifteen years, they are obligated to hold it until the end. This is not true. These assets are extremely marketable. A lot of people and institutions are constantly buying and selling these securities.

When you buy or sell an adjustable-rate GNMA or FNMA, you will not pay a commission directly. The fee the broker receives, which is really the same as a commission but does not show up on the confirmation, is built into the price of the security. This "mark-up" ranges anywhere from one-fourth of a percentage point to 4 percent, depending upon the broker and the size of the order. Generally, the greater the purchase or sale, the smaller the built-in fee will be. Discount brokerage firms do not offer any better or worse rates than traditional, full-service firms when it comes to bonds, government obligations, GNMAs, or FNMAs.

Tracking Performance

If you own an adjustable-rate GNMA or FNMA, you can find out its value by looking at your brokerage firm statement or by telephoning the broker of record for a daily price quote. Verbal quotes will be much more accurate than the firm's statement, since these statements are computerized and based on the assumption that you own a block of these securities worth at least $1,000,000—a distortion not true with stocks. Since this is probably not the case, the actual value of your individual issues can easily be ten percent less than what your statement shows.

Determining the actual value of a mutual fund or unit investment trust that invests in adjustable-rate instruments is much easier. Newspapers list the price per share of these funds every day. Unit trust values can be found out by telephoning the unit trust company, or you can telephone your mutual fund group. Representatives at the unit trust or fund group can tell you the daily value as well as the high and low price per share (or unit) over the past week, month, year, or since inception.

Historical Performance

Adjustable-rate GNMAs and FNMAs have only been around for a few years. This does not mean that they are not safe or should be avoided. Remember, they are just a variation of regular GNMAs and FNMAs, which have been in existence for a few dozen years. Equally important, the vast majority of other investments cannot match their backing and security.

As far as performance is concerned, adjustable-rate securities have pretty much tracked interest rates and the general level of inflation since their inception. These investments are always laggards, since adjustments are made only twice a year. This lagging effect is good when interest rates are falling (you get to receive a higher-than-normal yield for several more months) and a slight negative when rates are increasing (since you will have to wait for up to six months to get the new, higher rate).

Because of their dual safety—government or "quasi-government agency" backed and with the security of each mortgage in the pool—adjustable-rate GNMAs and FNMAs have a perfect track record. No investor has ever had a monthly payment delayed. This does not mean that no one has ever lost money in a GNMA or FNMA.

Like most other debt instruments, you can end up selling a GNMA or FNMA for more or less than what you paid for it if interest rates have changed since the time of purchase. If rates have fallen, you probably have a profit built in; if rates have gone up, there will probably be a loss. In the case of adjustable-rate securities, such losses or profits are nominal, since the yield is changing to meet market conditions. Rates that adjust upward or downward translate into tremendous stability of principal. This is one of the attractive features of adjustable-rate GNMAs and FNMAs.

Tax Considerations

Interest from these securities is fully taxable. There is no local, state, or federal tax exemption. If you sell an adjustable-rate GNMA or FNMA for more than you paid for it, then you must report a capital gain; if there is a loss, it can be offset against other gains or used to reduce your earned income or portfolio income by up to $3,000 per year.

Portfolio Fit

These instruments are a very good choice for the conservative investor who wants more than what CDs, savings accounts, and money market accounts are offering. By accepting a minimal amount of volatility, the investor is assured of maintaining a yield that is current with interest rates as they go through their natural up-and-down cycles.

This would be an excellent place for money that was not needed on a monthly or annual basis to pay bills. It would certainly be an appropriate place to invest "emergency funds" or intermediate- or long-term monies. High-tax-bracket investors may be better off looking at tax-deferred or tax-free alternatives.

Risks

These mortgage-backed securities have no real practical risk. They are very safe, have a dual form of backing, have exhibited a stable and acceptable track record, and can adjust by a fairly large margin to take advantage of increasing interest rates.

Before buying any mutual fund that specializes in adjustable-rate mortgages (ARMs) ask if it contains interest-only mortgages (IOs)—a position of 5 percent or more could mean your ARM fund is a lot more volatile than you thought. Some ARM funds use IOs to boost yield, despite the fact that such instruments can fall close to 50 percent in a year.

Unique Features

What is special about this investment is that your rate of return responds to long-term interest rates. Very few other investments give you the opportunity of getting better-than-average rates with an upside potential in the case of an inflationary environment.

Comments

Although not well known by most investors, this is a sound choice for ultra-conservative and conservative investors. Moderate risk-takers may find such securities useful for the more stable parts of their holdings. High income-earners can shelter themselves from current taxes by making adjustable-rate GNMAs and FNMAs part of their qualified retirement plan.

Additional Information

There are only a few mutual funds and unit trusts that specialize in this area. Listed below are some of the best.

Franklin Trust Company
777 Mariners Island Boulevard, San Mateo, CA 94403. 800-342-5236.

Pilgrim Distributors
10100 Santa Monica Boulevard, 21st Floor, Los Angeles, CA 90067. 800-334-3444.

14
High-Quality Corporate Bonds

Stability of principal	✔✔✔
Stability of income	✔✔✔✔✔
Protection against inflation	✔✔✔
Total return	✔✔
Tax benefits	✔

Definition

What distinguishes a high-quality bond from other kinds of corporate bonds is its rating. The two major rating services, Moody's and Standard and Poors, consider the top four categories (AAA, AA, A, and BAA, in the case of Moody's; AAA, AA, A, BBB in the case of S & P) to be high quality. The higher the rating, the more likely the corporation will be able to meet its current and future debt obligations. Similarly, the higher the rating, the lower the risk and the lower the yield. As the chance for default or suspension in interest payments decreases, so does the risk. The default rate for high-quality corporate bonds is a small fraction of one percent.

The rating of a bond can change over time. A financially strong corporation can fall on bad times and have the rating on its outstanding debt downgraded by any of the rating services. A downgrading (such as A to BAA) or ratings boost (AA to AAA) may last for only several months or indefinitely. It is the rating services that decide what rating a corporation's bonds will receive; the issuer has no control and cannot influence the rating service.

How It Works

When a corporation issues bonds, it must decide whether or not to have its security(s) rated. A good rating will make the bond more marketable and, therefore, more desirable. A corporation may decide not to have its issue(s) rated for one or more of the following reasons: (1) There is a high degree of certainty that the rating will be poor (no reason to pay for something that will make your bond more difficult to sell); (2) the fee charged by the rating service, which can be $10,000 to $20,000 or more, may be too high in light of the face value of the outstanding bonds (it does not make sense to pay, say, $20,000 for a $1.5 million dollar issue); (3) the track record of the corporation, and its outstanding bonds, may be so well known that buyers are willing to buy the debt with or without a rating.

There are several rating services, but as a general rule all ratings are based on the following: the corporation's ability to pay its current debts, trends in sales and profit margins, the caliber of management and its efficiency, the corporation's position compared to its competitors in the same industry, the outlook of the entire industry, and projected growth, costs, profits, etc., of the corporation. The rating decision is mostly objective. Once a rating has been given, the corporation is always free to pay another fee to have the same, or other, rating service make a new analysis.

Corporations strive for a high rating because the interest paid out by the company (a cost of doing business) can amount to a large percentage of its overall expenses. A higher rating means that the company will pay less in interest if it issues new bonds in the future. A difference of one or two percentage points can end up saving, or costing, the corporation hundreds of thousands of dollars per year. The figure could turn out to be millions if the debt about to be issued amounts to a couple of hundred million dollars.

Once you buy a bond, its coupon rate (the amount of interest paid out by the corporation) is fixed. Thus, a corporation does not benefit from, nor is it harmed by, a change in ratings as far as its existing (outstanding) debt is concerned. However, a higher rating could benefit the corporation in the future and will probably reflect favorably on senior management as well as the board of directors. A company considered to be sound financially has more latitude when it comes to dealing with creditors, vendors, and employees. People like dealing with safe companies. No one likes to buy a product or service from a business that appears to be troubled and may not survive for more than a couple of more years.

Advantages
The advantage of buying a high-quality corporate bond is peace of mind. By buying a safe corporate bond, you will be getting a return that is 1 to 2 percent higher than a U.S. government obligation with a similar maturity. Like other kinds of bonds, high-quality issues pay interest semiannually. And like other bonds, if interest rates decline from the time when you purchased your bonds, their value will increase.

Disadvantages

The biggest disadvantage of these bonds is that their rating can go down, thereby decreasing the value if the bond were to be sold prior to its natural maturity. True, the rating may also go up, but when you have a bond that is already A or AA rated, its safety can go up only slightly, while the potential fall could be severe. Fortunately, rating adjustments are more the exception than the rule. Furthermore, the chances that a bond's rating will drop by two or more grades is highly unlikely.

A second and more common *potential* disadvantage has to do with changes in interest rates. As you have learned from previous chapters, when rates increase, the value of bonds (at least on paper) decrease. Interest-rate risk (or reward) can be minimized by buying bonds with a remaining maturity of seven years or less.

A third potential disadvantage is that many corporate bonds have a "call feature" that allows a corporation to force you to sell your bonds back to them prematurely. For more information, see "Disadvantages" in chapter 10, Municipal Bonds.

How to Buy and Sell

High-quality corporate issues can be bought or sold through a securities firm. Several banks also offer similar brokerage services. A great number of mutual fund groups have high-quality portfolios that can be purchased or sold with a phone call. Unit trusts are still another alternate form of ownership.

It takes only a couple of minutes to buy or sell individual bonds, a unit trust, or shares of a high-quality corporate bond fund. The price is determined by the general level of interest rates.

You can buy high-quality corporate bonds with maturities ranging from just a few months to up to thirty years. Usually, the longer the maturity, the greater the yield (since such bonds are more volatile). A high-quality bond is not immune to interest-rate swings. When rates go up, all bonds, even those issued by the U. S. government, will go down in value; how much they decline depends upon how much interest rates have risen and upon the *remaining* maturity of the bond. A thirty-year bond *issued twenty-five years ago* is no more volatile than a five-year bond issued yesterday.

Tracking Performance

The prices for thousands of corporate bonds are shown each day in the newspaper. A faster way to determine the value of a high-quality corporate bond is to see how the bellwether thirty-year U.S. government bond is doing. If you notice that its yield is falling, this means that its price is rising and so is the value of your bonds. Conversely, when you hear or read that the yield on government bonds has gone up, this means that bond prices are down. You can also telephone your broker occasionally and have him or her give you prices.

If you own shares of a corporate bond fund, the buying and selling price of the shares are in the newspaper in the mutual fund part of the business section. Unit trust prices are not quoted in the paper, but values can be determined by telephoning the toll-free number of the unit trust company.

Historical Performance

The track record of high-quality corporate issues is similar to that of U.S. government securities. From 1975 to 1981, long-term bonds lost almost half of their value. During the 1980s and early 1990s, these same corporate bonds saw substantial appreciation. By the late 1980s, the losses incurred during the late 1970s had been wiped out.

If interest rates remain level during the 1990s, then bonds, bond funds, and unit trusts should be safe, displaying only modest changes in price. However, if there are wide swings in interest rates during the decade, all bonds, including high-quality issues, could end up being more volatile than stocks. If you anticipate such changes in interest rates, stick with bonds, funds, and unit trusts with maturities that average seven years or less. Such maturities are considered short to intermediate and do not change drastically in price.

Tax Considerations

Interest from corporate bonds is fully taxable on a state and federal level in the year in which it is received or reinvested. Corporations, mutual funds, and unit trusts all issue 1099s, so make sure that you report all of the interest received or reinvested.

The only way to avoid taxation of corporate bond interest is to buy such securities within a retirement plan such as an IRA or pension plan. If you have children, you can make them a gift of the bonds, and the interest will be subject to special tax breaks. Under the current tax law, for the tax years ending in 1992 and 1993, the first $600 of interest, dividends, or capital gains generated under a child's social security number is free of federal taxes, regardless of the parents' tax status. For the tax years 1992 and 1993, the second $600 of this income is subject to a tax of 15 percent. These brackets, which are currently $600, are subject to change depending on the inflation rate, but the current rule is that the brackets only adjust in $50 increments; over $1,200 the parents' tax rate applies. Once the child reaches age fourteen or older, the first $600 is still tax-free, but then the rest of the child's income is taxed at the rate of a single individual. For example, for 1992, if the child had no earned income (e.g., salary), then after the first tax-free $600 of income, the next $21,450 would be taxed at the 15 percent rate—which for many children would be significantly lower than their parents' rate.

Besides interest, there is the issue of capital gains or losses. If you buy a bond for one price and sell it for another, the difference is a capital gain (if the sales price is higher than the original purchase price) or capital loss (if the net proceeds are less than the cost). Any such gain or loss must be reported on your tax return. If you sell or redeem a bond for exactly the same price you paid for it, there is no taxable capital gain or loss.

Portfolio Fit

Bonds are an important part of one's holdings. Often they can add a great deal of stability when the stock or real estate markets are uncertain. It is very uncommon for both high-quality bonds and stocks to decline in value the same year.

One of the nice features of high-quality corporate bonds is that they pay interest whether or not real estate, the economy, or the stock market are performing well. If you own part of a unit trust or individual bonds, your yield will not fluctuate. You receive, or reinvest, the same amount every six months (every month, if you are in a unit trust). High-quality issues provide a reliable source of income. The increase or decrease in value referred to throughout this chapter is of greatest importance to someone who plans on selling his or her bonds prior to their maturity.

Risks

The biggest risk of owning high-quality issues is that you will sell them before they mature and at a time when interest rates are higher than they were at the time of purchase. Since the rating is good, the chance of default is virtually nil.

Unique Features

The only thing that is special about corporate bonds is that you have lent money to a specific corporation. If you own part of a unit trust or shares in a bond fund, then you have loaned money to a large number of companies. In return for the use of your money, the corporation agrees to pay you (or the unit trust or mutual fund) interest every six months. When the bond matures, the issuer further promises to pay back the face value of the bond. The face value may be more or less than what you paid for the bond. Corporate bonds are redeemed for $1,000 a piece at maturity. If you paid more than $1,000 for the bond, then you will experience a "loss" at maturity. Conversely, if you paid less than $1,000, you will have a capital gain upon redemption.

I put the word "loss" in quotation marks because bonds are often bought at a premium in order to get a higher current yield. The higher income every six months can end up easily offsetting any "loss" at maturity. It is often better to have more now and accept a little bit less later, what is known as the time value of money.

Comments

Most investors will be better served by owning U.S. government bonds. The desired maturity of any bond depends upon your circumstances and whether you believe interest rates are going to go up or down during your period of ownership (presuming you would act on such an event). Since there is usually little difference between the yield on similar maturing government and high-quality corporate bonds, take the safer investment. With government securities you never have to worry about a downgrading, payment of interest, or repayment of principal. Equally important, during periods of panic, when the marketplace temporarily believes world disaster is at hand, government issues will increase in value as people flock to quality.

Additional Information

Neuberger & Berman Management
605 Third Avenue, 2nd Floor, New York, NY 10158-0006. 800-877-9700.

Newton Funds
411 E. Wisconsin Avenue, Suite 340, Milwaukee, WI 53202. 800-242-7229.

Pacific Investment Management Co.
840 Newport Center Drive, Suite 360, Newport Beach, CA 92660.
800-927-4648.

Sanford C. Bernstein
767 Fifth Avenue, New York, NY 10153. 212-756-4097.

15
Fixed-Rate Annuities

Stability of principal	✔✔✔✔
Stability of income	✔✔✔✔✔
Protection against inflation	✔
Total return	✔
Tax benefits	✔✔✔✔

Definition

A fixed-rate annuity is a contractual relationship between the investor (you) and an insurance company, similar to the relationship between you and a bank when you invest in a CD. For the ability to use your money, the insurance company gives you a set rate of return for a specified period, usually one, three or five years. At the end of the contract, the investor is free to withdraw part or all of his or her money, transfer it to another annuity issuer, or "roll it over" with the same company, accepting their then-current rate of return. Money taken out of an annuity prior to its contract expiration date may be subject to a penalty. As you can see, in many ways a fixed-rate annuity is very similar to a bank CD. With most companies, this penalty cannot eat into your principal.

Just as with bank CDs, a variety of fixed-rate annuities are offered by the insurance industry. Some insurance companies offer competitive rates with small penalties that disappear within a few years. A few annuities have no premature withdrawal penalties or a penalty that ends after one year. Other issuers guarantee only sub-par returns and very high back-end penalties that go on for a decade or longer.

Money invested in an annuity grows and compounds tax-deferred, making this a somewhat unusual investment vehicle. Fixed-rate annuities are also one of the few investments you can go into in which your principal is guaranteed each and every day.

How It Works

Let us suppose that you want to invest your money somewhere and you want to know exactly what rate of return you will be getting and how long that rate of return will remain in effect. Let us further assume that you also want to make sure that your principal remains intact and that it can be gotten to at any time. In such a case, an annuity is something you should look into.

Suppose you had $10,000 you wanted to invest somewhere safe. You looked at bank CDs but were unimpressed by the interest rate they were offering, and you did not want to incur a penalty in an emergency that could eat into part of your original investment. You also looked at money market accounts and U.S. Treasury Bills, but did not want the interest rate to fluctuate during the next couple of years. You then hear about annuities.

You discover that the annuity is paying a 1- or 2-percent higher rate than bank CDs or other, similarly conservative, investments. If the annuity is paying, say, 7 percent for five years, this means that at the end of one year your account will be worth $10,700 ($10,000 x 1.07). At the end of the second year your investment will be worth $11,449, $12,250 in three years, $13,108 in four years and $14,026 at the end of five years, when the guarantee ends.

Once the five-year period contracted for has ended, the insurance company sends you a letter telling you that the new rate for the next year will be, let us say, 8 percent. If you do not notify the company within the next thirty days, the entire account will automatically be rolled over and your investment, principal plus all of the interest accumulated during the previous five years, will begin earning 8 percent. However, you may discover that 8 percent is not as high as you can get from another annuity company or from your local bank or brokerage firm. If this is the case, you simply contact the company that holds your money and tell them either to send you a check or to transfer the money to a different insurance company. That is all there is to it.

If the company you are using continues to offer what you consider a good rate, you never have to do anything. At the end of each guarantee period, which may be anywhere from one to ten years, the annuity issuer will send you a letter informing you as to the new rate for the next period and pointing out that if you do nothing, the investment will continue. If the description in this or the previous paragraph sounds confusing, keep in mind that CDs work exactly the same way.

Is it always this easy and painless? No. Some companies will charge you a penalty for a couple more years after the guarantee period ends. This means that the initial rate may be, say, 7 percent and the renewal rate an unacceptable 5 percent. Refusal to renew the contract for the next couple of years at 5 percent could mean that you would have to pay a penalty to get at your money; there is even a chance that the IRS could get involved and level its own, separate penalty (see "Disadvantages").

Advantages

People buy fixed-rate annuities for five reasons: safety of principal and interest, a specific rate of return, the ability to make withdrawals of interest or principal at any time, tremendous tax benefits during accumulation and when withdrawals are made, and no initial or ongoing fees or commissions.

Safety of principal is the reason why tens of billions of dollars are invested in annuities each year. No one has ever lost a dime in a fixed-rate annuity. Such a track record is only equaled by investments backed or insured by the U.S. government or one of its agencies.

When you go into a fixed-rate annuity, there are no surprises. The insurance company or broker will tell you exactly how much money you are going to earn. Unlike some other investments, the rate of return does not change weekly or monthly. To calculate how much money you are going to earn, simply use a basic calculator and multiply your principal (the amount of money you are going to invest) by the quoted interest rate. The resulting figure represents how much your account will grow during the first year.

If the annuity has a guaranteed rate for two or more years, take your principal plus the interest earned from the first year, add the two figures together, and then multiply this combined number by the stated rate of return (for example, $10,000 + $500 interest x 1.05). This will show you how much the account will earn or "grow" for year two; the process can be repeated for as many years as the guarantee lasts. If the company tells you that the guarantee period is seven years, you will get the rate they have promised you, compounded, for each of the next seven years (for example, $5,000 x 1.07 x 1.07 x 1.07 x 1.07, etc.), no matter what the stock market does, how much the prime interest rate goes up or down, or how profitable the insurance company is.

While you own an annuity you are free to make withdrawals. You do not have to give a reason as to why part or all of the interest or principal is needed. Withdrawal requests must be in writing. By law, most companies must send you a check within seven days, and a check can often be sent out Express Mail or wired even faster. Some companies let you make withdrawals several times a year; others only once a year.

One of the principle reasons people invest in annuities is their tax benefits. Money in an annuity grows and compounds tax-deferred (the interest income). The advantage of postponing taxes, or even avoiding them, in some cases, can be tremendous. As an example, if you are in a 33-percent tax bracket (state and federal combined) and an investment is paying 9 percent, you are really only netting 6 percent once taxes have been paid each year. A 6-percent after-tax return means that it takes money twelve years to double. As an example, $10,000 will grow to $20,000 at the end of twelve years and then double again, to $40,000 at the end of the second twelve-year period. Contrast this with a fixed-rate annuity paying the same 9-percent rate. Since the money is growing tax-deferred, the account is increasing in value faster. At the end of only eight years, the same $10,000 will be worth $20,000. At the end of sixteen years, this $20,000 will have grown to $40,000. Finally, at the end of the next eight years (after the same twenty-four years as the taxable investment), the $40,000 will have doubled once more to $80,000. As you can see, $80,000 is a lot more appealing than $40,000 (the same 9-percent return, but one that is taxed each year). The taxation of annuities is discussed under "Tax Considerations."

Finally, when you buy an annuity, you do not pay any commissions or fees. One hundred percent of your money goes to work for you immediately. Nothing is taken out for a broker or paid to the insurance company. The advisor or person who sells you the annuity may receive a commission from the insurance company, but any such dollar benefit is paid by the insurance company; it does not come out of the client's pocket.

Disadvantages

As you might have guessed, no investment is this good without having some strings attached to it. The five disadvantages of fixed-rate annuities are: (1) the rate offered may not be competitive; (2) there is a fluke chance that your principal, and any accumulated growth or interest, could be tied up for a few years if the issuer becomes troubled; (3) money taken out during the insurance company's penalty period may be subject to penalty; (4) withdrawals of interest (growth) prior to age $59\frac{1}{2}$ are usually subject to a 10-percent IRS penalty; and (5) there is no guarantee that the renewal rate will be competitive.

Hundreds of companies offer annuities. Some issuers offer high rates of return, others have low rates. Annuities that advertise less-than-competitve rates are not necessarily any more financially secure or better than companies with high rates. Often the salesperson or advisor who is trying to put you into a low-yielding annuity has not done any comparison shopping, or is a "captive" broker limited in the number or kinds of annuities he or she can offer, or is receiving special compensation (a higher fee or commission).

Although extremely remote, there is always a chance that the insurance company backing your fixed-rate annuity will run into financial difficulty in the future. For this reason, if you have a large sum of money, say $100,000 or more, you should split it up and invest in two or more fixed-rate annuities. The other way to counter this disadvantage, as well as the one described in the previous paragraph, is to make sure you do your homework. Review annuities offered by several companies, studying the rating(s) as well as the rate of return being offered.

The issue of financial insolvency in companies that issue annuities has been greatly exaggerated. Nevertheless, to be on the safe side, limit your exposure to any one insurance company, just as you would if you had over $100,000 to invest in a bank. There are only a few states that do not have a guaranty fund. (Fees are charged annually by the state's insurance commissioner and used to protect policyholders.) Every state that does have such a safety net limits its liability. In the case of annuities, protection is normally limited to $100,000.

When a company does run into money problems and the state is forced to suspend its operations, what usually happens is that the issuer is required to take certain steps. If these measures are not successful, or if the losses are just too severe, other insurance companies will usually step in. The competition hopes to be able to take over the faulting company's assets and all of its contract owners. It is for this reason that a state guaranty's fund is rarely used; the private sector comes to the rescue. The successor bidder does not bail out a troubled peer out of the kindness of its heart. In return for preserving their account, contract owners must accept the victor's terms. Typically, this means that investors' monies are tied up for three to five years, and the interest rate during this period may not be as high as the then-going rate. Withdrawals during this "reorganization period" are sometimes subject to severe penalties. The odds of an insurance company going bankrupt are about one in two hundred.

Speaking of penalties, when your advisor checks out different contracts for you, make sure he or or she tells you the penalty schedule. In particular, you will want to know what the free withdrawal privilege is, what the bailout provision is, and what penalty percentage could be imposed and how long it lasts.

The *free withdrawal privilege* refers to how much you can take out each year without cost or penalty. Most annuities allow you to take out up to 10 percent each year for free. If you buy a one-year "CD/annuity," your entire account can be liquidated at the end of the year without cost. Otherwise, most companies charge about a 5-percent penalty for excess withdrawals. What this means is that if you have a $10,000 annuity that is now worth $11,000, you can take out $1,000 for free. Amounts in excess of $1,000 will be penalized 5 percent. Thus, in this example, if the contract owner needed $1,500, he or she would take out $1,000 for free and then pay a $25 penalty for the remaining $500 (5 percent of $500).

The bailout provision is a clause designed to protect you against the insurance company's offering you a low renewal rate. To see how this works, let us go through another example. Suppose you invest in an annuity that has a 5-percent penalty for the first five years and a guaranteed rate of 8 percent for the first three years with a "7-percent bailout." At the end of three years, the insurance company notifies you that the renewal rate for years four through six will be 6.9 percent. Since 6.9 percent is less than 7 percent, this means that you can withdraw all of your money, or transfer it to another insurer, without cost, fee, or penalty. This penalty-free election is due to the fact that when you first went into the investment the insurance company essentially said, "Look, we are going to give you 8 percent for three years. At the end of three years, if we don't give you at least 7 percent, you can get out, without cost, without giving us a reason." If, instead, the renewal rate was 7 percent or higher, you would either have to accept the new rate or be subject to whatever penalty was remaining (5 percent in this example).

The penalty for annuities ranges anywhere from 0 to 10 percent. The most common penalty, 5 percent, either declines by 1 percent each year for five years or remains level (5-percent penalty if excess withdrawals are made during *any* of the first five years). When it comes to penalty schedules, there is quite a variety. Even though close to 80 percent of all people who invest in annuities never make withdrawals, this is still something that should be checked out. Nevertheless, out of fairness to the annuity industry, it should also be pointed out that if an emergency does arise, presumably the investor has other sources of capital that can be tapped without cost or penalty.

How to Buy and Sell

Although annuities are offered only by insurance companies, this investment is sold and marketed by banks, brokerage firms, and financial planners. Since there is no cost or fee involved, your decision as to what person or firm you choose should be based on variety (how many companies or policies do they represent), competence (how knowledgeable the advisor appears to be) and integrity (whether you feel this person is honest and will tell you all of a contract's advantages and disadvantages).

You can purchase an annuity directly from an insurance company, but there is no advantage to doing this; in fact, it may be a *disadvantage*. What I mean by this is that the company knows nothing about you. They cannot guide you as to whether you should favor a one, two, or three locked-in rate (contract), and they will not tell you about what the competition is offering.

The investment is made by filling out a one-page application and making out a check directly to the insurance company. You begin earning interest as soon as the insurer has received the application and check. The contract, which also doubles as your confirmation, is sent out about three weeks later. Annuity contracts are more extensive than mutual fund or stock confirmations, and this is why it takes so long to get the initial acknowledgement.

By law, every annuity contract includes a "seven-day-free-look" provision. Once you receive your contract in the mail, you have up to seven days to return it to the insurance company and get a full refund. Investors rarely do this, but it is nice to know that you have a chance to review the contract before making a final commitment.

Every annuity application asks you to list the names of three parties: the owner, the annuitant, and the beneficiary. The owner is usually the person who is making the investment. The owner, or investor, decides how much to invest and which annuity to invest in. The owner also decides who the annuitant and beneficiary are.

The annuitant's lifespan is the "measuring life" for the annuity contract. That is, the annuity investment continues until you, the owner, decide to liquidate the account or when the annuitant dies (an event you obviously cannot control). Thus, the annuitant is like the person named as the insured in a life insurance policy. The annuitant you list on the application can be yourself, your spouse, a friend, a neighbor, or a relative.

The beneficiary is the person you list on the application who will receive the proceeds from the annuity (its then-current value) upon the annuitant's death. If the account is fully liquidated by the owner before the annuitant's death, the beneficiary gets nothing. As you can see, the beneficiary of an annuity is similar to the beneficiary of a life insurance policy—neither gets, or is entitled to, anything until a specific person dies. You can list anyone you want as the beneficiary (yourself, your spouse, your children, a living trust, etc.). Prior to the annuitant's death you are also free to change beneficiaries.

Tracking Performance

Statements are only sent out once a year. If a contract owner wants to know the value of his or her account during the year, a phone call can be made to the insurance company. Most companies have toll-free telephone numbers.

There is really no need to check a contract's value prior to receiving the annual statement, since you cannot lose money in an annuity; it literally goes up in value each day.

Historical Performance

The rate offered by annuities goes along somewhat with the prime interest rate. As you might imagine, contract rates have also varied quite a bit over the past several decades. Since interest rates steadily dropped throughout most of the 1980s and early 1990s, this means that initial and renewal rates offered by annuities also dropped by several percentage points.

For the most part, annuity rates have been higher than those offered by bank CDs in the past. There is no indication that this trend will change in the near future.

When you buy a fixed-rate annuity, your rate of return is locked in for the guarantee period. This rate remains level during this period whether you take out some of your money or liquidate the entire contract.

Tax Considerations

Their tax benefits are a chief reason people buy annuities. These benefits come in two forms: during accumulation and during withdrawal. When you invest in an annuity, your money grows and compounds indefinitely. In fact, you do not have to make a single withdrawal while you and/or your spouse is alive. Unlike a qualified retirement plan, such as an IRA, Keogh, or profit-sharing plan, there is no age limit as to when you must start taking money out.

Between 70 and 85 percent of all investors who buy annuities never end up taking money out of them. For most people, then, the question becomes, What happens when the account is inherited by a spouse, children, or other beneficiaries? If your spouse inherits the account, he or she is never required to make any withdrawals. If the beneficiary is someone other than your spouse, the IRS does not require the account to be liquidated by the beneficiary(s) for up to five years. During this five-year period, the new owner does not have to make any kind of sporadic or regular withdrawal. He or she is free to wait until the last day of the fifth year and then close out the account. Remember, spouses are not under any kind of five-year or other deadline.

Money withdrawn by an heir, spouse, child, friend, etc., is not subject to any IRS *or* insurance company penalty. Death of the annuitant is not considered a "voluntary" event, and it is for this reason that any remaining penalties are waived.

Withdrawals of income and/or growth are fully taxable; distributions of principal are never taxed. Unfortunately, you do not have a say as to what part of the annuity is being liquidated. Whether you call it accumulated growth or income, this is what comes out first. As an example, if a $25,000 initial investment grew to $40,000, the first $15,000 would be fully taxable. It makes no difference whether that entire $15,000 came out at once or whether $1,000 was taken out this year, $700 taken out the following year, etc. Once all of the account had been depleted except the original $25,000, taxation would cease and the final $25,000, in this example, would be considered a return of principal and therefore not subject to any state or federal income taxes or penalties.

You cannot go to the IRS or to the insurance company and ask them to distribute your principal first (unless you have an annuity you purchased before 1981). On the positive side, only the withdrawals of interest or growth are subject to income tax (and a 10-percent IRS penalty if money is taken out before age $59\frac{1}{2}$). Money that remains in the account is not subject to a penalty or tax and continues to grow tax-deferred. There is only one way to avoid taxation of all of the withdrawn income or growth: annuitization.

Annuitization is something you must request. When you annuitize, you are telling the insurer (and the IRS) that you want to liquidate the entire contract over at least a five-year period. The period you choose can be longer than five years, but it cannot be shorter if you want to receive some tax benefits. Upon receiving a request for annuitization, the insurance company makes a computation and determines your exclusion ratio. The exclusion ratio shows how much of each distribution is considered to be a return of principal (not taxable) and how much is growth and income (fully taxable). Thus, if your agent tells you that your exclusion ratio is going to be, say, 85 percent, then only 15 percent of each check you receive will be taxable. These potentially tremendous tax benefits continue until 100 percent of the investor's principal has been received. Depending on how long the owner has opted to annuitize, this could take anywhere from five years to a lifetime. The longer the annuitization period, the smaller the exclusion ratio will be.

There are two potential disadvantages to annuitization: having the payout schedule locked in and a future accumulation rate that is usually less than a competitive rate. Let us look at each of these points separately. First, once you begin annuitization you cannot stop the process. Therefore, if someone opted for a lifetime payout schedule (monthly payments lasting until one or more people die—such as lasting until both the husband and wife are deceased), he could not later change his mind. It makes no difference whether there is a death, a bankruptcy filed, or another unforeseen emergency; the timing and the amount of the payments will not change in any way. Secondly, once annuitization is selected, the growth rate on the account balance that has not yet been distributed will not continue to grow at a fair rate. If your insurer was paying you 7 percent, this rate will probably stop once annuitization begins, and the rate from that point forward will most likely be in the 4-to-5-percent range. This is not always the case, but it is more the rule than the exception. A few companies offer a very competitive yield during annuitization. If your insurer does not offer a competitive rate, keep in mind the following points: the rate you have received up to this point (the value of the account) will not be affected, and you do not have to annuitize with your current contract carrier; the contract can be exchanged tax-free to another insurance company.

Investors are never required to annuitize. It is a selection that should be chosen only if: (1) tax-advantaged income is now needed, (2) the company selected is quoting a fair and competitive rate and (3) it is understood that once the process begins, it cannot be stopped, altered, or amended.

Portfolio Fit

There are no safer investments than those backed by the U.S. government, guaranteed by the government, or guaranteed by an insurance company. It is the historical and financial safety of the insurance industry that makes fixed-rate annuities such a safe bet.

Annuities are a clear choice for the investor who is looking for the utmost in safety and a competitive or better-than-average return (yield). Insurance company and IRS penalties mean that this is not a good alternative to highly liquid investments such as money market accounts, T-bills, and CDs that mature in just a few months.

Because of their pre-$59\frac{1}{2}$ penalty (which is waived by death or disability), annuities should be used chiefly by investors who are within a few years of this age or older. This 10-percent IRS penalty makes annuities a poor choice for a younger person or a couple who does not have the patience to live with this investment for several years. Factoring in any penalty and the eventual taxation means that a younger person needs to keep his or her money in an annuity for at least five years to make this a better investment than things like CDs and money market funds.

Risks

Fixed-rate annuities face the same risk that most of the investments shown in this book possess: purchasing-power risk. Fortunately, their historic rates of return, coupled with faster growth due to tax-deferral, means that this investment has a much better chance of outpacing inflation than most of the more traditional, safe investments.

A second risk is the chance of losing part of the accumulated account value due to an insurance company and/or IRS penalty. These penalties can eat into part, and occasionally all, of the interest gained in the account but cannot cut into the investor's principal. Any penalty can be completely eliminated by making sure that withdrawals are equal to or less than the free withdrawal privilege provided by the insurer, and that money needed before you reach age $59\frac{1}{2}$ is taken from sources other than annuity holdings.

The final risk, company financial troubles, can also be minimized or eliminated by restricting your purchases only to insurers who possess a high rating from two or more of the rating services. This risk is very small or unlikely to begin with, but headline stories in the early 1990s generated concern in the investment world, a concern that has now been quieted by revised rating standards and greater investor understanding.

Unique Features

The most unusual feature of fixed-rate annuities is that they have been around in this country for over a hundred years and no one has ever lost a dime. This perfect track record is only matched by certain insurance products and securities backed or guaranteed by the U.S. government. However, unlike government obligations, one's principal (initial investment plus any ongoing contributions) is guaranteed every day; when you own a government bill, note, or bond, face value is only guaranteed if the investment is held until maturity.

Annuities are the only investment in the world for which you cannot outlive the income. By opting for lifetime annuitization (which could be over the life of you and/or your spouse, child, parent, friend, etc.) the investor will receive monthly income until he or she dies. In the case of a couple, married or otherwise, the contract can be set up so that payments remain level until the second partner or friend dies.

Tax-deferral and annuitization are also special features. No other interest-bearing investment provides accumulation that is not taxed indefinitely. Annuitizing a contract is something that is only found with annuities and certain retirement accounts. This ability to make withdrawals that are, in the eyes of the IRS, part principal and part interest or growth is quite special and meaningful.

Finally, this is the only investment with a penalty that cannot eat into principal. Thus, you could invest $250,000 in a fixed-rate annuity and know that tomorrow, next week or next month, you could call the whole thing off and get back a check for at least $250,000, no matter what the IRS or the insurance company penalty might normally be.

Comments

There are few things in this world as safe and secure as fixed-rate annuities. The ability of an investor to choose among rates of return that are guaranteed from anywhere from a single quarter up to ten years makes this a flexible and appealing investment. Moreover, this is the only investment with which you can lock in a rate of return for life (by annuitizing).

Over $50 billion was invested in annuities last year. This is a very popular investment that is still not understood by the majority of investors or brokers. The great majority of all portfolios should include at least one annuity.

Additional Information

There is only one book exclusively devoted to annuities. It covers both fixed-rate and variable annuities (variable contracts are described in a separate chapter later in this book). For more information about this book, *All About Annuities*, contact your local bookstore or the publisher, by writing or telephoning:

John Wiley Book Publishing
605 Third Avenue, 10th Floor, New York, NY 10158. 212-850-6000.

There are several sources that track fixed-rate annuities. These sources can provide you with extensive financial information about the insurance company and its rating, along with a general commentary. A few of these sources will also show you the current rate of return that is being guaranteed.

For more information contact:

Best's Retirement Income Guide
c/o A.M. Best Reports, A.M. Best Road, Oldwick, NJ 08858. 908-439-2200.

Comparative Annuity Reports
P.O. Box 1268, Fair Oaks, CA 95628.

16
Whole Life Insurance

Stability of principal	✔✔✔✔✔
Stability of income	✔✔✔✔✔
Protection against inflation	✔✔
Total return	✔✔
Tax benefits	✔✔✔✔✔

Definition

Insurance is a form of risk transference: you pay an insurance company a premium and they in turn agree to accept a certain kind of risk. In the case of life insurance, the insurer pays a death benefit if the insured dies while the policy is in force. The *insured* is the person whose life is being insured; the *insurer* is the company that accepts the risk. The *owner* is the person who pays the premium. The person, persons, or entity that receives the death benefit is known as the *beneficiary*. The terms, conditions, and provisions of this agreement are spelled out in the *policy*.

Whole life insurance is made up of two parts: term insurance and a savings plan. A portion of each premium paid by the owner goes to pay the insurer for accepting the risk (of having to pay off when the insured dies) and the balance goes into an account, which is referred to as the policy's *cash value*. The size of the cash value depends upon the amount of premium dollars contributed to it and how the monies are invested by the insurance company. The contract owner is free to withdraw part or all of the cash value at any time; he or she does not have to die before cash values are taken out.

How It Works

As long as the policy is in force, the life insurance company is obligated to pay the face value of the policy upon the insured's death. This contract remains intact as long as the owner (who can also be the insured) makes premium payments to the insurance company according to the schedule set forth in the policy. The relationship between the policy owner and insurer ends if either party gives written notice to the other. If a policy is terminated, the insurance company is obligated to send the contract owner any accumulated cash value, as well as a pro-rata share of the most recent premium payment.

The death benefit is paid as soon as the insurance company is notified, in writing, that the insured has passed away. A certified copy of the death certificate is all the proof that need accompany the written request. The amount of money received by the beneficiary is the greater of the policy's cash value or face value, not a combination of the two. As time passes, the insurance company's risk decreases as the policy accumulates a greater and greater cash value.

How the cash side of the policy accumulates depends upon whether the insurer offers any investment options. In the case of *traditional* whole life insurance, the growth rate is declared by the insurance company each year, the figure is non-negotiable, and there are no choices. In essence, the insurance company is investing the cash portion of each premium and accepting the investment risk. In return, if the investment does better than expected, the insurance company benefits. To the extent that it underperforms the rate declared to the contract owner, the insurer suffers the loss.

In the case of whole life insurance, there is also what is known as variable life. The word "variable" means that the contract owner is able to choose, among several different investment portfolios, how the cash portion of each premium payment is to be invested. Usually the owner is able to invest in one or more of the following: growth (U.S. stocks), growth and income (conservative U.S. stocks), foreign (international stocks), government bonds, and a money market account.

In the case of variable life, it is the policy owner who accepts all of the risk and all of the reward. If the investment does well, the cash value increases; if there is a loss, it drops. The insurance remains intact no matter how the cash value portion performs, since such monies are segregated by the insurer whenever a premium payment is made.

Advantages

There are four advantages to whole life insurance. First, you are buying protection. In fact, this is the only way to protect yourself financially if something were to happen to the person who is supporting you (or perhaps paying half of all the household expenses, including the mortgage). Second, in the case of traditional whole life insurance, the cash value is conservatively invested and the rate of growth is known each year. In the case of variable life, you can choose from several different investments. Third, the policy can be canceled by you at any time. The need for life insurance may diminish or completely disappear. Or you may find that a competitor offers a better policy. Fourth, the cash portion of a whole life policy grows and compounds tax deferred. With certain policies, money can actually be taken out tax-free (see "Tax Considerations").

Disadvantages

Life insurance has three disadvantages. First, there are a lot of people who own life insurance but do not need it. They are attracted to the accumulating cash value and tax benefits but fail to realize that this is an expensive way to get tax-deferred or tax-free income. Whole life insurance is only a good deal if the insurance is actually needed. The second disadvantage is that the cash value may not grow at the rate you expect it to. Insurance agents, stockbrokers, and financial planners like to show cash value *projections* over the next five, ten, twenty, and thirty years, yet these are not guarantees. Projected values are based on a certain set of circumstances, something that may or may not occur in the future.

There are possible third and fourth disadvantages. If you want to take money out of your policy (known as borrowing part of the cash value), you may end up paying the insurance company an annual fee for such withdrawals. This can be avoided or minimized, depending upon your insurance company. Finally, if your insurance advisor does not do his or her homework, you can end up with a product that is not competitively priced. You may be overpaying for insurance and/or getting a poor rate of return on the accumulated cash value.

How to Buy and Sell

Once it is determined that a life is to be insured and quotes are received from several different insurers to make sure you get the best coverage for your money, you and your insurance advisor need to sit down and decide what your priority is. Do you want the greatest death benefit possible for your premium dollar or do you want the accumulated cash value to be as big as possible? You cannot have it both ways. Some policies offer inexpensive insurance, thereby allowing more of each premium dollar to go toward the investment portion (cash value). Other policies provide nominal cash value growth but heavily emphasize (increase) the death benefit.

To determine whether you even need life insurance, ask yourself this simple question: If person X were to die, would the financial quality of my life, now or in the future, decrease? If the answer is "no," there is no need to insure that person's life. If the answer is "yes" (for example, this person supports me and/or my children; if this person were to die I could no longer afford to live in this house, or my kids could not afford college, or the estate taxes and/or lack of liquidity are such that I need cash right away if death were to occur), then you need to determine how much coverage is needed.

An illustration may be useful.

If, for example, your spouse spends $50,000 supporting you and your household (the kids, mortgage payments, groceries, medical bills, etc.), then you will need a lump-sum figure that, when conservatively invested, will provide $50,000 of income each year (perhaps more to offset the effects of inflation). Your next step would be to find out what conservative investments are currently yielding. If ten-year government bonds are offering an 8 percent return, then you will need $625,000 ($50,000 divided by 8 percent). If you consider twenty-year municipal bonds to be a safe investment, and they have a current yield of 7 percent, you will need $714,286 worth of life insurance ($50,000 divided by 7 percent).

Whatever amount you and your advisor determine to be sufficient, do not forget to include a hedge for inflation. After all, $50,000 today will not have the same purchasing power in three or five years, much less ten to thirty years from now. Therefore, you may want to increase the projected coverage by 25 to 50 percent and invest this "excess" amount if death does occur so that it can grow and be used later.

If you are looking at insurance as more of an investment, then you will want to concentrate on those policies that have a high guaranteed rate of return and a history of good returns. A moderate or somewhat aggressive investor will also want to look at variable life products to determine the track records of the different investment portfolios.

There is no market to sell your insurance policy. The insurance contract is based on the age and sex of the insured; you cannot substitute a different party. If you want to insure a second party, then you will need to buy another policy. If insuring the original insured is no longer desirable, simply cancel the policy, bearing in mind that the resulting cash value received would then trigger a tax event. If you no longer like the company you are dealing with, find another and have the cash value transferred over. This is known as a "1035" or "tax-free" exchange. Such exchanges avoid income taxes.

Life insurance policies can be purchased from anyone who has an insurance license. Most stockbrokers, financial planners, and investment advisors, as well as insurance agents and brokers, will be able to get you several quotes and present you with different options.

Tracking Performance

The only way to see "how you are doing" is by telephoning the insurance company and finding out your policy's current cash value. Most insurance companies have a toll-free phone number. In the alternative, the person who sold you the policy can also get you a current quote. Life insurers will send you out a statement at least annually; some companies will provide you with a quarterly statement.

Historical Performance

Whole life insurance has been around for over a hundred years in this country. It has existed for several hundred years in other nations. So far, no one has ever lost a dime in a life insurance policy. Insurance companies have a perfect track record, matched only by the U.S. government as far as its ability to honor its obligations.

Until the mid-to-late-1970s, life insurance companies were notorious for offering a low rate of return on the accumulated cash values. Over the past ten to twenty years, this has all changed. With increased consumer awareness and more investment latitude, most insurers now offer very competitive rates. These returns often equal or exceed what you can get from a bank CD or money market account, yet your policy is completely safe. Today, the rate of return you are likely to get is similar to the general level of interest rates, such as the prime lending rate or the rate of return from twenty-year government bonds.

Tax Considerations

Four times during the life of a policy there is a tax consideration. First, you cannot deduct the premiums you pay in. Second, while the policy is in force, the cash value is not taxed, no matter how large it may get. Third, if the owner decides to borrow money out of the contract, the money received may or may not be taxed. In the case of policy loans, taxation depends upon how long the policy has been in force, on the amount of money taken out, and on the amount and frequency of premiums paid in. Fourth, when the insured dies, proceeds are received free from local, state, and federal income taxes.

If the insured was also the owner of the policy, then the value of the account is included in the decedent's estate in order to determine whether there is an estate tax liability. This is only a concern if the deceased's estate ends up being greater than $600,000 and more than $600,000 is being left to someone (or ones) other than the surviving spouse. You can leave your spouse an unlimited amount of money, including the proceeds from any life insurance policy, and there is no estate tax.

Portfolio Fit

Life insurance is somewhat like auto insurance: if you drive a car, you need car insurance, and if the standard of living of one or more people would decrease as a result of your demise, you might want to invest in life insurance.

The investment portion of a whole life policy, the cash value, should be invested (traditional or variable life) according to your risk level and time horizon. The longer you expect to keep the policy, the more likely it is that at least part, if not all, of the cash value should be invested in an equity portfolio (if offered and if you are a moderate-to-aggressive investor). Otherwise, you should stick with traditional life insurance, knowing exactly what you can expect. No matter what kind of policy you buy, the rate of return on your investment (the premiums paid in) becomes astronomical if death occurs during the first several years. The rate of return can still be good if you live a long time and the cash value is growing at a competitive rate.

Once again, do not buy whole life insurance unless coverage is needed. Too much of each premium dollar goes toward the insurance part of the policy to make this a great investment. On the other hand, if you need the protection, it must be included in your portfolio. The only time life insurance can end up being a good investment, even though the insured has not died, is if the policy is kept in force for at least ten, and more likely fifteen to twenty years. Once several years have passed and agent commissions, the cost of insurance, and administrative expenses have been absorbed, then some policies can provide a nice return.

Risks

There are only three risks to owning life insurance. First, death occurs and the policy is not current (no death benefit). Second, if variable life is chosen, the investment portfolios you selected do not perform well. The third risk, company failure, is highly unlikely. The insurance industry has an excellent reputation, despite the headline stories we saw in 1991. No industry is more stable than the life insurance industry. In fact, the only thing more financially secure is the U.S. government, and only because it has the power to print money.

Unique Features

Life insurance is the only way to protect yourself from someone else's death. The death benefit can be used to pay estate taxes, as a ready form of cash, or as an investment used to generate income for one or more years.

When properly structured, variable life insurance is the only way you can directly participate in the stock and/or bond market on a *tax-free* basis. The "seven-pay test" (the way to get great returns that are truly tax-free) is fairly complex to explain. If you are willing to take some risk, this may be the way for you to go. Contact an insurance expert.

Comments

Traditional whole life insurance can only be considered an investment if it is held for at least fifteen to twenty years. This is because all life insurance products include the cost of having someone else accept the risk of your dying (or whoever the insured is), commissions paid to insurance agents, and administrative expenses. If this is something you can live with for a lengthy period, your average annual rate of return should approach the return offered by long-term government bonds. The difference with life insurance is that you are also getting a tax-free death benefit. In return, you will have to be patient. The yield on this asset can be minor, or even negative, if it is terminated after only a few years.

Additional Information

Life Insurance: A Consumer's Handbook
c/o Indiana University Press, 10th and Morton Streets, Bloomington, IN 47405. 812-855-4203.

American Council of Life Insurance
1001 Pennsylvania Avenue NW, Washington, DC 20004-2599. 202-624-2000.

National Insurance Consumer Organization
121 North Payne Street, Alexandria, VA 22314. 703-549-8050.

17
Zero Coupon Bonds

Stability of principal
Stability of income
Protection against inflation ✔✔
Total return ✔✔
Tax benefits ✔

Definition

The U.S. government, municipalities, and corporations issue bonds to raise money. In return for borrowing your money, these entities promise to pay you a certain rate of return and the face amount of the bond upon its maturity. Bonds come in several different maturities, ranging from two to thirty years.

Zero coupon bonds are one kind of bond. They are distinguished from other kinds of bonds in that they pay no interest, there is no coupon—hence the name "zero coupon." Instead, these issuers promise to pay you the full face value when the instrument matures. The difference between your purchase price and maturity value represents compounded interest. It is for this reason that zero coupon bonds sell for a price less than par, also known as face value. The rate of return you receive depends upon the general level of interest rates and the maturity of the security. For the most part, the longer the maturity you are willing to accept, the greater the yield you will receive. At the time of purchase, your broker will be able to tell you the rate of return you have locked into. A zero coupon bond sold prior to maturity may result in the investor receiving a higher or lower yield than what was quoted, as shall be explained further on.

How It Works

Zero coupon bonds are issued in increments of $5,000; you can buy as many zero coupon bonds as you like. If, for example, you paid $14,000 for bonds that had a face value of $100,000, you would get the entire $100,000 if you held the bonds until they matured, which would probably be in twenty to thirty years, in this example. Alternatively, you may decide to sell these same bonds a few months or years from now for, say, $16,000. The difference between these two figures represents interest. By the way, a zero coupon bond that was purchased for $14,000 and later sold for $16,000 is not necessarily a better or worse investment than a $14,000 investment that later matures for $100,000.

The reason why $14,000 growing to $16,000 may be a better deal than $14,000 growing to $100,000 has to do with *yield to maturity*. In other words, if I only have to wait a year to make a $2,000 profit, this may be better than having to wait thirty years to make an $86,000 "gain" ($14,000 compounding to $100,000). In order to make sure that you are not fooled or misled, always ask your stockbroker, before the purchase, what is the yield to maturity. In other words, you want to know what kind of compound interest rate you are receiving. Then you can compare it to the rate of return offered by other bonds, bank CDs, or money market instruments.

As an example, if the yield to maturity is 8 percent and you are going to invest $100,000, your account will have an accreted value of $108,000 at the end of twelve months. At the end of the second year, the accreted value will be $108,000 x 1.08, etc. Accreted value is different from market or liquidating value (see "Disadvantages").

When it comes to zero coupon bonds, *yield to maturity* shows you the investment's rate of return and the rate of return on the interest payments that are being automatically reinvested. You do not receive interest checks from zero coupon bonds; instead you get what is referred to as *accreted interest*. This is just an abbreviated way of saying that your account, or investment, is being credited a certain specific rate of return.

Advantages

Zero coupon bonds have several advantages. First, you know exactly what you will end up with if the bond is held to maturity. Second, the rate of return on the investment can be easily determined so that it can be compared to other investments either before you make the investment or while you own it (to decide whether you want to sell it before it comes due). Third, it is an easy investment to own. By this I mean that there is nothing for the investor to do; there are no interest payments that have to be reinvested—"interest payments" automatically go back into the bond. Fourth, you have a wide range of returns, degrees of safety, and maturities from which to choose from. Fifth, zero coupon bonds can be sold at any time; you do not have to hold them to maturity. Finally, they have the potential for appreciation. Let us examine each one of these advantages in detail.

When you buy a bond, bank CD, stock, or money market account, you may know what your initial rate of return will be, but you have no idea what your reinvestment, or "rollover," rate will be. The bank CD you buy tomorrow may have a 6-percent locked-in rate of return, but you do not know what return you will receive on the interest that accumulates each year. When you take that $100 or $1,000 of interest out at the end of one or two years, will you be able to get 6, 4, 8, or 3 percent on that "new" money? The answer, of course, is that no one knows what interest rates will do in the future. The same thing is true when it comes to the reinvestment of bond interest, stock dividends, and money market accounts. However, this is not the case with zero coupon bonds. Here the investment is structured so that the accrued interest automatically goes back into the bond at a rate of return that is known when you buy the bond.

When you buy an investment, it is nice to know what you can expect. Investors have routinely heard over the years that they got an X rate of return instead of the expected Y rate of return because something unexpected happened: a stock-market crash, a jump in interest rates, a slowdown in housing starts, a rise in the price of oil, etc. When you buy a zero coupon bond, none of these things matters. There is no excuse, nor is there a need for one. Because of the "automatic reinvestment" feature, you can learn what this investment will return this year, next year, and even for the next decade by asking the person who is selling you the security what the yield to maturity is.

The third reason people like zero coupon bonds is that they are easy to maintain or own. You do not have to worry about what the investment will eventually be worth and you do not have to concern yourself with what you should do with the semiannual interest payment (there are no regular interest payments).

Another advantage to these bonds is that you can select from a wide range of options. You can buy zero coupon bonds that mature in just a few years (in a few weeks or months, if purchased in the secondary market) or in a few decades. The maturity you decide upon should depend on your need for a specific amount of money at some future date and your perception as to what interest rates will do. (If rates go up, bonds go down, and vice versa.) The kind of bond is another consideration. Some zeros are issued by corporations, others by municipalities, and still others by the U.S. Government. Safety presents further choices. Some zeros are rated much higher than others. Generally, the lower the rating, the greater the risk—and the greater the return potential.

The fifth advantage of zero coupon bonds is their high degree of *marketability*. This means that they can be bought and sold at any time. If you buy a zero bond that matures in, say, ten years, you can sell it tomorrow, a month from now, or a year from now. This is an important feature in the event of a financial emergency.

The final advantage of these bonds is that they appreciate in value when interest rates fall. If you invested $10,000 in a zero coupon bond last year that had a yield to maturity of 8 percent and a maturity date of 2010, that bond would be worth approximately $10,800 (the original purchase price plus $800 of accreted value). However, if interest rates fell 1 percent (a drop in the prime lending rate from 8 to 7 percent), the bond would appreciate close to $1,400. The new value of the zero coupon bond would be $12,200 ($10,000 + $800 + $1,400). The bond could be sold at this time for $12,200. A sale a week, a month, or a year from now may end up being for a price less than $12,200 since interest rates may be higher in the future (when rates go up, bonds drop in value). The longer the maturity, the greater the volatility in price, up or down.

The issue of volatility or changes in value may not be important to many investors. Some people simply want to know the interest rate that is being offered and the value upon redemption. The fact that the bonds may be worth more or less than the initial purchase price plus accreted interest is not important. Most people who buy bonds, any bonds, have no desire to sell prior to maturity. They bought the bonds in order to receive a certain rate of return. A sooner-than-expected sale may mean that the proceeds would not be enough to buy another, new investment that provided the same yield; such a sale could even result in a loss (see "Tax Considerations").

Disadvantages

Like other investments, this one also has its disadvantages: there is no current income stream, the "phantom income" that you do not receive may be taxable, the issuer could default, and a sale before maturity can result in a loss. Let us look at these disadvantages more closely.

If you are an investor in need of *current* income, then this investment is not for you. Unlike regular government, municipal, or corporate bonds that pay interest every six months, zero coupon bonds pay no current interest. Lack of current income may also result in an *opportunity cost*. What this means is that if you are receiving regular interest from bonds, CDs, or money market accounts, you can reinvest such payments into other, perhaps higher-yielding investments, particularly if interest rates have been moving upward over the past several months or years. This "lost" opportunity cost could turn out to be a benefit, however. If interest rates are remaining level or moving downward overall, you will be glad that you are in zero coupon bonds, where there is no reinvestment option—where the reinvestment rate or yield was determined at the time of purchase.

Perhaps the biggest disadvantage to zero coupon bonds is that the accreted interest, although it is not received or really seen by the investor, is still taxable in most cases. There are ways to counter such current taxation, and these methods are described under "Tax Considerations."

The third potential disadvantage has to do with issuer default. This is not a likely event, since the U.S. government guarantees all the zeros it issues and municipal bond issues are backed by the taxing power of the municipality or are supported by some kind of revenue-generator (a toll-bridge, airport fees, etc.). In fact, very few *corporate* zero coupon bonds ever run into trouble. Nevertheless, the best way to counter this unlikely disadvantage is to buy only highly rated corporate or municipal bonds. Bonds that are described as "investment grade" or "bank quality" represent the safest categories of bond rating services: AAA, AA, A, and BAA.

Even though the chances of default in the case of corporate or municipal bonds is probably one in a couple of hundred, such an event should still be taken seriously. This is why ratings are so important. If a zero coupon bond does default, the investor may lose not only part or all of his or her principal but also any accumulated interest. Since there is no chance of a U.S. government bond defaulting, these securities are not rated; government obligations are safer than AAA corporate or municipal bonds.

The last potential disadvantage of zero coupon bonds has to do with *interest-rate risk* (the way a bond can go up and down in value if interest rates in general move down or up). The term "interest-rate risk" may not be a fair description, since a drop in rates means that the bond's market value increases, hardly a negative event. It is true, though, that if rates increase, the value of bonds drop. The amount of potential increase or decrease depends upon three things: the coupon rate of the bond, the *remaining* maturity of the bond, and how much interest rates have changed.

The higher the coupon rate, the less susceptible a bond is to changes in rates. A 6-percent corporate bond will not move up and down as much in value as a 5-percent corporate bond with a similar maturity. Since zero coupon bonds have a 0-percent coupon rate, they are the utmost in volatility. The remaining maturity of the bond will also effect its market-price volatility. A bond with twenty years left until it matures will be wilder than a bond with only five years left. Finally, the change in general interest rates will affect the bond market.

As a general rule, a 1-percent change in interest rates (such as the prime lending rate) will result in an 8-percent change in the value of a long-term bond (a much smaller change if the bond matures in ten years or less). As an example, if you owned a bond that had twenty-five years left until it matured and you discovered that interest rates had recently had two one-half-point increases, the bond that was recently worth $1,000 would now be worth about $920 ($1,000 x .92 percent). A zero coupon bond is anywhere from two to three times more volatile. In this example, this means that the $1,000 bond would be worth somewhere between $840 and $760 ($1,000 x .84% or $1,000 x .76%). This is a paper loss and would only be realized if the bond were sold prior to maturity.

How to Buy and Sell

You can buy or sell zero coupon bonds from a brokerage firm or through your financial advisor. Zero coupon bonds come in increments of $1,000 face value (their value if held to maturity); minimum purchase is $5,000 face value. The amount of money you invest will always be less than face value, since this difference represents interest.

The institution you buy your bonds from will send you monthly or quarterly statements showing the approximate value of your zeros. This "market value" will reflect what the zero would be worth if it were sold at this point in time. The next statement may show a higher or lower price, since the statement (market price) will reflect accreted interest for the period plus or minus any decrease or increase in value due to changes in interest rates (the bond market).

If you decide you want to buy or sell some zeros, you may place your order over the telephone. The broker will then make the transaction according to your instructions. As an example, an investor could phone a stockbroker or financial planner and say, "Buy some zero coupon bonds that are going to mature in twelve years (or she might give a range of ten to fifteen years) with a quality rating of AA (but I'll consider A or AAA bonds) and I am looking for a yield in the 8-percent range." Or someone might phone his stockbroker and say, "I have $50,000 face value of 7-percent zero coupon U.S. government bonds that have a maturity date of 6/30/98. Sell them at the market price."

It takes less than five minutes to buy or sell zero coupon bonds. Once the transaction is completed, the broker should telephone you back and confirm the purchase or sale. He or she would phone back and say something like, "I just sold fifty U.S. government bonds for you at a price of $960 per bond. Total sales price was $48,000." When the broker quotes you these figures, this represents what you will be receiving (or paying, in the case of a purchase); no commission charges are tacked onto the figure. If a commission is being charged, this will be added to the price of the bond and you will simply see a net figure—unlike stocks, which almost always show a commission or ticket charge on the confirmation.

Tracking Performance

Zero coupon bonds are not quoted daily in the newspaper or in financial periodicals. However, government, corporate, and some municipal bonds are. By seeing how similar "regular" bonds ended the day, you can get a fairly good idea as to whether your zeros went up or down. If you own a zero coupon government bond with twenty years until it matures, you can look in the paper and see how regular twenty-year governments performed. If these bonds are up one-half point for the day (1 point = $10, so $\frac{1}{2}$ point = $5), then *each* of your zeros that has a similar maturity has probably increased approximately $10 for the day (since they are about *twice* as volatile).

A second way to track performance is to review the monthly or quarterly statements sent out by your brokerage firm. A third way is to call two or more brokerage firms to obtain current quotes in order to find out the current market value of your holdings.

Tracking the performance of zero coupon bonds is not a major concern for most investors, since they have no interest in selling the bonds prior to maturity. Regardless of such an objective, one should still consider a sale if it is perceived that we are at somewhere near the low end of the interest rate cycle. (When rates fall, zeros increase in value; if you believe rates are not going to fall any more, then a sale at such a point would result in the maximum possible profit.)

Historical Performance

Zero coupon bonds have only been around for about a decade. The relative newness of this investment does not mean that it has not been tested or that it possesses some special kind of risk. After all, corporate, government, and municipal bonds have been around for over a hundred years, and zeros are issued by these entities.

Since their introduction in the early 1980s, zeros have performed extremely well. This is because interest rates fell dramatically in the 1980s. As you may recall, the prime rate hit 21.5 percent briefly in 1981 and was less than 8 percent by the end of 1987. Indeed, the 1980s were the best decade bonds have ever experienced. If regular bonds did so well, imagine how zeros performed, with their enhanced volatility. For most years during the 1980s and early 1990s, zeros racked up total return figures (accreted interest plus appreciation due to interest rate decreases) that were quite impressive. Although no one can say for sure, it is doubtful that zero coupon bonds will do nearly as well in the 1990s, since it is unlikely that rates will fall by even a few more points.

Tax Considerations

When discussing the taxation of zeros, three areas must be looked at: What kind of zero is it? Is this asset being sheltered? And are there any gains or losses at the time of sale? Let us examine each of these three points.

First, there are three kinds of zeros: corporate, government, and municipal. Interest accreted to municipal bonds is not taxable on a federal level. If you own a municipal bond that was issued in your state of residence, chances are that it is not subject to state income taxes either. Government zeros are free from state and local taxes, but not from federal income taxes. If your account shows, say, $859 of accreted interest for the year, you must report this entire figure on your federal income tax return. Accreted interest from zero coupon corporate bonds is fully taxable on a state and federal level. Interest from these bonds is reported the same way that interest from your other accounts, such as money market funds or bank CDs, is shown.

The only way to avoid current taxation from the accreted interest of government or corporate bonds is to place these securities inside a retirement plan such as an IRA, Keogh, 401(k) plan, pension, 403(b), or profit-sharing plan. This is how most people like to own these kinds of zeros, since no one likes to pay taxes on something she does not "see" or currently enjoy.

The final tax consideration concerns selling your zero for a profit or a loss. This is not always easy to determine, since the sales price includes principal and accreted interest, plus a premium (if rates have dropped) or minus a discount (if rates have gone up).

Portfolio Fit
Since the accreted interest is currently taxable (a 1099 is issued at the end of each year), corporate and government zeros should only be part of a qualified retirement plan or as part of a variable annuity (a later chapter covers variable annuities). Interest from *municipal* bonds is generally exempt from taxes, so this kind of zero should only be owned *outside* of an annuity or retirement plan. (Money withdrawn from a retirement plan or annuity is fully taxable, no matter what its source, to the extent that it represents growth, interest, and/or dividends; principal may or may not be taxable.)

Sheltering zeros from current taxation makes this an attractive choice for someone who wants a locked-in rate of return for the reinvested interest and principal. It is this feature, and the safety factor, that make zeros a frequent selection for a child's college fund or retirement. Under the current tax law, for the tax years ending in 1992 and 1993, the first $600 of interest, dividends, or capital gains generated under a child's social security number is free of federal taxes, regardless of the parents' tax status. For the tax years 1992 and 1993, the second $600 of this income is subject to a tax of 15 percent. These brackets, which are currently $600, are subject to change depending on the inflation rate, but the current rule is that the brackets only adjust in $50 increments; over $1,200 the parents' tax rate applies. Once the child reaches age fourteen or older, the first $600 is still tax-free, but then the rest of the child's income is taxed at the rate of a single individual. For example, for 1992, if the child had no earned income (e.g., salary), then after the first tax-free $600 of income, the next $21,450 would be taxed at the 15 percent rate—which for many children would be significantly lower than their parents' rate.

Zero coupon municipal bonds are used by investors who have no need for current income (at least not from this source) but want to make sure that a specific dollar figure is available at maturity.

Zeros can also be used by aggressive investors. If someone is betting that interest rates are going to fall by one or more points, this person should buy long-term zero coupon bonds. If rates do fall, the capital gains can be quite high. (A two-point drop in long-term rates translates into a 32-to-48 percent profit.) If rates go up instead of down, the loss is also quite high. In order to enjoy such profits or sustain such losses, the bonds would have to be sold after the drop or rise. In the case of falling rates, an investor who waits too long, until rates have started to climb, may find this handsome profit partially or fully eroded. If rates rise, the paper loss can be wiped out if the investor remains patient and waits for a subsequent drop in interest rates.

The strategy described in the paragraph above is not for the impatient or faint of heart. Surprisingly, although most people realize that they cannot guess what the stock market will do next, they seem to be certain as to what will happen to interest rates. Do not fall into this trap. If the best money managers, economists, and financial writers have only a mediocre record in this area, what makes you think you can do better? After all, this is their full-time job, and they have access to information that you will probably never see and may not even understand!

Risks

Like other debt instruments, zero coupon bonds are subject to purchasing-power risk. Locking in an X rate of return for the next ten or twenty years may sound dandy, but you are not going to feel very happy if the price of goods and services increases by 2X during this period. For instance, people who bought zeros several years ago for a child or grandchild's education found out, after the damage had been done, that college costs increased at twice the rate of inflation during the 1980s. Debt instruments often do not keep pace with inflation. How would you like to own something that had only half its purchasing value when it came time to pay tuition or some other expense?

A risk rarely talked about when it comes to bonds of all kinds is the *call risk*. A great number of municipal and corporate bonds, including zeros, include a provision allowing the issuer to "call them away" from the investor at a certain price. What this means to the investor is that a corporation or municipality can force you to sell the bond back to them at a certain date. Fortunately, most bonds have *call protection* for the first ten years after issuance (when the bonds were first issued, not necessarily when you first bought them). This means that they cannot be called away during this period. Phrased another way, you are the only one who can decide whether the bonds should be kept or sold during this time.

A call feature is only a concern if you paid a premium for the bond and it is called away in just a few years, or if you were hoping for a large capital gain. Furthermore, a call feature only becomes an issue when interest rates are falling. Corporations and municipalities will not call in a bond if they have to turn around and issue new bonds at a higher yield. Zero coupon government bonds do not have a call feature. In fact, this entire risk can be eliminated, or at least factored in, by simply asking the broker whether the bond has a call provision and if so, what its features are (when it can be called away and at what price).

The other risk of owning zeros is found only with municipal and corporate issues. This is the risk of default. When you buy one of these kinds of zeros, ask your advisor or broker what the rating is; normally you should stay away from anything that is rated less than "investment grade."

Unique Features
The compounding, or "leverage" effect is what makes zeros so special. The idea of investing $50 or $100 and ending up with a $1,000 is rather appealing. However, do not get caught up in this "magic"; find out what the yield to maturity is *before* you make any purchase.

The other unique aspect of zeros is that we are being taxed on something we are not receiving, the accreted interest. To some, this may seem unfair, but then again, no one is forcing you to buy zeros. (Accreted interest from *municipal* zeros is tax-free.) If it makes you feel any better, the concept of "phantom income" is also found in other, more sophisticated investments.

Comments
Zeros are not a favored choice for several reasons. First, the idea of locking in a rate of return when we live in a world of ever-increasing prices is not appealing. With more traditional bonds, money market accounts, and CDs, at least we can reinvest the interest into higher-yielding items. Second, unless you are buying issues backed by the U.S. government, the issue of default becomes more of a concern; at least with regular bonds, if there is a default, all of the previously received interest is yours to keep. Third, most investors are not aware of how many zeros have a call feature (common with municipal and corporate issues; not a feature of governments). If a zero is called away, the yield to maturity can be much lower (and occasionally higher) than expected. Finally, the marketplace for zeros is not as open as it could be. If a sale occurs prior to maturity, the markup (built-in commission or spread between the buy and sell price) can be quite high. A markup of three to five points means that the client is getting that much less and a broker, or bond trader, that much more.

Additional Information

Benham Distributors
1665 Charleston Road, Mountain View, CA 94043. 800-472-3389.

LPL Financial Services
7911 Herschel Avenue, Suite 201, La Jolla, CA 92037. 800-748-5552.

18
High-Yield Corporate Bond Funds

Stability of principal   ✔✔✔
Stability of income   ✔✔✔✔
Protection against inflation   ✔✔✔✔
Total return   ✔✔✔
Tax benefits   ✔

Definition

Close to 90 percent of all corporations would be forced to issue high-yield, also referred to as "junk," bonds if they were to raise capital by issuing debt instruments in the marketplace. Junk bonds are a name given to bonds that are not rated "investment grade." These are securities with a rating of less than Baa (if you were using the rating system of Moody's) or BBB (if you were using Standard & Poors).

Bonds are issued by corporations in order to raise money. If the issuing corporations were more financially secure and had been around longer, they would issue investment grade, also known as "bank quality." Since the great majority of corporations in America do not have the financial clout to issue AAA, AA, A or BAA rated bonds, they are forced to issue "junk." Investors are attracted to high-yield bonds because of their better-than-average rate of return.

In reality, there is a big difference between "junk" and "high-yield" bonds, even though these terms are frequently used to mean the same thing. *Junk* bonds were those debt instruments used for corporate takeovers (trying to buy another company with paper instead of sweat, hard work, and cash). *High-yield* bonds really represent those securities that have had a long track record of overall reliability for the timely payment of interest and principal; they also represent those bonds that have had comparatively few defaults.

High-yield corporate bond funds, within the context of this book, are simply mutual funds that seek a high current income while keeping an eye on preserving principal. These are the funds that are willing to sacrifice a little bit of the current income (accepting, say, 10 percent instead of 12 to 14 percent current income) in return for bonds at the high end of the "junk" bond spectrum—B or BB-rated bonds instead of CCC, CC or C-rated securities.

How It Works

Virtually any corporation can issue bonds. The public decides whether it is going to buy these bonds. Major rating services evaluate the current and projected financial stability of these companies and issue ratings that range from AAA down to D (for "in default"). Some bonds are not rated because the issuing corporation or municipality was not willing to pay the rating service fee, which can end up costing tens of thousands of dollars.

One of the biggest determinants will be the bonds' rating. Poorly rated bonds appeal to a much smaller, more aggressive, investor base. Since there is less demand for these securities, the issuing corporations must enhance their yields to attract buyers. The resulting yields, also known as coupon rates, are anywhere from two to six percentage points higher than corporate bonds that are considered extremely safe (say 13 percent versus 9 percent).

The investor receives interest income from these bonds as long as he or she owns them. If the bonds are sold prior to their maturity, the sales price may end up being more or less than what was originally paid for the securities. If the bonds are held until maturity, the issuer will pay the holder full face value. This, by the way, is true with all bonds, including government and municipal.

In the case of high-yield bond funds, there is a wide range of current income, quality, and total return. You cannot condemn the entire stock market because some stocks went down last week or last year, and you cannot paint the entire high-yield bond market with a single brushstroke. The world of bonds is not black and white; it cannot be compartmentalized with a simple description such as "investment grade" or "junk." There are several shades of grey, and it is important that you understand the distinctions, for some of these "shades" can provide you with some handsome returns.

Advantages

High-yield bonds have two advantages: a better current return and reduced volatility most of the time. Again, people who buy these securities expect something extra for taking on more financial risk. Financial risk refers to the possibility that the corporation may go into bankruptcy, foreclosure, or reorganization. As scary as this sounds, only 1 or 2 percent of the outstanding corporate bond market experiences such troubles each year. Equally important, those that do are often able to turn themselves around and show a profit as well as pay off all bondholders.

The second advantage, reduced volatility, has already been described in other chapters that deal with bonds. Briefly, lower fluctuations in value are beneficial to an investor who may want to sell his bonds prior to their maturity. If your underlying principal does not go up or down very much in value, there is a greater chance that you will be made whole at the time of sale. Volatility, however, is a two-way street. When interest rates are falling and bond prices are going up, you will have wished that you owned these kinds of bonds. It is only when rates are *increasing* that you want to own more stable securities. Junk bonds have less interest-rate risk than other bonds, such as government or high-quality corporates.

With high-yield bond funds you also get the advantage of ongoing, professional management (that can get rid of a bond before it becomes greatly troubled), reduced risk (since you own part of a very diversified portfolio), and the ability to switch to other funds within the same family with a simple phone call. The price per share (value) of high-yield bond funds is also reported in the mutual fund section of the newspaper each day.

Disadvantages
High-yield bonds have four disadvantages: credit risk, price changes during poor or uncertain economic periods, interest-rate risk, and "call feature" risk. Credit risk has already been examined, so we shall first focus our attention on price changes.

When the U.S. economy is going through the initial or middle stages of a recession, high-yield bonds may drop in value. This is because there is a perceived, and sometimes real, concern that corporations that are not among the strongest in financial terms will default or suspend their obligations. During the later stages of a recession, such as in 1991 and early 1992, junk bonds experienced tremendous gains. Some high-yield corporate bond funds were up over 40 percent for 1991, easily beating out all other kinds of bond funds and even outperforming several categories of stock funds.

The third potential disadvantage is price changes due to interest rate movement. This is potentially a significant risk if interest rates increase dramatically, albeit somewhat less of a risk than it would be for higher grade bonds.

The fourth potential disadvantage is the potential "call feature" on individual bonds within the fund. This is not a major risk because these types of bonds are generally of six to ten years in duration.

How to Buy and Sell
Junk bonds are bought and sold just like any other kind of bond: individually, in a bond fund, or as part of a unit trust. Mutual funds and unit trusts that are heavily loaded with junk issues are usually easy to spot by their names. Names like "XYZ High-Yield Bond Fund" or "ABC Enhanced-Re-

turn Unit Trust" often translate into, "We own at least a moderate, if not a lot, of lower-rated securities."

Investors who buy individual high-yield bonds should only do so if they are intimately familiar with the issuing corporation or are willing to keep on top of the financial news. Otherwise, stick with funds and unit trusts. These organizations are staffed with people who understand the workings of this marketplace and generally know what is a good buy and what should be dumped. When you compare funds and unit trusts, do not be tempted by higher-than-expected current yields. Look at *total return* figures for each of the last several years. By factoring in the value of the underlying bonds, you will quickly be able to see which funds and trusts are stocked with "good-quality" junk and which have very poorly rated issues (but capture investors by advertising a very high current income or yield).

Although high-yield bonds are not as popular as high-quality securities, they can still be bought or sold within a few minutes. Like other bonds, junk bonds are most commonly traded in increments of five (such as a face value of $5,000, $10,000, $15,000, etc.). Thus, when you buy a bond, you must normally purchase five, ten, fifteen, etc., at a time.

Tracking Performance

You can find out what your bonds are worth by telephoning the broker who sold them to you. If you own a bond fund or unit trust you can also telephone the group directly and get a buy or sell price quote for the day. (The purchasing price is often referred to as the "asking price" and the selling price is known as the "bid price.") The price you are quoted for a unit trust or fund is the *previous* day's closing price. The price you receive will be the *current day's* closing price, something you will not know until after the sale. Do not be alarmed. Daily changes, particularly when it comes to high-yield issues, are usually not very substantial. In fact, you may be surprised to learn that the price went up, not down. When you buy or sell individual bonds, the price you are given is the actual price you will pay or receive.

When individual issues are sold, they are sold for market value plus *accrued interest*. (Bonds accrue interest every day for up to six months, when the accrued interest is distributed to the bondholder.) This accrued interest is simply the interest to which you were entitled for owning the bonds during the most recent six-month cycle. When you buy bonds, you will most likely also be buying them with accrued interest. This means that you are, in a sense, prepaying interest to the former owner. It also means that if this happens, you will be owning these same bonds for less than six months and then receiving a full six months' worth of interest. If you do not understand what "accrued" or "prepaid" interest means, do not worry; it should have no impact on your decision as to whether you should own any kind of bonds.

Historical Performance

You may be surprised to learn that during most periods of time, junk bonds have outperformed high-quality corporate, municipal, and U.S. government securities. Their return has been better on a current-yield, or return, basis as well as on a *total return* basis (current income plus appreciation or minus depreciation). Even for the past ten years ending 1991 or 1992, junk bonds had better returns, despite the beating most junk bonds took during 1989 and 1990. You may remember this as a time of "merger mania" and "leveraged buyouts," a period when individual and institutional investors seemed to be buying junk bonds no matter how shaky they were.

Let us examine in greater detail what happened during the later part of 1989 and during 1990. First there was adverse legislation. In the summer of 1989, Congress essentially outlawed the savings and loan industry from investing in the high-yield market. This placed the S & L industry, then holder of 11 percent of all outstanding high-yield securities, under tremendous selling pressure. Second, there was regulation. The National Association of Insurance Commissioners, the regulatory body of the life insurance industry, tightened quality requirements for life insurance portfolios and restricted the use of high-yield credits. That forced life insurers, who then owned 30 percent of all outstanding high-yield bonds, to step back from this market. Third, there was negative publicity. Press reports on the bankruptcy of Drexel-Burnham-Lambert, the largest underwriter of high-yield bonds, in February 1990 shook consumer confidence and spurred large cash outflows by mutual fund companies. Finally, there was the Persian Gulf War. When Iraq invaded Kuwait in August 1990, the financial markets started feeling the beginning of a recession in the U.S. economy.

When measured by *total return*, there certainly have been periods of time when safer securities performed much better than their high-yield brethren. This is particularly true when you look at certain one-, three-, and five-year periods. Yet, over most of these same time horizons, and particularly when you look at ten-year periods of time or longer, junk bonds are normally the winner when compared to other U.S. bonds.

To see how these bonds have fared over shorter periods of time, let us look at all of the five-year periods beginning with 1982. (These figures are based on the Lipper High-Yield Universe Average—an index of high-yield bond funds compiled and tracked by a neutral advisory source.) The figures that follow are total return numbers; they are not annualized.

1982-1986	+121.1%
1983-1987	+75.4%
1984-1988	+69.1%
1985-1989	+52.3%
1986-1990	+11.1%
1987-1991	+36.5%

There are certainly high-yield bond funds that have fared better (and worse) than this index. As an investor, your goal should be to select a fund that has consistently rated in the top third of its universe—the high-yield bond universe, in this case—by looking at some mutual fund advisory services or books, such as my *The 100 Best Mutual Funds You Can Buy* (1993).

Tax Considerations
The interest received from high-yield corporate bonds, whether through individual issues, a mutual fund, or a unit trust, are fully taxable in the year in which they are received. You will receive a 1099 form from the issuer, fund, or trust each year; reinvestment of interest payments or some other diversion will not mitigate the taxation of corporate bond interest.

Capital gains and capital losses are once again an issue. If the bonds are sold for a profit (more than you paid for them, minus any accrued interest), this results in a *capital gain*. If the sale proceeds are less than your purchase price, there is a *capital loss*. Capital losses offset capital gains, dollar for dollar. Thus, if you sell ABC stock for a $70,000 gain and you also sell XYZ bonds for a $40,000 loss and JKL bonds for a $10,000 loss, you will only have to pay taxes on $20,000 ($70k - $40k - $10k).

Portfolio Fit
Since junk bonds throw off a substantial amount of *current* income, they are most effectively used, for tax purposes, in a qualified retirement plan or within a variable annuity. (Variable annuities are described in detail in another chapter.) They are also appropriate for investors in a low tax bracket who may or may not be able to shelter such income.

The second issue concerning portfolio fit is the patience and risk level of the investor. If you are ultra-conservative, you should avoid junk bonds. If, on a scale of one to ten, you are a two through seven (the higher the number, the higher the risk you are willing to accept), then high-yield bonds should make up to 15 percent of your portfolio. Someone above a "seven" will not find high-yield bonds exciting enough (unless we experience another 1991).

High-yield bonds perform best and are certainly more stable if they are held for at least five years. Such a holding period will help amortize any future disasters, such as what was experienced in 1989 and 1990. However, it is very doubtful that these bonds will go through losses as severe as this in the future. Now that the marketplace has seen what can happen to junk bonds, it is likely to learn from its past excesses and weed out those issues based on unrealistically rosy predictions.

Risks
As you might suspect, the biggest risk with high-yield bonds is that of default. No one likes to own a bond that has stopped or suspended paying interest. More importantly, no one likes to have his or her principal in jeopardy of not being paid back. Again, however, the number of junk bonds that default is very small compared to the thousands that perform just fine; and losses from defaults are rarely 100 cents on the dollar. At least one study shows that investors get back approximately 70 cents on the dollar when this worst-case situation occurs.

Unique Features
The only truly unique thing about junk bonds is how they are perceived by the public: high return but also high risk. The fact is that these bonds can provide valuable additional income for individuals and couples who rely on their investments to supplement other sources of income.

On a similar note, it is odd to think of the world of bonds as black or white, of a security as either investment grade (bank quality) or junk. The reality is that there are several shades of grey. Some of those shades of grey can translate unexpectedly into a safe and rewarding investment, especially when mutual funds are used.

Comments
You and I know that the world is not full of absolutes. Not every stockbroker is just a salesperson, not every doctor is rich, and not every lawyer is smart. The same is true with the world of investments. Historically, stocks have been and continue to be a great investment, but there are hundreds of equities that have lost money over the past decade. Few people in California ever thought real estate prices could actually go *down* until just a couple of years ago. Junk bonds sound risky and many of them are; this does not mean that certain categories of "junk" are not safe and a good deal.

Good investments are just like a good marriage or relationship: they take work. In the case of investing, you must do your work. If you do not or cannot spend the necessary time, you can hire a professional by buying into a mutual fund or unit trust. Do not automatically exclude high-yield bonds just because of the bad publicity they received a few years ago. What the press never told you was that well over 95 percent of these bonds have never been in trouble. Besides, if you relied on yesterday's news, you would have missed out on stocks in the 1980s and early 1990s—and you will probably never buy CDs or government bonds again because they are not particularly attractive right now. As more than one famous, and rich, investor has counseled, "Buy when everyone else is selling."

Additional Information

No brokerage firms or nationally known publications stand out from other sources when it comes to high-yield bonds. Most large firms have sufficient resources in this area, and this may be the source you should contact. There are, however, mutual fund groups that have consistently done well in this area. These funds have demonstrated, year in and year out, that they are willing to sacrifice a little current yield for quality. The names, addresses and toll-free telephone numbers of some of these companies are listed below.

Kemper Financial Services
120 S. LaSalle Street, Chicago, IL 60603. 800-621-1148.

Liberty High-Income Bond Fund
Liberty Center Federated Investors Tower, Pittsburgh, PA 15222.
800-245-5051.

Lutheran Brotherhood Securities Corp.
625 Fourth Avenue South, Minneapolis, MN 55415. 800-328-4552.

Nicholas Family of Funds, Inc.
700 N. Water Street, Suite 1010, Milwaukee, WI 53202. 414-272-6133.

19
Foreign Bonds

Stability of principal	✔✔✔
Stability of income	✔✔✔✔
Protection against inflation	✔✔✔
Total return	✔✔✔
Tax benefits	✔

Definition

Foreign, also known as "international," bonds are issued by corporations and countries other than the United States. As with their U.S. counterparts, investors receive interest payments twice a year and the face value (principal) upon maturity. The bond is guaranteed by the issuing corporation or government.

How It Works

When you buy a bond, you are buying two things. First, you are buying a certain degree of safety. The quality of your investment depends upon the financial strength of the issuer. Outside rating services can help you determine the security of the instrument. Second, you are buying a current income. Bonds normally pay interest on a semiannual basis. When you sell your bonds, you may end up receiving a price identical to, higher than, or lower than your purchase price. Thus, bond ownership can mean possible appreciation of principal.

When you buy a foreign bond, you are buying the same things just described, but with one additional factor: you are also "buying" the country's currency. This means that your income checks will vary depending upon the currency's conversation rate to the U.S. dollar. If the foreign currency is up 2 percent against the dollar, your check will be 2 percent higher. If, during another period of time, the currency has dropped 3 percent against the dollar, your income will also drop 3 percent. Principal value at redemption or sale is also affected by currency movements.

For example, if you bought a German government or corporate bond five years ago when it took, say, four deutschemarks to equal one U.S. dollar, and now it takes only 3.6 marks, then your original $10,000 purchase is now worth $11,000. This is because the deutschemark has increased in value by 10 percent against the U.S. dollar by the end of these five years. Phrased another way, it now takes fewer marks to equal a dollar. While you own a German bond, you are also, in a sense, owning deutschemarks.

Advantages

Owning foreign bonds has five advantages. First, they provide a current stream of income. Second, when properly purchased, they are also very safe. Third, there is appreciation potential, either from a drop in interest rates (remember, when rates fall, bond prices go up, and vice versa) or an increase in the country's currency value against the dollar. Fourth, portfolio risk is reduced because your holdings are now more broadly diversified. Finally, you have more buying opportunities by going overseas. There are more securities to choose from when it comes to maturity, quality, and yield.

Disadvantages

There are four possible disadvantages to owning international bonds. First, as with any other corporate bond, there is always the chance of default, not only of interest but of principal. This negative can be eliminated by buying foreign government bonds from stable countries. The second potential disadvantage has to do with currency fluctuations, which has already been discussed. This second point is not necessarily a disadvantage. A currency "risk" can turn into a currency "reward" if the currency appreciates in value.

There are also the interest rate and "call feature" disadvantages as previously discussed in chapters 10 (Municipal Bonds) and 14 (High-Quality Corporate Bonds).

How to Buy and Sell

Foreign bonds can be bought through your broker or by investing in a unit trust or mutual fund directly. The purchase and sale price is always quoted in U.S. dollars. Those dollars are then exchanged for the foreign country's currency, and then the bond is purchased. You do not make the exchange. The brokerage firm, unit trust company, or mutual fund group does this for you. Billions of dollars of currency are exchanged each day. Many of these entities are well-versed in such exchange procedures.

Tracking Performance

There is no easy way to track *individual* foreign bonds. If you own shares of a mutual fund that invests in foreign or global bonds, the price per share of the fund (and thus the value of the international bonds in its portfolio) is quoted daily.

If for some reason you want to own individual bonds, do not be overly concerned about getting exact daily quotes. You may be able to get a sense of the direction of the bonds (whether they are appreciating or dropping in value) by seeing how foreign bond funds are doing in the newspaper or by telephoning your broker occasionally. There is a good chance that your broker will not have hourly prices, since many quotron machines (what brokers use to get up-to-the-second quotes on stocks and bonds) do not include the service that covers international securities.

Finally, your monthly or quarterly statements will give you an approximate value. When viewing these statements, bear in mind that bond quotes (or approximate valuations) are usually 1 to 8 percent higher than their real current market value (sometimes the price difference is even greater). This is because the tracking services on which brokerage firms rely price (or value) bonds with the assumption that everyone owns at least $1,000,000 worth of that specific security (U.S. or foreign). Smaller "lots" trade at lesser prices.

Historical Performance

The track record of foreign bonds has been quite impressive over the past one, five, and ten years. Consider the results of the Salomon World Bond Index (made up of foreign and U.S. bonds with remaining maturities of at least five years), compared to the Shearson Gov't/Corp. Bond Index (high-grade U.S. corporate bonds and U.S. government obligations):

TIME PERIOD	WORLD BOND INDEX	U.S. BOND INDEX
one year	+21.8%	+14.2%
five years	+10.7%	+10.2%
ten years	+14.8%	+13.3%

(note: these are average annual compound rates of return for periods ending 6/30/92)

As you can see, foreign bonds have done better over every one of these time periods. In fact, the results would be even more impressive if a pure foreign bond index were used instead of a world bond index.

Tax Considerations

Interest from foreign bonds, like that of their U.S. counterparts, is fully taxable in the year in which it is credited to your account (or mutual fund) or sent out to you. The brokerage firm you deal with will send you out a 1099 form at the beginning of the year that will reflect the interest paid or credited to your account during the previous year. Mutual fund and unit trust companies send out similar statements.

As with foreign stocks or international (or world or global) funds, a certain amount of tax is also withheld by other governments. At first investors think this means they are being taxed twice, once by the country from which the bonds are denominated and again by the United States. (In return for the privilege of being a U.S. citizen, you must pay taxes on income, interest, or capital gains earned in other countries, including Swiss bank accounts and offshore operations.) Although it is true that you will be paying taxes twice (the foreign country or mutual fund will withhold a certain percentage), your total tax liability is not increased, however. Why? Because the U.S. has reciprocal tax treaties with most nations in the world. This means you are given credit, dollar for dollar, for any tax withheld by a foreign country. In short, your U.S. tax liability for interest, income, dividends, etc. is reduced to offset any such taxes paid or withheld elsewhere.

As an example, say you owned some Italian bonds that paid you the equivalent of $100 a year, and you noticed that the Italian government was withholding $15 of that interest. Your U.S. tax liability on that $100 would normally be $28, (assuming you are in the 28-percent federal tax bracket). However, since $15 has already been withheld by a foreign power, your U.S. tax liability for this interest is now only $13 ($28 minus the $15 already paid).

You should be aware that a few countries, such as Mexico, do not have a reciprocal tax treaty or agreement with the United States. In these isolated cases you will be paying tax twice, with no credit or deduction on your U.S. return for taxes paid to these countries.

Portfolio Fit

One of the real beauties of foreign bonds is that they often move in a direction different from U.S. stocks. The results for both investments over an extended period of time can be quite impressive. From July 1, 1982 (a month or two before the great bull market of the 1980s began), through June 30, 1992, a $50,000 investment in the Salomon World Bond Index grew to just under $200,000, while a similar investment in the S & P 500 grew to just over $270,000. U.S. stocks performed better, but they also experienced about 50 percent more risk than a global bond portfolio.

Risks

When you invest in foreign bonds there are three risks: risk of default, interest-rate risk, and currency risk. These risks are described in detail in chapter 26, "Foreign Stocks." Let me summarize them here.

The risk of default is your biggest concern. If the underlying issuer (the foreign government or corporation) goes bankrupt or for some reason refuses to pay interest or principal back, the investment is obviously quite troubled. Fortunately, this kind of risk can be eliminated by making sure that you deal only in highly rated foreign bonds, or in foreign bond funds that concentrate on highly rated bonds, or in bonds issued and backed by strong governments.

Interest-rate risk is a concern whether you own U.S. or foreign bonds. When you own foreign bonds or bonds that are part of an international mutual fund, you are concerned with what is happening to interest rates overseas. Specifically, you are interested in fiscal policy in the countries you own bonds in. If these governments are encouraging spending and so have a policy of lowering rates, your bonds will appreciate in value. If, on the other hand, the foreign government is trying to break the back of inflation by raising interest rates, the value of your bonds will suffer until they mature or monetary policy changes.

Currency risk, like interest-rate risk, is something that can help or hurt you. As odd as it may sound, when you own foreign bonds, you selfishly hope that the country's currency will appreciate against the U.S. dollar. If it does, all other things being equal, your bonds will increase by that same currency appreciation rate. If you own French bonds, for instance, and the franc appreciates 4 percent against the U.S. dollar, your French bonds will go up exactly 4 percent, assuming that interest rates or the French bond markets have not changed. The reverse is also true. If the currency in which your bonds are denominated drops against the dollar, you will suffer a similar loss. However, part or all of this loss can end up being offset by the bonds' appreciating due to foreign interest rate drops.

Unique Features

What is unique about foreign bonds is the currency risk or reward that goes along with the investment. You are subject to this risk or reward even if you own the bonds indirectly through a mutual fund or unit trust. The currency risk can be minimized, and sometimes avoided, by certain hedging strategies that you can employ on your own. Some mutual funds also actively pursue such an "insurance policy." However, do not think that any such strategy is free or that it will protect you 100 percent against a strong U.S. dollar. Such techniques cost money (money that comes out of your pocket either directly or as an expense of the mutual fund, which in turn is passed onto you in the form of higher operating costs), and do not always work out exactly the way they are supposed to—meaning that the hedging may only end up protecting part of the portfolio.

Comments

Foreign, global, or international bond funds are highly recommended for almost every investor. High-tax-bracket people will want to shelter the current income, if possible, through a retirement account or variable annuity. People in a low bracket will find the current income and historical track record quite appealing.

One of the real beauties of "going global" is that you are reducing the overall risk of your portfolio while probably enjoying higher rates of return. It is true that foreign bonds from stable economies do not outperform U.S. bonds every year, but they have been winners over the last five, ten, fifteen, twenty, and twenty-five years.

Only a small percentage of U.S. investors have taken the opportunity of owning foreign or international bonds. It is time that you did so too. Individual foreign bonds or bonds from just one country (unit trusts, which are somewhat similar to mutual funds, sometimes put together portfolios of bonds from one or two countries and sell such units to investors) are not recommended, even if they are professionally managed. The risk level increases quite a bit when you start betting on how *one* country's currency will fare against the U.S. dollar.

Additional Information

Huntington Investments
251 S. Lake Avenue, Suite 600, Pasadena, CA 91101. 800-354-4111.

MFS Service Center
P.O. Box 2281, Boston, MA 02107. 800-225-2606.

Scudder, Stevens & Clark
175 Federal Street, Boston, MA 02110. 800-225-2470.

Van Eck Securities, Inc.
122 E. 42nd Street, 42nd Floor, New York, NY 10168. 800-221-2220.

20
Short-Term Global Bond Funds

Stability of principal	✔✔✔✔
Stability of income	✔✔✔
Protection against inflation	✔✔✔
Total return	✔✔
Tax benefits	✔

Definition

A mutual fund is a portfolio of securities, such as stocks, bonds, and/or money market instruments (T-bills, commercial paper, bank CDs, etc.) that are professionally managed. When you invest in a mutual fund, you are pooling your money with thousands of other investors. There are several different kinds of mutual funds: money market, growth, municipal bond, corporate bond, aggressive growth, gold, etc. As the investor, you decide which fund or series of funds your money will be invested in. As you can probably gather, some mutual fund categories are much safer than others. Money can be added or taken out of a mutual fund at any time.

Short-term global bond funds, sometimes referred to as short-term global income funds, are a relatively new kind of mutual fund that has only been in existence for a few years. Yet these funds are safer than any other category of funds except money market funds and short-term U.S. bond funds. What makes them so safe is the investments in the portfolio; all of them are quite conservative.

How It Works

When you buy shares of a mutual fund, you end up with a very small interest in every security in the portfolio. If there are a hundred different securities in the mutual fund portfolio, you will now own a very small fraction of one percent of each of those assets. If the value of those securities increases in a day, week, month, or year, you will also benefit. This benefit is seen as an increased price per share.

In the case of bond funds, including short-term global income funds, investors, also referred to as "shareholders," are concerned with the price per share (the value of their underlying principal) and the *current yield.* Some bonds in the portfolio might be yielding 9 percent, others may be paying 8.5 percent, and still others may offer a return of 8.75 percent. When all of these securities are combined, the average yield may be 8.67 percent; this represents how much your investment will "grow" or yield for the year *if* the average yield in the portfolio does not change. This is not a very likely event, because bonds, notes, and other instruments in the mutual fund portfolio are maturing all of the time. When these securities come due, it is the manager's responsibility to find something else immediately that will give as high a return as possible, given the risk parameters of the fund. Unlike a bank CD, you do not have to "roll over" a mutual fund investment; the fund manages everything for you.

Short-term global bond funds go out and buy U.S. and foreign bonds and notes that are maturing in just a few months or years. Management's goal is to get investors a higher rate of return than they would normally get from a portfolio of U.S. bonds, CDs, or money market instruments. Since their introduction almost four years ago, short-term global income funds have consistently outperformed bank CDs, money market accounts, and most short-term U.S. bonds.

Advantages

People buy short-term global bond funds for safety, to get a better-than-competitive rate of return, to have a portfolio whose yield will stay competitive with whatever current rates might be in the future, and for convenience.

Convenience always plays an important role when it comes to investing. True, you and I could probably go to the library and learn about short-term bonds and notes—how they are traded, where to purchase them in different countries, how to understand the safety ratings, etc.—but that would take weeks of extensive homework. Even then we would not have the experience of a seasoned trader or manager. More importantly, we would also lack the objectivity to make rational decisions in the face of a minor catastrophe or emergency. When you invest in mutual funds, all of these things are taken care of for you.

The portfolios of short-term global bond funds are made up of some securities that are maturing in a few days, a few weeks, a few months, and, in the case of some items, perhaps as much as a year or two. A portfolio of short-term securities is like owning CDs that mature every six or twelve months. As interest rates start to move up, the CD investor does not have to wait very long before he or she can renew the CD and get the new, higher yield. When rates are moving down, however, CD investors are stuck with the lower rate when their CDs come due. Like the CD investor, the short-term global bond fund owner hopes that rates will stay the same or go up.

As instruments in the global bond fund come due, they must be replaced with whatever competitive instruments are then paying, for better or worse. On any given day or month, the overall change in the portfolio is modest, since only a small portion of the fund is being replaced at any one time; over a six- or twelve-month period the resulting yield difference can be a few percentage points. For example, at the beginning of 1991 several short-term global income funds had yields of over 10 percent; a year later, the same funds were offering yields in the 8.5-to-9-percent range. This one- or one-and-a-half-point drop was minor in comparison to what happened to bank CD rates during the same period; they dropped from around 8 percent to under 4 percent. So short-term global bond fund yields do change, but generally not as quickly or radically (for better or worse) as CD or money market rates.

The comparatively high rate of return offered by these funds is what makes them so popular. Even though they are only a few years old, short-term global bond funds have attracted well over $10 billion worth of sophisticated and unsophisticated money. Certain instruments, such as junk bonds and long-term foreign bonds, offer a higher yield, but the risk profile of these other securities is radically different.

Perhaps the greatest selling point of short-term bond funds is that they have a safety factor somewhat similar to bank CDs while offering a rate of return approximately double that offered by banks and savings and loan associations. What makes these funds such a conservative investment is quality, maturity, and currency hedging.

Most short-term bond funds can invest only in securities such as CDs, commercial paper issued by corporations, and government-backed obligations that are either rated AA or AAA or are supported by the full faith and credit of a major government (country). These are the three highest ratings possible. The quality of the investments in which the fund can invest is clearly spelled out in the fund's sales literature and/or prospectus. I have yet to hear or read about anyone who is not happy with the high quality of securities found in these funds.

The second reason these funds are considered safe is maturity. As you now know, bond *values* go up and down with interest rates. When rates go up, bonds drop in value; when rates fall, bonds increase in worth. The degree of movement (how much the bond goes up or down in value) largely depends upon its remaining maturity; the greater the remaining maturity, the more the bond's price will change. Thus, a bond that only has two years or less until it matures will be affected to a very small degree if the prime interest rate climbs a full point. A ten- or twenty-year bond, however, may rise or fall in value by 6 to 8 percent if long-term rates change by a full percentage point.

Because short-term global income funds have such a short-term maturity (several funds have an average maturity of well under a year), *interest rate risk* is a very minor concern. Phrased another way, investors in these funds will not benefit much (their price per share will not go up more than a few cents a share) or get hurt very much (share price will not fall by more than a few pennies), no matter what happens to interest rates. Furthermore, any such short-term "windfall" profit or loss is often quickly erased during the following week or month.

The final reason why these funds are considered conservative is *currency hedging*. Do not let this phrase intimidate you. Currency hedging simply means that the portfolio's managers have gone out and bought a sort of insurance policy to protect the fund's assets during those periods when the U.S. dollar is strong and other currencies (those represented in the portfolio) are weak. When you invest in a global fund, you are investing in securities—in this case short-term bonds and notes—that are bought and sold in different currencies. If the fund buys some United Kingdom two-year Treasuries, the manager must take U.S. dollars and convert them into British pounds before the purchase can be made. When these British notes mature, pounds are then converted back to dollars. Depending upon the exchange rate between the dollar and pound at the time, the fund can benefit or be harmed by the conversion. Currency hedging protects fund investors like you and me against unfavorable conversions.

If you do not understand currency hedging, do not despair. Many fund managers do not use currency hedging, because it has been demonstrated that over longer periods of time (ten or more years), it does not benefit investors. If short-term swings are important to you, however, simply ask your advisor or telephone the mutual fund directly and find out whether they use hedging and to what extent. If you want to get really specific, ask what the monthly high and low price per share has been for each of the last twelve months. This will give you an excellent idea of the share price volatility. By viewing these numbers, you can see whether these minor fluctuations are something you can live with. You will find that after share prices dip by ten or twenty cents they usually, if not always, rebound by similar price-per-share increases within just a couple of months.

Keep in mind that the objective of management is to try to make sure that the price per share does not vary more than a couple of percentage points up or down. These funds are not set up so that investors will make some kind of killing (or get killed) on share-price appreciation (or depreciation).

Before you buy a short-term global income fund, your advisor will be able to tell you the current rate of return. This rate will change during the year. Do not be alarmed by this. It is much more conservative to be in an investment that is sensitive to interest rate changes (and moves up and down with them), than to lock into a guaranteed rate of return offered by a five- or ten-year bank CD or government obligation. A "changing rate" is safer, because a locked-in rate is only better if rates go down. If rates move up, the locked-in rate may no longer be a good investment and may even fail to keep pace with inflation.

You can make additional contributions or withdrawals from these funds at any time. Additions or subtractions can be done directly through the mutual fund or through your investment advisor. Funds often charge a $5 fee for partial or full redemptions and exchanges.

Disadvantages

There are three disadvantages to owning short-term global bond funds: price-per-share fluctuation, a yield that changes, and the *perception* that investing in anything "foreign" is risky.

We live in an age of a global economy. We do not buy just U.S. cars (many of which contain foreign parts); most electronic equipment is produced and assembled overseas, and many domestic corporations, such as Coca Cola and Ford Motor Company, derive the majority of their income from overseas operations. In fact, fifteen of the largest world corporations are based outside of the United States. Investing in foreign securities, particularly those that are considered "short-term," is only slightly riskier than investing in a comparable portfolio of U.S. assets. In fact, over lengthy periods of time, such risk difference is negligible. However, when you take part of your portfolio and invest it in foreign securities, your overall risk level drops. This increased safety is due to the fact that world markets (stocks, bonds, interest rates, real estate prices, etc.) do not move up and down in tandem very often. Going "global" (owning some U.S. and some foreign securities) means that when part of your portfolio is "zigging," another part will be "zagging." These sometimes opposite moves help to cancel out or downplay overall volatility. Study after study has clearly demonstrated the risk reduction benefits of owning both U.S. and foreign securities.

This first "disadvantage," in other words, is only in the minds of brokers and most investors. The reality is that a global portfolio is actually better than a pure foreign or U.S. set of assets. By owning a short-term global bond fund along with investments like CDs, money market accounts, government bonds, etc., you will be doing yourself a favor, not a disservice.

The changing yield, or return, of short-term global bond funds could be a disadvantage or it could end up benefiting you. By being in something whose yield adjusts with, for instance, CD rates and money market accounts (except more slowly), you will get more during periods when interest rates go up. A "changing yield" is only a disadvantage if rates are falling and your yield on the short-term global bond fund also falls, although it will not fall as fast or as far as most other investments. Thus, this second "disadvantage" may not be so bad after all.

The final disadvantage is another "maybe." You may buy into one of these funds at $9.50 a share and then sell out a year later and receive $9.75 a share, plus interest. Or, you may buy into a fund at $6 a share and sell out six months later at $5.90 a share. The ten-cents-per-share loss will probably be more than offset by the extra interest you received during these six months; nevertheless, even minor price-per-share changes can be a little disconcerting for the ultra-conservative investor. Doing your homework and finding out the complete price-per-share history of the short-term global bond fund you are thinking about buying will go a long way in relieving any concern you might have now or in the future.

How to Buy and Sell

Several mutual fund families now offer short-term global bond portfolios. In fact, even a few variable annuities (described in another chapter) offer these kinds of accounts. You can invest in mutual funds directly by sending an application and check right to the fund. Brochures, applications, and prospectuses can be obtained by telephoning the fund's toll-free telephone number or through your brokerage firm.

Some short-term global income funds charge a commission; others are "no-load" (they do not charge a commission), and others have a *contingent-deferred sales charge.* A commission, also referred to as a load, is a fee paid to the mutual fund and/or brokerage firm you end up using. The commission you are charged for these kinds of funds generally ranges from 1 to 3 percent. Thus, if you went into a short-term global income fund that charged a 2-percent commission, $200 of a $10,000 investment would be the sales charge. This means that if your "$10,000 investment" were cashed in right away, you would net $9,800 ($10,000 minus $200), plus any accrued interest, plus or minus any price-per-share appreciation or depreciation. Price-per-share appreciation over a several-month period can easily make up this 2-percent charge. The important point to keep in mind is that the commission, although described in the fund's prospectus, is somewhat hidden; it is not reflected in your confirmation or any annual fund statement.

A no-load fund does not charge a commission. This means that if you invest $10,000, the full $10,000 is going to work for you. Some "no-load" funds, unlike a fund that charges an upfront commission, charge a redemption fee of up to 2 percent for liquidations made during the first few years after purchase. Although this is not common, the prospectus describes such a feature *if it exists.*

A contingent-deferred sales charge, sometimes referred to as a "back-end load" or "contingent-deferred sales load" (CDSL), means that 100 percent of your money is going to work for you immediately. Interest in the account can be withdrawn at any time without penalty. However, withdrawals or liquidations of principal during the first few years after purchase will result in a penalty, or charge, being imposed on the principal amounts being taken out. (No penalty is levied against money that remains within the fund or the fund family.)

The obvious question is, what kind of short-term global bond fund should you go into? Well, that all depends on the circumstances. If a broker or advisor is rendering you valuable advice, he or she should be fairly compensated. If your advisor cannot add any value (he or she knows the same or less than you do), then you are wasting your money paying any kind of commission. In such cases, no-load funds should be carefully looked at.

Some investors think that by dealing directly with the mutual fund group, or family, they will avoid or minimize any commission or back-end penalty. This is not true. These charges do not vary whether you buy the fund through a discount broker, through a financial planner, or by sending your money straight to the fund.

Commissions and fees are, and should be, a real concern. Nevertheless, do not lose track of the big picture: quality, yield, volatility, service, and expertise.

Tracking Performance
Short-term global bond fund prices, like those of other mutual funds, are quoted every day in the newspaper. If you cannot find your particular fund, contact the fund or your broker and find out how it is abbreviated (for example, "st. glb. inc."). You can also telephone the mutual fund on any day to find out the current price per share and yield.

Historical Performance
These kinds of funds have only been in existence for three or four years. The yield, or return, has ranged from a high of close to 11 percent to a low of just over 7 percent. Some funds have been able to maintain a narrower range, say 10 to 8.5 percent. The instruments or securities found in these funds have been around for decades; certain kinds of bonds and notes have been around for over a hundred years. For this reason you do not have to be fearful that you are in something "new" or untested. After all, money market funds have only been in existence for twenty years, yet no one has ever lost a dime in any one of them.

On a *total-return* basis, short-term global income funds have had annual returns that have been as high as 15 percent and as low as 5 percent. Total return refers to the portfolio's annualized yield plus price-per-share appreciation or minus share devaluation. As an example, if you went into the XYZ fund at $10 a share and it had a return that averaged out to 8 percent for the year, you might think that your total return was just 8 percent. This would be true only if the price per share was exactly $10 a share a year later. If, instead, the price per share was $10.50, your total return would be 13 percent (8 percent current yield plus 5 percent share appreciation).

The reason there has been a fairly high range between the total return of some of these funds is that some portfolios are better managed than others and some do not practice currency hedging. Over any given year, hedging can add several points to the total return picture. But hedging loses most, if not all of its value, when viewed over a ten-year period of time or longer. The fact that a fund had a 5-percent total return one year (let us say that it had a 9-percent yield but experienced a 4-percent drop in value), does not mean that it will not have a total return of 8 or 12 percent next year. The simple fact is that some funds are more consistent and stable than others.

Tax Considerations

Short-term global bond funds have no tax advantages. Interest from these accounts is fully taxable whether monthly checks are sent to you or payments are automatically reinvested. All international interest-bearing bonds and notes are subject to a foreign withholding tax, but such taxes are credited to you when you file your federal income tax return. This means that you are not being discriminated against; your tax liability is not increased or decreased by being subjected to a foreign country's tax, unless you are not paying any income taxes to begin with.

Portfolio Fit

Short-term global income funds are an ideal substitute or addition to that part of your portfolio that you want to be "liquid" and quite conservative. These funds experience less price-per-share, or unit, changes than GNMAs, government bonds, or long-term municipal bonds. They are certainly more conservative than all categories of stocks, including utilities, and virtually all intermediate- or long-term bonds or other bond funds.

These funds fit nicely into an income-oriented portfolio. The current yield is top-rate for a conservative fund. These funds can only be considered "growth-oriented" if the investor reinvests the interest so that he or she ends up with more shares each month.

Since money can be quickly taken out of these funds (some even have check-writing privileges), they are also a good choice for a quasi-emergency fund (something just a tad less liquid than a bank account or money market account).

Risks

For practical purposes, the only risk that should concern most investors is the currency-rate risk. Risk of default and interest-rate risk are both virtually zero. Currency rate risk can be somewhat effectively managed if the fund uses hedging or if the investor is patient and waits out what are usually temporary price swings in currencies.

Unique Features

What makes these funds unique is that they are invested in debt instruments (CDs, commercial paper, T-bills, T-notes, etc.) from overseas countries. All short-term global bond funds work pretty much the same way. The differences lie in which countries are chosen, the weighting given to each country, and whether any currency hedging takes place.

Comments

Short-term global bond funds are somewhat special. Their combination of an appealing current yield and general price stability make them a very appealing alternative for the CD, money market, or T-bill investor who was used to getting a much higher return. They also offer a welcome change for any bond investor who has seen his or her portfolio suffer in value when interest rates move up. No doubt about it, these funds should be part of almost everyone's portfolio.

Additional Information

Several mutual fund groups offer short-term global bond funds. If there is a particular fund group you are used to doing business with, you may wish to contact them directly by phone or letter. Listed below are just a few of the better performers over the past couple of years.

Alliance Fund Services
P.O. Box 1520, Secaucus, NJ 07096. 800-221-5672.

The Pilgrim Group
10100 Santa Monica Boulevard, 21st Floor, Los Angeles, CA 90067.
800-334-3444.

Prudential Mutual Fund Services
Attn: Administrative Services, P.O. Box 15015, New Brunswick, NJ 08906.
800-648-7637.

Scudder, Stevens & Clark
175 Federal Street, Boston, MA 02110. 800-225-2470.

Part III

◆ ◆ ◆

Equity Instruments

21
Residential Real Estate

Stability of principal   ✔

Stability of income

Protection against inflation   ✔✔✔✔

Total return   ✔✔✔

Tax benefits   ✔✔✔✔✔

Definition

Within the context of this book, residential real estate refers to one's primary residence or home. A home can be defined as a single-family structure, condominium, or cooperative. The term includes the structure and any underlying land.

How It Works

The value of residential property, like commercial and industrial properties, is largely dependent upon location. The value of the land is an important part of the value and in some cases, such as oceanside towns on the West Coast, can even be worth more than the actual structure.

The purchase or selling price will mostly be determined by what other houses in the immediate vicinity have sold for recently (not their listing price). These "comparables" are what appraisers and real estate brokers are looking at when determining prices for either listing purposes or loan applications. The value of the house you are thinking of buying (or selling) is increased or decreased depending upon how it measures up to the comparables in the neighborhood. For example, if other similar houses have a one-car garage and your home has a two-car garage, it could be worth a couple of thousand dollars more, depending upon the part of the country you are talking about. A recently remodeled kitchen or bathroom can also add several thousand dollars to the asking price. Conversely, if the majority of

153

homes in the area have swimming pools and yours does not, the listing price may have to be reduced to reflect the lack of a pool. However, in some neighborhoods a pool can actually reduce the resale value of your property and narrow the market of potential buyers.

Advantages

Home ownership has three advantages: psychological comfort, appreciation potential, and tax deductions. The third advantage, tax deductions, is discussed under "Tax Considerations."

Owning a home carries a kind of satisfaction, an inherent pride that cannot be valued monetarily. Until you buy your first house, you cannot fully appreciate the difference between renting and owning. These feelings are different for each one of us and impossible to measure, but not to be underestimated, nevertheless.

A second reason people buy homes is—they hope—to own something that keeps pace with inflation.

Disadvantages

There are three things to be concerned about as you ponder whether you should own a home. First, it will cost you more than you expect. I do not mean things like closing costs, escrow fees, and the like. I mean things like replacing appliances, having the place painted every few years, maintaining a yard, etc. Second, you should not buy a home purely as an investment. If this is your sole motivation, then you are making a big mistake, for one simple reason: There is no guarantee the house will appreciate in value, and if you end up selling such a large asset for a loss, it may have a profound effect on your financial security. As a side note, real estate experts acknowledge that the typical American home, once adjusted for inflation and home improvements, peaked in value in 1985. The price of homes in this country, again adjusted for inflation and improvements, has actually been declining for close to a decade. Third, from a strictly financial perspective, home ownership makes sense only if you assume a modest or moderate rate of appreciation. And then it only makes sense if you accept paper profits. Let us go through an example to see what I mean.

Let us say that you were renting a California house for $1,500 a month and were thinking about buying a similar home. Such a home would sell for about $400,000. If you continued to rent, your only out-of-pocket expense would be the $1,500 rental payment. The rental tax credit is of negligible benefit. Now, if you owned a home, you could write off virtually all of your payments. But such write-offs are not as good as you think.

First, you would not be able to buy the house at all unless you had about $80,000 for a down payment. Assuming you had it, and used it, you would then have $80,000 less to invest in something else. For the sake of illustration, let us assume you sold an investment that was averaging a 10-percent rate of return. Now you no longer have $8,000 a year coming in or being reinvested in something else. This is the first hidden cost of home ownership: what the down payment money could have been invested in. Second, you are going to have to finance the balance. A $320,000 mortgage will run you about $3,000 a month in mortgage payments. You can write off almost all of the $36,000 a year of payments, but even in a 40-percent tax bracket (state and federal combined), your after-tax cost for those payments is going to be $21,600 (60 percent of $36,000). Next, there is the issue of property taxes, water, and sewage. These fees will cost you about $5,000 a year. Finally, there is the question of maintenance. Let us be modest and assume that this is only going to run $2,000 a year.

So far, the picture for ownership does not look good. Our expenses and "lost opportunity" costs are in the neighborhood of $36,600 ($8,000 loss from a previous investment that was liquidated to come up with the down payment, plus $21,600 worth of after-tax mortgage payments, plus $5,000 for property taxes and local utilities, plus $2,000 for maintaining the building and land). At this point it costs $36,600 a year to own something we could have rented for $18,000 ($1,500 a month times twelve months of the year). Subtracting the difference leaves a net cost of $18,600 to own this home. As long as the house appreciates by at least this difference each year, home ownership is a good financial decision—at least on paper. The equivalent appreciation rate ($18,600 divided into $400,000) is just under 5 percent. Thus, as long as the value of the house goes up by at least 5 percent per year, ownership is the smart choice—assuming we can continue the cash outlay while being able to live with an offset that is only on paper—the appreciation.

How to Buy and Sell
Residential housing can be purchased for all cash (non-leveraged) or with a down payment and mortgage (leveraged). Buying anything with borrowed money is riskier than using your own funds, but most people do not have enough cash to make the purchase outright. Using outside funding can increase your profit or loss due to the effects of leverage. Let us go through an example to see how leverage (borrowed funds) can be either our best friend or our worst enemy.

Suppose you somehow had $200,000 to invest and were deciding whether to buy a second house for rental income and eventual capital gains upon sale. If an all-cash purchase was made and the house appreciated $60,000 in value over the next few years, you would enjoy a 30-percent profit (before any selling commissions or closing costs). If, instead, the property dropped in value by the same amount, there would be a 30-percent loss.

Assuming the same 30-percent gain or loss, a leveraged purchase, assuming 20 percent down ($40,000), would translate into a 150-percent gain ($40,000 x 150% = $60,000) or a 150-percent loss. All of us would gladly accept such a gain, but when was the last time you jumped at an investment that was described as, ". . . and there is a chance you can lose all of your money ($40,000, in this example) plus owe us another 50 percent ($20,000)"?

As you can see from this example, using leverage to buy anything can be exciting or dangerous. Obviously, most people are forced to buy their primary residence and residential-income property by using an outside lender, relying on traditional financing, or having the seller carry back a mortgage. My only point is to show you what can happen when you borrow someone else's money.

The best way to buy and sell property is by looking at other properties in the area that have sold in the recent past. These "comps" can be obtained by contacting a real estate office that has access to a multiple-listing service or that specializes in the immediate neighborhood. Finding out what other properties are currently being *advertised* for may only give you a rough idea of comparable properties, for two reasons. First, the asking and eventual selling prices can be two very different figures. Second, unless you are experienced in real estate, you may not be able accurately to compare the property you are thinking about buying or selling with other properties. (One garage is finished, the other is not; one house has extensive landscaping, the other does not; etc.)

You do not need to use a broker or real estate agent to buy or sell a home. Purchases and sales by owners are becoming more and more commonplace. However, these professionals can provide valuable services and should not be dismissed lightly. The agent has experience that you lack. The real estate office has access to figures and clients that you do not. Most importantly, an agent or broker can probably negotiate price better than you can. This person is more objective and usually has a sense as to how far a buyer or seller can be pushed. These representatives can also make sure that the chances of a future lawsuit are minimized by using the correct forms and making the proper inspections and disclosures.

The commission you pay a broker is negotiable. If you are having trouble selling a property and the normal commission is 6 percent, you might want to raise it to 7 percent to give the agent an added incentive. You could also give the listing broker (your representative) 3 percent and have the multiple-listing service show a 4-percent commission to the buying broker. This 33-percent increase in commission, from 3 to 4 percent, may be enough to get other brokers to begin showing the property more.

Commissions can also be lowered. If your home does not sell during the listing agreement period, the broker's request for a renewal may be just the time to renegotiate things. Or, if the property is listed for, say, $180,000, and you receive an offer for $175,000, you can always go to the agent and say that you will take $175,000 if she will reduce her commission from 6 to 4 or 5 percent.

Tracking Performance

As mentioned above, you can find out what a property is worth by looking at what comparable properties have sold for in the recent past, assuming conditions have not gotten much worse or better. For more generic and/or national figures, the National Association of Realtors (NAR), which is often quoted in news stories, has an extensive data base of selling prices by region or using national averages.

Historical Performance

Until the late 1960s, home ownership was considered a poor investment. In fact, it was generally acknowledged that if you bought a home and lived in it for a number of years, there was a good chance you would sell it for less than you paid for it. People continued to buy because of the tax advantages, in lieu of paying rent, and as a place to raise a family.

Beginning in the late 1960s, the prices of homes began to take off, as did the price of other goods and services. Moderate and high levels of inflation were seen everywhere in the mid-1970s to the early 1980s. Appreciation continued until the end of the 1980s, as more and more households saw both mates working. The boom years of the 1980s, coupled with dual paychecks, gave real estate prices quite a boost.

Looking back from almost any year until the late 1980s, if you asked someone what was the best investment to own, the answer was almost always "real estate." This was not the correct answer, but the public's perception was that you could not lose with real estate. Generations grew up seeing real estate do only one thing—appreciate. Almost everyone was convinced that it was *the* investment because the numbers were so high. After all, buying a house for $70,000 and selling it ten years later for $350,000 seemed like a far better investment than investing $7,000 in a mutual fund and watching it grow to $45,000. The house seemed like the better deal because the dollar figures were higher. Never mind that a great number of stocks saw much better percentage gains; people were not investing $70,000 in the market as they were in a house.

As the 1980s began to end, many people saw something they never thought could happen: the price of personal residences actually began to fall. Million-dollar homes were being routinely sold for $600,000 in the early 1990s. Condominiums that fetched $75,000 in the early 1980s were worth the same $75,000 twelve years later—a loss, when you consider inflation.

As we approach the mid-1990s, a couple of things seem obvious. One, real estate will probably not begin appreciating any time soon at the rate it did during much of the 1970s and 1980s. Both spouses are now working; where will the next injection of income come from? Two, people will not speculate with real estate as quickly and easily as they did during the "can't lose" years. The losses that all of us have seen in the past few years will be etched in our memories for at least another five years or so. Third, as investors become more knowledgeable about other avenues for their money, the personal residence will come to represent a smaller portion of people's net worth.

Tax Considerations

There are four things to keep in mind when you own a home. First, the interest portion of any mortgage payment is fully deductible. In fact, it is one of the few non-business deductions still remaining. Second, certain expenses such as remodeling can be added to the original cost basis (the purchase price plus all closing costs) to reduce the taxable gain when the home is sold. Third, gains can be deferred if a new home is purchased within two years of the sale of the existing residence and if the new purchase price is equal to or greater than the net proceeds from the last sale. Fourth, if you are fifty-five years or older, you can exclude, one time, up to $125,000 worth of gain (profit) from taxes. Fifth, ongoing expenses such as maintenance, painting, gardening services, etc. are generally not deductible. Finally, if you sell your home for less than you paid for it, you cannot deduct the loss from your taxes. Unlike other investments, Uncle Sam wants to tax you on the gains but will not share in any losses.

Portfolio Fit

Although a number of investments have done better than real estate in the past, this is still a favored category. Until you get into the $300,000+ range, residential housing is generally not as volatile as most investments. As a practical matter, you have to live somewhere. The economics of ownership may not be as appealing as being a renter, but the pride of home ownership is hard to beat.

By doing some basic homework, you shouldn't get hurt owning your primary residence. The overwhelming majority of investors, however, should stay away from buying a second or third rental property. Since real estate is the most expensive asset owned by most people, an already top-heavy portfolio would become even more so if a second or third property were added.

Home ownership is part of the American dream, but certain facets of this desire need to be explored. A first-time buyer needs to sit down and consider whether the down payment and/or monthly payments will make him an economic prisoner—whether things like dining out and vacations will have to be eliminated because there is no longer enough money. The security factor may increase if both spouses are working or if the single owner has a secure and sufficient source of income. Buying a house when things are tight or a major lifestyle change is occurring (new job, divorce, death of a mate, etc.) should normally be avoided.

Risks

Perhaps the biggest risk of buying a home is location. There is always a market for quality, and when it comes to real estate, the location of the property is what determines the quality. We live in a world where better is translated into bigger, but not when it comes to property values. You are always better off selecting a smaller home in a great neighborhood than opting for a mansion in a deteriorating section.

The other concern you should have when buying a home is affordability. You should not buy any investment or property if it is going to force a major change in your lifestyle. Making a profit over the next five years is an appealing thought, but not if it forces you to cut back on things you are used to.

Unique Features

Residential housing is unique because it offers tax benefits not found with most other investments. The interest portion of any mortgage payment is deductible, and the structure can be depreciated if the property is used for business purposes. Real estate is also an investment almost universally favored by people around the world.

Comments

Because of the multiple benefits of home ownership, residential real estate is a recommended investment. However, most people should not own more than one property. Every business is a business. If you plan on owning more than one property at a time, realize that mistakes will be made as you go through the learning curve.

Additional Information

Appraisal Institute
875 N. Michigan Ave, Suite 2400, Chicago, IL 60611-1980. 312-335-4100.

Commerce Clearing House
4025 West Peterson, Chicago, IL 60646. 312-583-8500.

Mortgage Basics for Home Buyers
Citicorp, Public Affairs Department, Box 0630, New York, NY 10043. 800-321-2484.

22
Common Stocks

Stability of principal	✔
Stability of income	✔✔
Protection against inflation	✔✔✔✔
Total return	✔✔✔✔✔
Tax benefits	✔✔✔

Definition

Common stocks represent an ownership interest in a corporation. You cannot buy shares of a company unless someone is willing to sell them to you. Similarly, once you own shares, they can only be sold if there is a buyer. In the case of most publicly-held stocks there is an active market, and shares are traded by the thousands or tens of thousands Monday through Friday. Where the shares are traded depends on where the stock is listed. The biggest stock exchange is the New York Stock Exchange (NYSE), which accounts for about 75 percent of all U.S. exchange activity. The American Stock Exchange (AMEX) accounts for close to a fifth of the activity, and the remaining regional exchanges, located in places like San Francisco and Boston, account for the balance. Several thousand stocks are not traded on a formal exchange but instead are bought and sold "over-the-counter" (a network of market makers). This system, referred to as the OTC market, is largely computerized by a sophisticated network known as NASDAQ. All stocks traded on a formal exchange or NASDAQ are easily tracked through stock retrieval systems such as Quotron.

How It Works

A corporation has two ways to raise money: by borrowing or by selling people an interest or partial ownership in the business. Corporations borrow money from financial institutions or by issuing bonds. Ownership interests are sold by issuing stock.

If the existing owners of a corporation decide to "go public," this means that they are willing to sell part of the business in return for cash. The sale is made to the public via underwriters and institutional bankers who help structure the stock offering, including the price per share, the number of shares to be issued, what brokerage firms will be involved in the sale of the securities, etc. A corporation that has already issued shares in the past is considered to be a "public company," since part, most, or all of the ownership is now in the hands of the shareholders. Such a business has already "gone public" but can usually still issue additional shares of stock to raise more capital. An example may help to clarify the concept of ownership.

Suppose you own a corporation with three other friends. The four of you decide that you want to expand your operations and that you need to raise quite a bit of money. You do not want to borrow the money, because servicing such a debt, by paying interest on either bonds or a bank loan, would increase your costs of doing business. Instead, the group of you agree to raise $6 million in working capital. After making some contacts and having some appraisals done, you discover that your corporation will have a market value of $10 million (after raising $6 million of new capital). This means you will need to sell off 60 percent of the business in exchange for the infusion of new money.

Investment bankers structure the deal so that a total of 600,000 shares will be offered at $10 per share (for simplicity, let's not consider the marginal effect of underwriting, legal, and accounting costs). If all of the shares are sold and $6 million is raised, you will still own 10 percent of a business that has a market value of $10 million. Each of your three partners will also own 10 percent of the business.

This example makes it sound easy to raise money, but it is not. First, you must have a group of investment bankers and underwriters who believe that your business is worth X amount of money and who are willing to help you sell off a small, moderate, or large percentage of the business to the public. The "public" could end up being mutual funds, pension plans, money managers, individual investors, brokerage firms, or anyone else who believes in the future of the corporation.

The mere fact that you and a group of organizers want to sell shares of stocks (or bonds) does not ensure that anyone is going to buy into the company. The marketplace (the public) may feel the price per share (or bond) is too high, that the future prospects for the business are not good, or that a new offering is a poor idea in light of recent market or economic news. On the other hand, people may be very excited about your product or service and believe that you are the next Apple Computer, GM, or McDonald's. Determining what the price per share should be and how many shares should be issued—in short, what the value of the business is—is done by the investment bankers. They usually have a pretty good pulse on what is good or bad and what the marketplace is looking for.

Once a company has gone public, it can issue additional shares of stock at any time in the future, as outlined by its corporate charter. The corporate charter can be amended or changed with the requisite number of votes from the shareholders—the people or entities that now own the company. Any such shares issued in the future can easily be priced, since one share is worth just as much as any other share and therefore new shares will be based on the market price of the shares currently trading.

Advantages

Owning common stocks has two advantages: appreciation potential and dividend income. Most people buy stocks for growth; they hope that they can buy shares for X dollars per share and later sell these same shares for X + Y. Historically, stocks have been one of the best hedges against inflation. A large number of stocks also pay dividends.

When a publicly traded corporation makes a profit, it can either pay out part or most of that profit in the form of a dividend to its shareholders or retain the money for internal growth—increased advertising, production, or research and development, for instance. The decision as to what should be done with corporate profits is made by the corporation's board of directors. These board members are elected by the shareholders.

Disadvantages

Owning common stocks has three disadvantages: your principal can be lost if the price per share declines; there is no guarantee that a company will pay, maintain, or, later, increase its current dividend; and the decision to buy or sell is frequently an irrational one.

When people buy stock they do so because they think the price per share will go up. But often the prices of individual stocks or the entire market average will go down, at least for the short term. The chance of losing money is not seriously considered. Hundreds of millions of dollars are made and lost each day in the stock market. Fortunately, if a stock drops in price, the loss is only a "paper loss" until the shares are actually sold. Similarly, if the price per share rises from what you paid, the profit is also on paper only. You do not actually make or lose any money from price increases or decreases until you sell part or all of your shares.

As mentioned, some stocks pay dividends and others do not. Paying dividends does not make a stock good or bad. In the past, some of the best-performing equities (stocks) have paid an attractive dividend, while other top performers have never paid any. In general, the greater the dividend, the less risk there is (and presumably the less reward). This is because a dividend payment can partially or fully offset a depressed stock price. If you own shares of a company that pays a 4-percent dividend and the stock drops 10 percent during the year, your real loss is only 6 percent. However, if the same stock drop occurred with a company that paid no dividend, the loss would be exactly 10 percent (you paid $10 a share for XYZ stock and it is now worth $9 a share).

Owning stocks can be an emotional decision, appealing to powerful instincts of fear and greed. People like to buy stocks when prices are going up and often sell when things look gloomy. Rationally it is obvious that shares should be bought when prices are down (we like to buy other things on sale; why not stocks?) and sold when a moderate or large profit has been made.

How to Buy and Sell

If an investor is in need of current income, he or she will normally be attracted to high-dividend-paying stocks. The term "high-dividend-paying" is a relative one and depends upon what other investments are yielding. A 4-percent dividend looks attractive if bank CDs or money market accounts are only paying 4 to 5 percent, since the common stock also has price appreciation potential. Bank CDs and money market accounts do not have any such appreciation (or loss) potential. Certain industries, such as utility and energy companies, are known for paying higher dividends than other kinds of stocks. When interest rates are high and conservative investments are paying 6 to 8 percent or more, a "high-dividend-paying" stock may be one that has a dividend in the 5-to-6-percent range.

Investors who are not in need of current income may be attracted to growth companies, those corporations that pay either no dividend or some nominal amount (like 1 or 2 percent). Companies that are able to retain more of their earnings, instead of paying them out to shareholders, have more cash available for growth. Such expansion should lead to greater profitability in the future. The more profitable a corporation is, the more likely the price per share of its stock is going to climb.

Tracking Performance

There are two prices for every stock: the *bid* price and the *ask* price. The bid price represents what you would get for the stock if you had shares to *sell*. The ask price is the price you would pay if you wanted to *buy* shares. The ask price is always higher than the bid price. The difference between the bid and the ask price is known as the "spread." This spread, or difference, is what the market maker keeps as a profit. The market maker is the person who inventories the stock on the exchange, the one your broker or brokerage firm would go to if shares were being bought or sold. Every stock has a market maker. This person stands ready to buy or sell shares. Market makers play an important role in the stock market because they can help stabilize prices during periods of panic. Market makers are usually not affiliated with any broker or brokerage firm.

The difference between the bid and the ask price is normally 12.5¢ (an eighth of a point) for widely traded stocks such as GM, IBM, McDonald's, etc. For less-frequently traded stocks, the spread is usually 25¢ per share (a quarter of a point). The greater the spread between the bid and the ask price, the greater the likelihood that the stock is not particularly popular or widely traded. Thus, when you see a bid-ask spread of a half-point (50¢ per share) or more, you can assume that this is a "thinly traded" stock and is therefore probably quite volatile (risky). It may be difficult to sell if the price were to begin to collapse. A large spread between the bid and the ask price does not benefit the buyer, seller, broker, or brokerage firm. In fact, it may not even benefit the market maker, since wide price movements put his or her inventory of the stock at greater risk.

Common stock prices are found every day in your local newspaper, *The Wall Street Journal*, and *Investor's Daily*, and weekly in *Barron's*. Full-service and discount brokerage firms can be contacted during normal business hours for telephone quotes. You can also directly subscribe to a quotation service at home or at work if you have a computer and telephone modem or FM receiver.

Historical Performance

The track record for common stocks as a whole has been excellent. This investment has outperformed real estate, bonds, bank CDs, art, rare coins, oil, gold, and any other investment you can think of. Long-term common stocks have been the best-performing investment category, and the future looks even brighter than the past. There is not a person alive who has not seen the market go up during his or her lifetime. Whether you are one year old or a hundred years, the market is higher today than it was when you were born. This is not true with most other investments. Think about it. Gold is trading at half its early 1980s high, silver is trading at less than one-tenth of its high, real estate prices are not likely to see their pre-1989 highs for several years— many areas of the country have had depressed real estate prices for over a decade—bond and CD yields are a fraction of what they were ten years ago, art, oil, and rare coin prices have collapsed. Yet stock prices continue to increase, as do corporate profits and scales of efficiency.

It is easy to understand what makes common stocks such a great investment by recalling that when you own stocks, you own part of a business. If the company does well, so will you. It is human nature to want to succeed. There are a lot of great corporations that you and I will never be able to own, but we can be partial owners by buying their stock. Of course, a number of corporations have not done well. The key, obviously, is to avoid the losers and load up on the winners, something that is easier said than done, despite what market gurus and newsletters might claim.

You can do well in the stock market by following two simple rules:

diversify and be patient. No matter what someone tells you, no matter how convincing the writer or speaker, no one knows what the stock market will do tomorrow, next month, or next year. Predicting how an individual stock will perform is even more difficult, requiring great doses of luck. We do know that the stock market has always moved in an upward fashion and that the line of advancement is not always straight up. Often, stock prices "stray" and move sideways or even drop. Yet the market always recovers and goes on to make new highs. Sometimes it takes a week, a year, or five years for that new high to be reached; this is why patience is important. But by diversifying and owning shares of several different stocks instead of just one or two, you will decrease your risk significantly.

To bring home the benefits of patience and diversification, consider the following two studies. If you had invested in the stock market for one year at any time during the past half-century, your chances of making money would have been over 70 percent. If that one-year holding period had been extended to three or five years, your chances of making money would have been over 95 percent. And for any ten-year period, (1973-1982, 1944-1953, etc.), your chances of showing a profit were 100 percent.

Turning to diversification, if you invest in one stock, rather than a diversified portfolio of ten stocks, your risk level is about five times greater without any significant increase in return. This is an example where risk (lack of diversification) is not commensurate with return. (Little, if any, return potential is added with a one- or two-stock portfolio).

Tax Considerations

When you own common stocks, two tax events are possible. First, if the stock pays a dividend, that cash dividend is taxable whether it is automatically reinvested, sent directly to you, or invested elsewhere. Dividends are taxable in the year in which they are received. As you will recall, not all corporations pay a dividend.

A few corporations do not pay a *cash* dividend but instead may pay a *stock* dividend, awarding you an extra share of stock for every X number of shares you already own. Stock dividends are not taxable until the specific shares (the stock-dividend shares) are sold. At the time of sale, the entire net proceeds of the stock dividend shares are fully taxable. For instance, if you paid $10 a share for a hundred shares of XYZ, received twelve shares of XYZ as a stock dividend, and later sold the twelve shares for $6 a share, you would show a net taxable capital gain of $72 ($6 x 12). If part or all of the hundred shares were also sold for $6 a share, you would have a capital *loss* of $4 per share ($10 purchase price minus the $6 selling price).

The second tax event occurs when shares of stock are sold. When you sell stock for less than you paid for it, a capital loss occurs, as in the previous example. If, instead, shares are sold for a profit, there is a capital gain. Gains and losses must be reported in the calendar year in which they are sold. Therefore, if you sell stock in February of 1993, your 1993 tax return (which you would file by April 15th of 1994) would show the transaction (a capital gain, loss, or break-even situation).

For tax planning purposes, you decide when a stock is to be sold. You may have a large built-in profit on XYZ stock but decide not to sell it this year because you are in a high tax bracket. Instead, you decide to sell it next year when you expect to be in a lower bracket. Similarly, you may own a real dog that has done nothing but go down. You decide to sell it this year for a capital loss in order to offset capital gains elsewhere. Capital losses can offset capital gains with no dollar limit; however, capital losses can only offset up to $3,000 a year of earned income (for example, salaries, tips, bonuses, and commissions) or portfolio income.

You cannot control the flow of dividends. If a corporation pays a cash dividend quarterly, you must accept it when it is paid. If you are the owner of the stock, you cannot try and divert a dividend or capital gain to your children or someone else who is in a lower tax bracket. The way to control the amount of dividends you own is either to buy stocks that pay little or no dividends or to own stocks within a qualified retirement plan or variable annuity. Both of these vehicles shelter dividends, interest, and capital gains from current taxation.

Portfolio Fit

There are two ways to own common stocks: individually or within a mutual fund. Virtually everyone should own common stocks. Most people should own common stocks within a mutual fund (or sheltered from taxes within a variable annuity).

Despite stocks' historical record, most people do not have the temperament to own individual stocks. Purchases are often made when the stock is reaching all-time highs, and sales are usually made at lows (after a stock market crash or "correction"). In general, people buy stock out of greed and sell out of fear; "The sky is falling!" "The nightly news says this is the worst drop in history and things may get worse!" As a side note, stay away from "hot tips" and the "sure things." Some of the worst-performing stocks I have ever seen were supposed to do great things—at least, that is what some financial guru or company employee told me.

If you decide to own individual stocks, make sure your portfolio is diversified. No matter how good your company looks or how hot a particular industry appears, a single stock should ideally represent no more than 10 percent of your holdings (5 percent is even better and safer), while a given industry—auto stocks, computer companies, health care, etc.—should take up no more than 20 percent of your assets (10 to 15 percent would be even wiser). These figures may seem too restricting, but consider for a moment how your life would change if the stock or industry collapsed. Although such an event may not affect your standard of living now, it could taint your views about owning common stock in the future—and that would be a big and far-reaching mistake.

No one can say with precision that 20 percent (the national average) or some other percentage of your net worth should be in common stocks or mutual funds that invest in stocks. The weighting should depend upon your risk level and time horizon. If your goals are long-term—to retire comfortably in fifteen or twenty years, send two kids to college in ten years, etc.—then your portfolio should be dominated by stocks (preferably mutual funds and/or variable annuities so that emotional buy-and-sell decisions are minimized), even if you are on the conservative side. On the other hand, if your time-frame is one or two years, stock ownership in any form should be minimal, unless you are a fairly aggressive investor. The longer your holding period, the more likely you will be to make money in common stocks.

Portfolio fit and the amount of money that should be earmarked for stocks also depend on the kind of stocks you are considering. Some stocks are considered conservative and comparatively safe, like those of utility companies; some are considered to be of moderate risk, like General Motors; some are considered somewhat risky, like Apple Computer; and some can only be described as a gamble (any start-up company).

As a broad generality, the amount of your portfolio that should be in stocks should range from 20 percent (retired and conservative) to 80 percent (middle-aged, working, investing money every year, and at least slightly aggressive). An older individual or couple may not be able to make up a loss in the market, but they also cannot afford not to have some kind of hedge against inflation. Someone in her forties or early fifties who plans on retiring in fifteen or more years has time on her side. Nevertheless, there are other good investments besides stocks.

Risks

In a strange sense, stocks carry two risks: owning them and *not* owning them. We have all heard about the risks of owning stocks, but few people talk about the risk of not owning stock. It's subtle, but it's there. You want to own stocks not because they are fun and exciting but because the price of goods and services goes up each year, and few other investments are as good a hedge against inflation.

When you buy a stock, or a mutual fund or variable annuity that invests in common stocks, you get no guarantee that it will go up in price. You can, however, get a pretty good idea as to how volatile the stock might be by asking the broker the top and bottom price paid for the stock over the previous year. A stock with a fifty-two-week range of twenty to forty-six is riskier than one with a range of ten to fourteen. Even so, there is no assurance that the stock will not sell for more than the previous high or less than its low. Some well-respected sources say that you should try and buy a stock when it is near its fifty-two-week low; other publications say that you can make money when a stock "breaks out" and starts hitting new highs (presumably this means that the best is yet to come). Neither school of thought can be considered the only rule to follow.

A distant secondary risk of owning stocks has to do with dividends. A company that has a history of paying dividends, perhaps even increasing dividends over the years, will probably continue to do so, but you have no recourse if the board of directors decides either to suspend or cut down the dividend. Stock dividends are not like bond interest payments, which are guaranteed by the issuing corporation.

Unique Features

Stocks are special because they offer you a chance to own part of almost any publicly traded company you like. The number of shares you own is limited to the size of your pocketbook. And, although an increasingly profitable company does not assure you of making huge stock profits, there is a strong relationship between the net income of a company and its price per share.

Common stocks represent the easiest, and perhaps the only long-term sure way, of making money. It is also easy to lose money in stocks. No one is forcing you to hold onto a stock after it has dropped in value, or preventing you from loading up on a "sure thing." The power of greed and fear is almost unlimited. This is one of the few investments in this book where it is possible to see substantial percentage drops in value unless diversification and patience are exercised. On the positive side, common stocks are the only investment that goes up most years and has consistently been a winner.

Common stock ownership is an example of an investment that can be a win-win situation. By that I mean you can buy a stock for, say, $10 a share and sell it for $13 a share; I can buy it for $13 and perhaps sell it later for $20. We both made money, unlike with some investments where someone has to lose before someone wins.

The most unusual thing about stocks may be the amount of misinformation and the number of wrong opinions. When stock prices are high, people say that there is going to be a crash or correction. When there is a crash or drop, the same people say that it is going to get even worse. Never lose sight of the fact that newspapers, magazines, and the radio and television shows that report the news are in a business. Their business is market share. Each of these sources is competing with the other to get more listeners, readers, or viewers. Good news has never sold; bad news and disasters always create interest. That is why one of the more harmful things affecting the stock market is the news media. The flow of information is crucial to our freedom, well-being, and business, but distorted news can be equally harmful, turning people off to what has and continues to be the very best investment—American (and foreign) enterprise. If you do not believe me, ask yourself when was the last time business was portrayed in a positive way on a television show? I will tell you the answer: It was about thirty years ago. The show was "Father Knows Best" (Mr. Anderson sold life insurance).

Comments

As you can see, I strongly favor common stocks. More specifically, I favor mutual funds and variable annuities that have common stocks in their portfolios. Can stocks be scary and uncertain at times? You bet. But so are a lot of other things in life: relationships, job security, health-care costs, the price of housing, etc. Do people lose money every day in stocks? Yes. But you would lose money in almost any investment if you panicked. If the loss is not due to price depreciation, then it is due to reduced purchasing power (buying less with today's dollars than you did yesterday).

Declaring that stocks are the best investment may sound boastful, tempting some readers to conclude that the author is an active stock trader. In fact I do not follow any individual stocks. On the contrary, my personality and background are such that I encourage people to own certain mutual funds and variable annuities.

Others are thinking that stocks cannot be the "best" because they have a friend who made a killing in real estate or on a piece of art. Ah, hindsight. Let me assure you that when it comes to citing gains after the fact, there is no chance that any investment can come close to matching common stocks. How many properties or other investments can you show me that have gone up over 1,000 percent in just a couple of years? Probably none. Yet there are dozens of examples of individual stocks that have done just that.

Additional Information

Merrill, Lynch, Pierce, Fenner & Small, Inc.
Marketing Communications, 800 Scudder's Mill Road, Plainsboro, NJ 08540. 800-637-7455.

New York Stock Exchange
11 Wall Street, New York, NY 10005. 212-656-3000.

Quick & Reilly, Inc.
26 Broadway, New York, NY 10004. 800-221-5220.

Spear Securities
1605 Cahuenga, Suite 204, Los Angeles, CA 90028. 213-962-7515.

23
Utility Stocks

Stability of principal	✔✔
Stability of income	✔✔✔
Protection against inflation	✔✔✔✔
Total return	✔✔✔✔
Tax benefits	✔✔

Definition

A utility stock represents partial ownership in a utilities company such as a water works, telephone company, or power plant. As a small owner of the corporation, you participate in the success or shortcomings of the business. If the utility is able to get a rate hike, increase its user base, or add services, shareholders normally benefit in the form of a larger dividend and/or increased value in the stock. Conversely, if the Public Utilities Commission (PUC) continues to deny requests for user costs, or if the utility company is unsuccessful in one of its ventures, like constructing a nuclear power plant, the price per share of the stock as well as the dividend may be cut.

Normally the utility company has a monopoly or near monopoly on the service in a particular geographical area. This "captive audience" is what makes utility stocks so popular. That, and the fact that people are likely to pay their utility bills before their income taxes, makes this investment unlike others.

How It Works

There are several ways to participate in utilities stocks. If you consider public telephone services to be a growing or stable industry, you can purchase the stock of one or more of the "baby Bells" or buy AT&T. If you want something more conservative, buying stock in an electric company may be more to your liking. Similarly, if you think electricity and gas bills are too high, you can profit by owning shares of the company that charges such "outrageous rates."

Advantages

Utility stocks offer several advantages. First, the trading range of most utility companies is fairly predictable; price changes are upward more often than downward. This means that no matter what price you pay per share, there is a good chance that when you go to sell your shares, you will see some moderate appreciation. Second, utilities offer some of the very highest dividends when compared to other common stocks. This is because the majority of the profits are paid out to shareholders instead of plowed back into the company for expansion or research purposes. Third, these kinds of stocks are quite popular. People like owning utility stocks because they are almost like owning a security that is part bond (the high current yield) and part stock (appreciation potential). In fact, utility stocks, preferred stocks, and convertibles are the closest thing you can get to bonds. Finally, unlike most other industry groups, utilities rarely, if ever, face competition.

Disadvantages

Next to the cost of fuel or power, the biggest expense incurred by a utilities company is normally the cost of debt. Utility companies typically have a great deal of outstanding debt that must be serviced. The interest paid on these bonds has a major impact on the company's net profits. Furthermore, since utility companies are known for paying a high stock dividend, a great deal of money is sent out quarterly or semiannually to shareholders and bondholders. Thus, the general level of interest rates has a tremendous impact on this industry.

As interest rates fall, utility companies are often able to refinance portions of their total debt at much lower levels. By paying out less in interest, they make more money available to shareholders or for corporate reinvestment. Conversely, when interest rates are high, utility profits are squeezed. This can depress the stock's price and may cause the company to lower its dividend. This is another similarity between utility stocks and bonds. Both are quite sensitive to changes in interest rates.

A disadvantage of electric utilities is that a provider of electricity may decide to venture into nuclear power, although having said that, it has been years since a new plant has been completed or proposed. The construction of these plants has been plagued with delays and huge cost overruns. And though the long-term monetary consequences of such an addition may be good for the utility company, the short- and medium-term effects can be devastating to both the stock's price and its dividend.

Although utility stocks as a group may have relatively low risk, you need to understand that risks in individual stocks can still be high. Companies with inefficient operations, mismanaged construction projects, hostile regulatory commissions, economically depressed service areas, or botched diversification schemes can and do have problems. Investors should not assume that a monopoly on the local power or gas business assures steady profits. Consider:

- Public Service of New Hampshire filed for bankruptcy in 1988, crushed by cost overruns on a nuclear plant and constant battles with regulators. It was the first utility to do so since the Depression.

- Of the ninety-seven electric utility companies followed by *Value Line Survey* (a well-respected stock advisory service), twenty-three of them, or nearly one in four, have reduced or eliminated common stock dividends in the last six years.

For these reasons, you should focus on mutual funds that specialize in utility stocks, leaving the selection process up to the pros. These are the people who will monitor not only the industry but the individual companies in the fund's portfolio.

How to Buy and Sell

Utility stocks can be bought individually or as part of a mutual fund. Several funds deal exclusively in utility stocks. If you are attracted to individual issues but want to make sure that the company you are considering deals only in hydroelectric power or fossil fuel, you can obtain such information and more by consulting such publications as *Value Line* or *Standard and Poors*. These publications describe close to two thousand different companies, including many utilities. They will tell you what kind of power the company uses, whether nuclear power is anticipated in the future, how successful the provider has been in getting rate increases in the past, how much outstanding debt it has, and future plans, hopes, and concerns.

Like most stocks and bonds, utility securities can be bought and sold through any brokerage firm.

Tracking Performance

Utility stocks are quoted daily in the newspaper; so are mutual funds that specialize in utilities. If you own several shares of several different companies, you can get a good and quick idea as to how you are doing by checking the general level of the Dow Jones Utility Average (DJUA). This index tracks the performance of twenty large utility companies.

Historical Performance

For something that seems a little boring, utility stocks have fared quite well over the past five, ten, fifteen, and twenty years. In the past, anywhere from one-third to one-half of the total return from these securities (and mutual funds that specialize in utility stocks) has come from the dividend. Surprisingly, the balance has been due to share appreciation.

Keep in mind that utility companies do best when interest rates and the cost of fuel are low. Although interest rates and fuel costs have seen some extremes, these ups and downs have still translated into a good, long-term track record for utilities. These stock often outperform bonds but are considered to be less safe when it comes to price stability. However, there have been periods of time when utility stocks have been less volatile than long-term government or high-quality corporate bonds.

Tax Considerations
Unless you are in a low tax bracket, utility stocks are best suited for qualified retirement plans such as IRAs, Keoghs, pension plans, 403(b) plans, 401(k) plans, and profit-sharing plans. Since utilities pay a higher dividend than most any other industry group, and all such dividends are taxable, only the price appreciation is deferred to future years.

Portfolio Fit
This is an excellent addition to almost any portfolio. High-bracket tax payers who do not currently own any utility stocks or mutual funds can reposition their retirement accounts or variable annuities to take advantage of this safe and reliable source of income and moderate growth. Low-bracket individuals and couples have more latitude.

Growth-oriented investors often shy away from utility issues, thinking they do not possess enough appreciation potential. Such people are not aware of the power of the dividend compounding year after year. There has been more than one ten- or fifteen-year period of time when the utility index has outperformed the S & P 500 and Dow Jones Industrial Average.

Risks
Investing in utilities carries four risks: tremendous rises in fuel costs, a company that branches out into nuclear power, denial of rate-increase requests by the PUC, and interest-rate hikes. Unfortunately, nothing can be done to anticipate any of these events. However, we have come to learn over the past ten and twenty years that what goes up, comes down.

In the early 1980s, energy experts were predicting oil at $50 a barrel. Instead, it got down to the $10 range, unadjusted for inflation, by the late 1980s—never coming close to $50. For this reason, the chances of a utility company constructing a nuclear power plant have decreased enormously from a decade ago. Utility companies are now well aware of public protests, cost escalations, and delays. Decisions on rate increases also tend to be somewhat political. The PUC may easily permit a rate hike one year and deny one a few years later. Interest rates work in the same way. Just when you and I think they cannot get any lower (or higher), the Federal Reserve makes an announcement contradicting what we and the financial gurus were predicting.

In other words, a patient investor does not really have to worry about any of these "risks." As in other stock categories, only even more so, utilities go up and down, but their long-term trend is always upward.

Unique Features

Having little, if any, competition, is a unique feature most businesses would like to possess. Imagine not having to worry about a new competitor or a better mousetrap. Granted, certain kinds of utilities have more competition than others, but that competition is almost always domestic and quite sparse. Furthermore, the demand for utilities is likely to climb each year for the next several decades. Our demand for electricity, water, fuel, and communications seems almost insatiable. As the population increases, so will our need for these services.

Comments

Utility stocks and mutual funds are a conservative way to participate in the U.S. stock market. For purposes of added safety, most investors are better off in utility funds, leaving specific security selection, analysis, and ongoing monitoring to full-time professionals. Even an investor who has the vast majority of his or her portfolio in debt instruments (such as bonds, CDs, and money market accounts) should have a modest portion in utility stocks. Such an investor would be better served getting rid of some of the debt instruments and buying into this conservative industry group. In fact, the only kind of investor who should probably avoid utilities is the very aggressive person who is trying to make a killing (but usually ends up getting "killed" instead).

Utility stocks and utility mutual funds can be an excellent alternative to fixed-income securities for current income and long-term protection from inflation. Some firms have admirable records in this regard: Dallas-based Central & Southwest, for example, has raised its cash dividend every year since 1952.

Additional Information

State Street Bank
Attn: ABT Fund, 3rd Floor, P.O. Box 8505, Boston, MA 02266-850.
800-553-7838.

Dean Witter Reynolds
Two World Trade Center, 71st Floor, New York, NY 10048. 800-869-3863.

Flag Investors Fund
135 E. Baltimore Street, Baltimore, MD 21202. 800-767-3524.

Liberty Utility Fund
Federated Investors Tower, Pittsburgh, PA 15222. 800-245-5051.

Value Line Investment Survey
711 Third Avenue, New York, NY 10017. 800-833-0046.

24
Balanced Funds

Stability of principal	✔✔✔
Stability of income	✔✔✔✔
Protection against inflation	✔✔✔✔
Total return	✔✔✔✔
Tax benefits	✔✔

Definition

A balanced fund is a kind of mutual fund. Like other kinds of mutual funds, balanced funds offer professional management, instant diversification, an ascertainable track record over any desired period, and services not found with other kinds of investments, like telephone exchange privileges, easy-to-understand statements, immediate liquidations, etc. Unlike other kinds of mutual funds, balanced funds invest in both stocks *and* bonds.

How much weight the balanced fund's manager places on stocks or bonds depends upon management's assessment of the economy, the direction of interest rates, and stock market optimism or pessimism. Normally, at least 30 percent of the fund's assets are in bonds, and some funds may end up investing the great majority of its assets in bonds and convertible securities for brief or extended periods of time.

How It Works

When you invest in a mutual fund, you are leaving the actual security selection up to the person or people who manage the fund. In a sense, you (and hundreds of thousands of other people and institutions) have hired them to manage your money.

Restrictions on how the money is invested are described in the fund's prospectus. In the case of balanced funds, the prospectus points out how much or how little the fund may invest in either stocks or bonds. The greater the range, the more latitude the manager has. If the prospectus states that at least 30 percent of the fund's assets will always be in bonds, the manager must follow this guideline, no matter how strongly he or she may feel about the stock market.

Advantages

Owning a balanced fund offers four great advantages. First, the chance that common stocks and bonds will both go down in value the same year is very small, since when one goes down, the other often goes up. In fact, over the past half-century, there have only been a few years when stocks and bonds both posted losses for the same calendar year. Second, since the portfolio is so well diversified, your money can be invested in just a couple of different kinds of mutual funds (balanced being just one category), and your resulting risk level will be quite low. In a way, you are admitting that you do not know which will do better, stocks or bonds. Third, the track record of balanced funds is surprisingly good. Although they are never the number-one performing category, they are often toward the top of the list. Equally important, they are never at the bottom of the list, which is what can happen to a pure stock or bond fund. Finally, if you ever get tired of this investment, you can always exchange it for something else, like a money market fund or government securities fund, by phone or letter.

Disadvantages

The reason balanced funds are not more popular is that they lack both the "sex appeal," or excitement, of a stock or aggressive-growth fund and the perceived safety of a government bond or money market fund. I say "perceived" because of the interest-rate and/or inflation risk that accompanies these two categories. Balanced funds are a hybrid security, neither fish nor fowl. The manager of a balanced fund never appears on the cover of *Money* or as a featured expert in *Barron's* or *The Wall Street Journal*. In a sense, the people who run these funds are the unsung heros of the investment world.

Financial advisors often gloss over, or fail to mention, the benefits of a balanced fund because it offers too simple a solution to the problem of diversification. These are not the kinds of funds you are going to boast to your friends about. During a stock-market crash these funds will fall, but not nearly as much as an aggressive-growth, small-cap growth, growth, or growth and income fund. Yet they will fall more than a high-quality bond fund. When the stock market is skyrocketing upward, balanced funds will also go up, but not at the same speed or to the same degree.

Another "disadvantage" of balanced funds is that they do not have as high a current yield as a bond fund. This is because part, perhaps a large part, of the portfolio is made up of common stocks that pay modest dividends in comparison to bonds. This "disadvantage" can be offset by setting up a systematic withdrawal plan (giving you monthly income) that equals or exceeds the yield of good-quality corporate and government bonds.

How to Buy and Sell

You can buy a balanced fund from a stockbroker, financial planner, brokerage firm, or bank officer (if your bank offers securities trading)—or directly from the mutual fund. Prospectuses, brochures, track records, and applications can be obtained by making a toll-free telephone call. A check or money order can then accompany your application and be sent directly to the fund group.

When you buy into a balanced fund (or any other kind of mutual fund), you end up owning shares of the fund. The price you pay per share depends upon how well the portfolio is doing the day the fund receives your money. As an example, the XYZ Balanced Fund may be selling for $8 a share one day and $7.95 the very next day. The cheaper the price per share, the more shares you will end up with.

Selling part or all of your balanced fund shares is even easier than making a purchase. To get out of the fund, you simply telephone the fund or contact your broker and give instructions to "sell all my shares and send me a check." Alternatively, you can sell just some of your shares—"Mary, sell $3,000 worth of my balanced fund"—or have part or all of the account exchanged for shares of another fund within the same fund family: "Hello, XYZ Fund Group? . . . Sell all shares of account number . . . and use the proceeds to buy into the XYZ growth fund. I understand that there is a $5 fee for this exchange." In most cases you can sell some or all of your shares without going through your broker. You simply telephone the fund and make the change. If you do not know your account number, give them your name and social security number and they can do the rest.

Tracking Performance

Like any other kind of mutual fund, the price of balanced funds (there are dozens of them) are quoted every day in the newspaper. The only thing you need to know is the name of the fund (they are listed alphabetically, first by fund family name, and then alphabetically within the fund listing). If you want to know the exact value of your account on any given day, you will also need to know the *current* number of shares you own. You may own more shares than you think. Most people have their dividends and capital gains from balanced funds automatically reinvested. This reinvestment feature means that more and more shares are being purchased for you each year.

If you do not wish to telephone the fund directly, you can also contact your broker or review your most recent statement. Mutual funds send out statements every time there is activity in an account: when you add money or make a liquidation, or when a capital gain or dividend is declared. By dealing with your broker, you will be able to learn of other investment opportunities and perhaps get a more objective idea as to what your overall financial or investment plan should be.

Historical Performance

The track record of balanced funds over the past one, three, five, ten, fifteen, and twenty-five years has been quite good. This kind of fund is a steady performer. There are certainly periods of time when bank CDs, government bonds, and money market funds perform better, but such occurrences are the exception, not the rule.

The performance of balanced funds cannot be described as "exceptional," unless returns are measured on a risk-adjusted return basis. Exceptional and exciting returns are reserved for mutual fund categories such as aggressive-growth, small-cap growth, growth, growth and income, and foreign stock. However, these are also the same categories that once in a while have returns that are "disappointing" or "negative."

Tax Considerations

Since balanced funds are mostly made up of common stocks and corporate bonds, they are fully taxed. You will pay income taxes on any dividends or interest payments declared during the calendar year. If the fund incurs a capital gain, the gain must also be reported.

The yearly tax consequences of your particular balanced fund is summarized for you on what is known as a "substitute 1099," a form sent to you by the mutual fund in late January or early February. This form summarizes, in just three or four small boxes, how much you must declare on your taxes. As odd as it might sound, you generally hope that the tax consequences will be quite high. A large tax liability means that you have made a lot of money. When it comes to mutual fund investing, the only way you do not pay taxes is if the fund loses money or breaks even for the year.

You can avoid current taxation by investing in a variable annuity that has a "balanced fund" as one of its options. Taxes would then only be due when a withdrawal is made.

Portfolio Fit

One or more balanced funds could easily represent up to two-thirds of an investor's portfolio. In fact, the only thing a risk-conscious person would need to add would be some international funds and a short-term bond (income) fund, or perhaps a municipal bond fund if the person was in a high tax bracket.

Balanced funds are a nice fit with almost any portfolio. They are not wild enough for the aggressive investor, yet they are appropriate for at least a modest portion of even a dyed-in-the-wool conservative individual or couple. They are a welcome addition to the portfolios of both young and old, offering a degree of safety plus a hedge against inflation.

Risks

Balanced funds will normally have a negative total return for the year approximately once every decade. As mentioned, there have been about five years in the past fifty when stocks and bonds both posted negative returns for the same year. A loss results in a balanced fund when interest rates go up by at least a few points *and* the stock market declines. When both of these events occur, the interest from the bonds added to the stock dividends may not be enough to offset any principal erosion.

The only other risk of investing in a balanced fund is the possiblity of selecting a poorly performing mutual fund or variable annuity. The chance of this can be greatly reduced if you are willing to do a little work. By seeking out a fund that has had the same manager(s) for at least the past five years, that has a track record of positive results on a year-by-year basis (rather than a lot of ups and downs compared to other balanced funds), and whose operating costs are in line with balanced funds in general, investors are likely to end up with a winner.

Unique Features

Unlike most other investments described in this book, balanced funds offer two kinds of securities: stocks and bonds. (Some of these funds also include preferred stocks, convertibles, and/or money market instruments.) By virtue of their "hybrid" status, balanced funds are always going to maintain a low profile compared to investments like gold, real estate, stocks, bonds, and money market funds that, at one time or another, will star as the number-one performer.

Comments

This category of investments should not be missed. You can participate in these great risk-adjusted returns (for current income and/or growth) either by buying shares of one or more balanced funds, within a variable annuity, or by creating your own "balanced fund." That is, if you already own shares of a growth or growth and income fund, you can buy shares of a corporate or government securities fund. If you already invest in a bond fund, reposition some of your money or assets and buy into a growth or growth and income fund.

Additional Information

Composite Research & Management
1201 3rd Avenue, Suite 1220, Seattle, WA 98101. 206-461-3800.

Dodge & Cox
One Sansome Street, 35th Floor, San Francisco, CA 94104. 415-434-0311

Capital Growth Management
P.O. Box 449 Back Bay Annex, Boston, MA 02117. 800-345-4048.

Pasadena Group
600 N. Rosemead Boulevard, Pasadena, CA 91107-2101. 800-882-2855.

25
Variable Annuities

Stability of principal	✔✔
Stability of income	✔✔✔
Protection against inflation	✔✔✔✔
Total return	✔✔✔✔
Tax benefits	✔✔✔

Definition
A variable annuity is a lot like a mutual fund. The investor divides his or her money up among one or more subaccounts. When you invest with a mutual fund group, you may choose one or more funds within their family. Variable annuities offer similar choices, but they are called subaccounts. Most variable annuities offer at least the following investment options: money market, government bonds, growth stocks, growth and income stocks and total return, or balanced (a portfolio of stocks and bonds). A fair number of variable annuities also offer global stocks, foreign bonds, zero coupon bonds, gold, high-yield corporate bonds, and a guaranteed, fixed-rate account.

Just as with a mutual fund, the investor is free to move money around among the different subaccounts offered. Total return or yield depends upon how well the portfolio performs. Your investment choices, and risks, are only limited by the number of different "funds" offered by the variable annuity company.

How It Works
Money invested in a variable annuity is segregated according to your application. The single check you write might be for $25,000 but divided up as follows: $10,000 growth, $5,000 balanced, and $10,000 international. The variable annuity company, just like a mutual fund group, would then divide up your portfolio accordingly. The person or team running the growth portfolio, for instance, would be notified that new money is now available—your

$10,000 plus money from other investors whose money was received that day. The management of each portfolio invests the money according to the parameters of the prospectus (meaning a growth fund refrains from investing in junk bonds) and the analysts' views of the market, specific industries, and select securities. All purchases and sales within the subaccount are determined by the manager(s). As with a mutual fund, the investor does not tell the people running the portfolio what to buy or sell.

Profits or losses are credited, pro rata, to each investor in the account. If you own just the international bond portfolio, you are not entitled to any of the gains, or losses, from the stock fund. Similarly, if your $10,000 represents .001 percent of the portfolio's total holdings, you are only entitled to .001 percent of the profits, losses, dividends, and/or interest. Mutual funds work exactly the same way.

Variable annuity subaccounts are professionally managed by individuals or teams. Many of these people also manage mutual funds you may be familiar with; often you can find a variable annuity that has a similar portfolio and identical manager as your favorite mutual fund.

There are three parties to every annuity contract: the contract owner, the annuitant, and the beneficiary. The *contract owner* is normally the investor. As the owner, you are free to add or take out money at any time and to gift or will your interest to anyone you like (just like a mutual fund investor). The *annuitant* is similar to the insured in a life insurance policy. A variable annuity continues until either the owner says differently or the annuitant dies. When the annuitant dies, either tomorrow or decades from now, the contract may be terminated by the annuity company, depending upon contract provisions. The *beneficiary* is the person who receives the proceeds from the subaccount(s) if and when the annuitant dies (unless the account was liquidated before the annuitant's death).

What normally happens is that one spouse is the owner and annuitant and the other spouse is the beneficiary. This way, if either spouse dies, the other is protected either by will, trust, or the annuity contract. After the death of the first spouse, the survivor who inherits the account can then change the beneficiary, perhaps naming one or more children as heirs.

All of this means tremendous flexibility. For most people, imagination is the only limitation.

Advantages
There are nine advantages to variable annuities: consistent performance, professional management, multiple investment options, administrative and bookkeeping benefits, tax deferral, accountability, probate avoidance, no fees or commissions charged, and a guaranteed death benefit.

Variable annuities generally have more consistent performance than their mutual fund counterparts because this kind of investment is considered more long-term than a mutual fund (fewer investors move money around). Additionally, the portfolio manager tends to be more fully invested—the need for cash reserves to deal with market panics is not as great. No matter what the investment objective, variable annuities tend to be a little more conservatively invested than their mutual fund counterparts.

The second advantage, shared by mutual funds, is professional management. Though the amount of money you have to invest cannot attract a top-quality manager, your money combined with that of thousands of other investors adds up to several tens or hundreds of millions of dollars. If a manager or team receives a fee of 0.5 to 1.0 percent per year, such a salary, based on a portfolio worth, say, $300 million, can hire some of the best money managers in the world at a cost to you of less than a dollar a year per $100 invested.

A full-time money manager can devote all of his or her attention to the selection of securities for your subaccount(s). These professionals are specialists with a very narrow focus. Unlike stockbrokers and financial planners, who are constantly dealing with administrative tasks, attending meetings, and handling client questions and problems, a money manager's sole responsibility is to turn in good results consistent with the risk level of the portfolio.

Third, just as an investor can distribute her investment among different members of a family of mutual funds, variable annuities offer several different investment choices. Sometimes these choices are even greater than with mutual funds. When you invest with any mutual fund company, Oppenheimer or Vanguard, for example, you are limited to the management style of that company, but many variable annuity companies allow you to choose among multiple companies. Thus, the XYZ Variable Annuity may offer the following choices: Fidelity Growth and Income, Oppenheimer Growth, Van Eck Metals, American Growth, and Henderson International. These variable annuities try to find what they consider to be the best money managers within one or more mutual fund companies.

Fourth, just like mutual funds, variable annuities offer investors the benefits of quarterly statements, toll-free telephone numbers, performance reports, exchange privileges within the family of "funds," systematic withdrawal plans if monthly income is needed, and the ability to add or take out money whenever you like. Unlike mutual funds, which charge a $5 fee to move part or all of your money from one fund to another, variable annuities let you make changes for free. In fact, there is no direct charge for any of the benefits described above.

The fifth benefit of variable annuities is tax deferral. This is discussed fully under "Tax Considerations."

Sixth, there is the issue of accountability. When was the last time a stockbroker said to you, "Oh, you don't want to invest money with me; several of my clients suffered large losses last year." The truth is, the majority of stockbrokers and investment advisors think they are great stock and bond pickers. Yet, as the saying goes, "If you're so great, why aren't you rich (why do you need my account)?" Unfortunately, there is no way to track the performance of a stockbroker. He or she may have a terrible track record and you would never know it . . . unless you experienced it first hand. Variable annuities, however, are different. You can find out how a particular subaccount (investment within the annuity "family") has performed over any time period you want by using one of several neutral sources available (see "Additional Information"). Alternatively, your advisor can telephone the variable annuity company and get performance figures.

The seventh advantage is that variable annuities avoid probate. When the annuitant dies, the beneficiary(s) automatically takes over the account, no matter what a will or trust might say. In this case the contract takes precedence over any other legal document. Probate can be minimized or avoided by having a living trust, but most people do not have one of these estate-planning devices. The costs and delays of probate can be nothing short of amazing, not to mention depressing.

Eighth, there is no commission charged to the investor. When you send in a check for, say $15,000, the entire $15,000 goes to work for you as soon as the annuity company receives the money, meaning faster growth of your investment.

Last but not least, there is a guaranteed death benefit. Variable annuities are the only investment that offers this guarantee. Here is how it works: At the time of the annuitant's death, the beneficiary (the person who inherits the account), which could be you, your spouse, children, friend, living trust, etc., is guaranteed to receive the initial investment (plus any subsequent contributions by the investor) or the account value on the date of death, *whichever is greater*. The only adjustment made is for any previous withdrawals by the investor. Let us go through an example and see how this benefit works.

Say you invested $100,000 in a variable annuity and decided to take a big risk by putting all of the money in the aggressive stock portfolio. At the time of the investment, you were fully aware that the subaccount could be wild, rising or dropping by large percentages each year. In fact, let us suppose your account history looked like this:

initial investment (6/16/92)	$100,000
value on 12/31/92	$120,000
value on 12/31/93	$185,000
value on 12/31/94	$250,000
value on 12/31/95	$194,000
value on 12/31/96	$103,000
value on 12/31/97	$81,000
value on 12/31/98	$47,000
value on date of death (3/6/99)	$29,000

As you can see, the value on the date of the annuitant's death (remember, the annuitant is similar to the person named as "the insured" in a life insurance policy) was $29,000. The beneficiary, which could be you, your spouse, etc., will receive $100,000 (due to the guaranteed death benefit). If, instead, the account was worth $780,000 on the date of death, the beneficiary would receive $780,000.

As you can see, variable annuities allow you to take a certain amount of risk, knowing that at least your loved ones will be protected if the stock or bond market collapses and you die (assuming you are named as the annuitant). You will not find this guarantee when you invest in stocks, bonds, real estate, or mutual funds.

Disadvantages

Variable annuities carry four disadvantages. First, there is no assurance that your investment or the subaccounts will appreciate. As with most other investments, there is a chance that you can lose money, unless you choose a money market or fixed-rate account. Second, if you take out more than 10 percent of the account's value each year, you may be subject to a penalty. With most contracts, this penalty disappears completely after the fifth, sixth, or seventh year. Third, there is a possible IRS penalty (see "Tax Considerations").

Finally, variable annuities are a little more expensive to operate than mutual funds. Typically, a variable annuity will charge a flat $30 annual contract maintenance fee as well as a management and administrative expense that is about three quarters of a percentage point higher than a similar mutual fund.

These "disadvantages," or charges, are a small price to pay for all of the advantages variable annuities offer. A talented investment counselor can help you sort out the right annuity, one that can give you returns consistent with your risk level.

How to Buy and Sell

All variable annuities are offered by insurance companies. They are *sold* through brokerage firms, financial planners, and investor advisors. An investment is made by filling out an application and making out a check to the annuity company. The application is easy to complete. You indicate the owner (you), the annuitant (the "insured"), and the beneficiary (who gets the investment if the annuitant dies—the beneficiary is normally you and/or your spouse, while either one of you is alive). You also indicate which investment portfolios (subaccounts) you want to go into and what dollar figure is to go into each. You can even indicate whether you want the money dollar-cost averaged into a particular position. As an example, under the "special instructions" section, you might fill out the application to read, "Initially place 100 percent of the money in the XYZ money market portfolio.

Thereafter, starting next month, take $\frac{1}{12}$ th out of the money market account and put it into the growth account. Continue this process until there is nothing left in the money market position and 100 percent in growth."

There is nothing else to do on the application besides dating and signing it. No medical questions are asked. Most variable annuities have an initial minimum investment of $5,000; additional contributions can be as low as $1,000. You can add money at any time without cost or fee.

Taking money out is even easier. You simply write the annuity company a letter requesting a specific dollar amount. Within seven days you will receive the money requested.

Tracking Performance

Daily newspapers do not track the performance of annuities. *Barron's*, a weekly financial publication for serious investors and advisors, lists the price changes and values of several hundred variable annuities. A few monthly magazines, such as *Money* and *Stanger's Investment Advisor* now track the performance of several subaccounts. *The Wall Street Journal* periodically carries an article about annuities and will list the performance of the top ten, as well as the worst performers in a specific category.

Another way to find out how you are doing is by contacting the issuing company (the variable annuity people). Almost all of these insurance companies have toll-free numbers that can give you automated information about your particular account and offer you the option of talking to a personal representative. Variable annuity companies also send out quarterly statements to all of their clients. These statements show the value of each subaccount (growth, government bonds, etc.) and a total for the entire contract (investment).

Historical Performance

The first variable annuities were offered to school teachers in the 1950s. The original variable annuity is still offered today, in fact, although its results can only be described as "fair." The things that variable annuities invest in, stocks, bonds, real estate, metals, and money market instruments have been around for a long time.

The performances of variable annuities are similar to those of mutual funds over the past several decades: most of them are average, some are terrible, and a modest number have done extremely well. As with a fund, the trick to variable annuities is to pick one that has a consistent track record, stable management, and a risk level you can live with. Over the past five and ten years, many of the more popular variable annuity subaccount categories (aggressive growth, growth, growth and income, international stock, and balanced) have performed very similarly to their mutual fund counterparts.

Tax Considerations

One of the chief reasons people invest in annuities is that their growth is tax-deferred. You do not pay taxes on any of the accumulated growth, interest, dividends, or trading profits until you take the money out. You do not even trigger a tax event if you move your money from one subaccount to another. For example, suppose you invested $20,000 in a variable annuity and divided it evenly in the growth and government securities subaccounts. At the end of the year, the account was worth $24,000. You would not pay taxes on any of the $4,000 profit. Next year, let us say, the account appreciated from $24,000 to $27,000. After this $3,000 gain, you decided that you needed $1,500. If you withdrew $1,500 in 1994, you would have to show $1,500 of taxable income on your 1994 return. You would not have to indicate any of the other accumulated profits in the account (since they have not yet been withdrawn).

If money is taken out of an annuity, taxes are only due on the growth or appreciation. Thus, if a $20,000 initial investment grew to $23,000, only the first $3,000 withdrawn would be taxed; the remaining $20,000 would be considered a return of capital and therefore not taxable, if withdrawn.

While the annuitant is alive, you are never forced to take money out of your account. You are certainly free to make withdrawals at any time, but you are not required to while the *annuitant* is alive. When the annuitant dies, the beneficiary must fully liquidate the account within five years from the date of death. During this five-year period, the new owner (the former beneficiary) is free to take money out or move it around among the different investment subaccounts (just like the flexibility you have within a mutual fund family). If the beneficiary is the spouse of the annuitant, then this five-year requirement does not apply. The surviving spouse can continue the contract as long as he or she desires—he or she is never required to make a withdrawal.

Money taken out of an annuity prior to the contract owner's reaching age $59\frac{1}{2}$ is subject to a 10-percent IRS penalty. The penalty applies only to the increased value in the account, not the principal. If a thirty-year-old invested $9,000 in a variable annuity and it grew to $9,400 and then a withdrawal of $400 was made, there would be a $40 penalty (10 percent of the $400 growth). This 10-percent penalty is waived if one of the following occurs: the annuitant dies, the owner becomes disabled, principal is taken out, or the owner is $59\frac{1}{2}$ or older.

One of the nice features of variable annuities is that they provide you with a little extra privacy. If you own tax-free bonds, the IRS now requires you to list the interest you are receiving, even though it is not taxable. In the case of annuities, there is no space to fill in or box to check to indicate that you even own an annuity, much less what its value is. In fact, the annuity company does not even send a notice or report to the IRS unless a withdrawal is made or the money is transferred to another insurance company.

As noted at the beginning of this chapter, all annuities are offered by insurance companies (but sold mostly through brokerage firms, financial planners and banks). If you ever become dissatisfied with the performance of your contract, you can transfer part or all of your account to another company. Known as a "1035" or "tax-free" exchange, this is a way to get a new investment without triggering a taxable event.

Portfolio Fit

Variable annuities are the perfect investment vehicle for an individual or couple who is not in the lowest tax bracket and who wants to accumulate money in an account for future use or to leave to loved ones. Variable annuities are preferred to similarly performing mutual funds if the investor is close to or over $59\frac{1}{2}$ (to avoid the 10-percent IRS penalty).

Despite the pre-$59\frac{1}{2}$ IRS penalty, young people can gain an edge by investing in variable annuities if the account grows at a decent rate and is allowed to stay intact for at least several years. Consider the following example of two investors, one who uses a variable annuity and one who does not (assume the following background):

a) both investors are in a 33-percent tax bracket (state and federal)
b) both accounts are growing at 15 percent per year
c) investor A's account grows tax-deferred (annuity)
d) investor B's account is fully taxed each year (mutual fund)
e) each investor begins with $100,000
f) no additional investment or withdrawals are made
g) the variable annuity account (investor A) is fully liquidated in ten years

VALUE AT THE END OF:	INVESTOR A	INVESTOR B
1 year	$115,000	$110,000
2 years	$132,250	$121,000
3 years	$152,088	$133,100
4 years	$174,901	$146,410
5 years	$201,135	$161,051
6 years	$231,305	$177,156
7 years	$266,001	$194,872
8 years	$305,901	$214,359
9 years	$351,786	$235,795
10 years	$404,554	$259,375
value at liquidation (the end of 10 years)	$404,554	$259,375
minus:		
the 10% IRS penalty	$30,455	—
taxes due (on the $304,554 gain)	$100,503	—
net to the investor	$273,596	$259,375

- The annuity investor would avoid the $30,455 penalty if he or she was $59\frac{1}{2}$ or older when the contract was liquidated.

- The annuity investor owes taxes on the $304,554 gain ($404,554 minus the initial $100,000 investment).

- The 10-percent IRS penalty is due on the $304,554 gain, not the entire account value.

- Investor B's account (the mutual fund) grew at 15 percent each year, but this figure was reduced each year by income taxes.

Annuities become a better investment than similarly performing mutual funds *after only a couple of years if you are old enough so that the 10-percent IRS penalty does not exist.*

Risks

There is only one risk associated with variable annuities, the risk that your investment does not grow in value. This risk can be minimized by investing your money in a conservative account, such as a money market portfolio or fixed-rate, where you get a locked-in rate of return for one year, just as with a bank CD.

Investing in any of the other subaccounts is just like investing in stocks or bonds, except you have professional management to help cushion any losses. The longer your investment time horizon, the greater the likelihood that you will make a good rate of return by being in a growth-oriented subaccount.

Unique Features

Variable annuities have two special features: tax deferral and a guaranteed death benefit (tax deferral is also found in retirement accounts, the cash buildup in a life insurance policy, and *fixed-rate* annuities). The power of compounding tax-deferred interest can be amazing, compared to investments like bank CDs and money market funds, which are taxed each year. The death benefit can end up benefiting you, your spouse, your child, etc., depending on who is listed as the annuitant and who as the beneficiary.

Comments

Variable annuities should be seriously considered by anyone who is at least fifty years old. Which investment categories (subaccounts) you end up selecting will depend upon your risk level and advice from your financial advisor.

This is one of the few investments you can make where you pay taxes only when you spend it, not when you make it. Often, variable annuities are referred to as "tax-deferred mutual funds."

Additional Information

Even though over $50 billion was invested in annuities last year alone (their growth rate is greater than mutual funds), only one book has been written exclusively about fixed-rate and variable annuities. I am proud to say that I am the author of that book. The other sources shown below are companies that offer variable annuities; they include some of the best-performing subaccounts (portfolios).

All About Annuities
by Gordon K. Williamson, published by John Wiley & Sons (1992).
800-748-5552.

American Legacy
P.O. Box 2205, Brea, CA 92622-2205. 800-421-0180.

IPO-STE
5th Floor, Pavilion East, P.O. Box 16609, Columbus, OH 43216.
800-321-6064.

Kemper Money Market Fund
120 South LaSalle Street, Chicago, IL 60603. 800-621-1148.

Phoenix Equity Planning Corp.
Bright Meadow Boulevard, Enfield, CT 06083. 800-243-1574.

26
Foreign Stocks

Stability of principal	✔
Stability of income	✔✔
Protection against inflation	✔✔✔✔
Total return	✔✔✔✔✔
Tax benefits	✔✔✔

Definition

Foreign, also known as international, stocks are issued by corporations based outside of the United States. Like their American counterparts, foreign stocks represent ownership in businesses. As a shareholder you own a small percentage of the corporation; if the company does well, so can you. All stocks are considered equities.

How It Works

Corporations around the world issue stock as a means of financing their operations. These companies receive the proceeds from the stock when it is initially issued. The money raised helps the corporation operate and, with luck, increases its size and profitability. Once traded, profits or losses sustained from stocks traded in the *secondary marketplace*, such as the New York Stock Exchange or The London Exchange, do not directly benefit or hurt the issuing corporation. The corporation benefits from the initial offering and any subsequent issuance of new shares, but not in daily trading—except to the extent that the company may later issue new shares of stock at a higher price, or to the degree that it, or its employees, holds onto some of the company stock.

People who buy shares of foreign stock can benefit by owning part of the corporation. Shareholders' net worth increases if the company's profits increase or if future prospects look good. The equity may also increase in

192

value if that country's stock market is moving up. Conversely, bad economic conditions, disappointing company earnings, the loss of a major contract or key employee, and a market crash or correction can all send the price per share of the stock downward.

Advantages

Foreign stocks offer four advantages. First, international issues help an investor reduce his or her risk through diversification. U.S. and foreign stocks do not move up and down together. While your U.S. securities are moving sideways or downward, your foreign issues may be increasing. Second, many foreign stocks pay quarterly dividends, which are passed onto the shareholders. Third, foreign stocks, like other stocks, may appreciate in value. That common stock for which you paid $25 a share may be worth $30 or $60 a couple of months or years from now. Fourth, since international stocks are traded on foreign exchanges, U.S. dollars must first be converted to the "currency of the realm" before a purchase is made. When the stock is sold, the transaction takes place in deutschemarks, yen, francs, etc., and then converted back into U.S. dollars. This currency exchange can mean extra profit for the investor.

Disadvantages

There are two disadvantages to owning foreign securities. First, you have no guarantee that the stock you choose will go up in value. It is possible, although highly unlikely, that it could drop by anywhere from 1 to 100 percent; some publicly traded U.S. and foreign stocks do fail, rendering the stock worthless. However, it is more likely that the stock will go up by several hundred percentage points over the course of five or ten years. Second, you may find that the foreign stock went up in value but that you have actually lost money because of a strong U.S. dollar.

How to Buy and Sell

Foreign stocks can be purchased from your local broker. This broker will either be affiliated with a firm that has offices overseas, or will have a relationship with a foreign securities company. The broker can find out the current price as well as the stock's fifty-two-week high and low.

Some international securities can also be purchased on American exchanges. These are known as ADRs (American Depository Receipts). ADRs make foreign trading a little easier, since a financial institution, usually a bank, transacts all of the buying and selling for the brokerage firm, collects dividends and interest, and converts all of these monies into U.S. dollars. The cost for doing all of this administrative work is nominal, because the banks are doing these tasks on such a large scale. The important thing to remember about ADRs is that they do not limit your exposure to a strong or weak U.S. dollar.

The easiest way to buy foreign stocks is through a mutual fund or variable annuity. These will take care of any foreign taxes due as well as monitor currency movements. Dealing in foreign stocks can be quite tricky; a professional management team is strongly recommended.

The strength or weakness of the U.S. dollar is important whenever you deal in foreign securities. If the value of the dollar increases, dividends or gains from a sale are worth less because it now takes more of that foreign currency to equal a dollar (say, 150 instead of 140 yen to the dollar). Since you are, in essence, trading in foreign currency whenever a dividend or sale occurs, you want that currency to be as valuable as possible compared to the dollar. When the dollar drops in value, it then takes fewer yen, francs, lira, etc. to equal a dollar—meaning that you will end up with more dollars.

The currency consideration is not something you have to worry about continually unless you are dealing with unstable currencies from countries like Mexico, Brazil, Israel, etc. The dollar goes up and down in value just as other stable currencies do. Ideally, when your foreign securities are sold, the currency is worth more on the day of sale than it was on the day of purchase.

"Currency risk" is usually blown way out of proportion. Many financial advisors seem to think that it can only harm the investor. The truth is, there is an equal likelihood that it will help, hurt, or have no impact. A gain from the sale of a foreign stock could be 18 percent and the country's currency might have risen 4 percent against the U.S. dollar during the period of ownership. In such a case the U.S. investor would have a total return of 22 percent. Conversely, if the dollar gained 4 percent against the foreign currency, the total return would be 14 percent. Normally, currency movements have only a modest impact, plus or minus, on returns or quarterly dividends. If you plan on holding the securities for five or ten years, the difference caused by currency fluctuations should be extremely slight, and certainly not worth worrying (or dreaming) about.

Tracking Performance

Individual foreign stocks are not reported in U.S. newspapers. To find out how you are doing, you will have to contact your broker. It may take your broker several minutes or hours to get a "current" quote. ADRs, which are traded on U.S. exchanges, are quoted in newspapers daily and are also part of computer quotation services. Almost any broker or investment advisor can get you a buy- or sell-price quote for an ADR within seconds.

Foreign stock fund prices are quoted in the newspaper each day. Like other kinds of mutual funds, the price of a foreign fund is not normally tracked during the day; daily prices are computed a few hours after the trading day. Quotes for variable annuities can be obtained by contacting the broker or by telephoning the company directly. Most annuity companies have toll-free phone numbers.

No matter what *vehicle* you use to own foreign stocks (individual issues, ADRs, variable annuities or mutual funds), the value of each position will be shown on a brokerage firm's monthly or quarterly statement. The firm can only show you the value of assets held by them; certificates in your physical possession or held by the fund or annuity are not included, since there is no way for the brokerage firm to know whether you still own the security.

Historical Performance

During most years, foreign stocks outperform U.S. equities. In fact, if you were to list the top-five performing stock markets from around the world for the last fourteen years, using a grid of seventy slots (5 x 14), you might be surprised to see the United States only twice on that grid. In 1982 we had the second-best-performing market, and in 1991 we had the fourth-best market. (All of these figures are in U.S. dollar terms, which means performance has been adjusted for whether the dollar was strong or weak.)

Performance figures for the last decade (1982-1991) also point to the benefits of owning international stocks. For the ten years ending December 31, 1991, the U.S. was ranked twelfth—fourteenth, if returns are shown in local currencies.

These figures do not mean that the U.S. is a bad place to invest. On the contrary, a diversified portfolio of U.S. stocks has had excellent results in the past and will probably perform even better in the future. Foreign stocks have done better only because they represent companies and countries that are often not as mature or as large as their U.S. counterparts.

Tax Considerations

When it comes to foreign securities, there are three tax considerations. First, when you sell the stocks for a price different from the purchase price, there is a capital gain or loss. Second, any dividends received or credited to your account are fully taxable. Third, the corporation's country has its own tax laws and/or treaty with the United States. The bad news is that the foreign country usually taxes all dividends, interest, and/or capital gains from companies located within its boundaries. The good news is that in most cases, any such taxes are fully credited against similar U.S. taxes. If the international country withholds 20 percent for dividends and/or interest, that entire figure will be deducted from your U.S. taxes for dividends and/or interest payments.

For this reason, the issue of foreign taxes withheld is actually a non-issue. All that happens is that a different country ends up keeping some of your profit or income instead of the U.S. taking it. This is because most countries have a reciprocal tax treaty with us: they keep part of the action from their securities and we keep part of the action when their citizens own

U.S. stocks. A few countries, such as Mexico, do not have such a tax treaty. In those rare instances, any foreign tax paid is lost; your U.S. taxes would not be reduced, and you would be paying a form of double taxation. There is nothing you can do about this except to avoid the small handful of countries that do not have this arrangement with us.

Portfolio Fit

Almost everyone should own some foreign stocks. If 30 percent of your total holdings (IRA, pension plan through work, regular account, spousal accounts, etc.) are in common stocks, then up to 60 percent of such stocks should be foreign issues. This means that up to 18 percent of your total holdings should be in international stocks and 12 percent in U.S. issues. Such a weighting would be appropriate for a somewhat aggressive investor. A moderate or conservative portfolio would tone that 18 percent figure down to 10 to 12 percent, with the balance, 20 to 18 percent, being in U.S. stocks. These figures would adjust upward or downward depending upon how much of your total holdings were already devoted to common stocks.

The reason why even conservative investors should have at least modest exposure to foreign stocks is that such a holding actually reduces your overall risk level. Foreign stocks alone compared to U.S. stocks are about 5 to 10 percent riskier; a *global* stock portfolio (foreign and U.S. stocks combined) has up to 51 percent *less risk* than a pure-U.S.-stock portfolio (Stanford University study). Other studies, which cover different time periods, point out that the risk reduction is only in the 20 to 35 percent range. However, I would recommend foreign stocks even if there were zero reduction in risk because of the potential for greater returns overseas. Any risk reduction is merely icing on the cake.

Risks

Some brokers and financial planners will tell you to stay away from foreign stocks. They will make comments like "too risky," "difficult to track performance," "don't know much about the company (or country)," "there are foreign taxes involved," or "currency risk." Well, we have already seen that foreign taxes and the currency issue are really non-issues. All of the other issues raised can be countered by using a mutual fund or variable annuity. The management at a fund or variable annuity will take care of everything for you. They buy and sell the stocks within the portfolio, pay any foreign taxes due, research the companies thoroughly before a purchase, and track results daily through their overseas operations or affiliations.

The only real risk of owning foreign stocks is market risk—stocks go up and down in price. Presumably you would not be foolish enough to own just a few different U.S. stocks but would instead own a diversified portfolio representing several companies and various industries. (This could be accomplished by owning shares of one mutual fund or units in one variable annuity). The same should be true with your foreign holdings. Do not own shares of stock from companies located in just one country. Instead, buy shares of a portfolio that includes equities from several countries and industries. Since no one knows what the next best-performing stock or industry will be, do not assume that you know what the next hot country will be.

Unique Features
Other than the fact that there is a currency exchange and possibly foreign taxes withheld, there is nothing special about foreign stocks. They do generally have greater appreciation potential, while being only slightly riskier; they also generally pay a smaller dividend than their U.S. counterparts.

What is perhaps unique or special about foreign stocks is that they allow you to broaden your horizons. We may prefer to buy things made in the U.S., but there are times when such a product does not exist or its foreign counterpart is better or less expensive. The same thing is true when it comes to international equities.

Comments
Of the twenty largest corporations in the world, fifteen are foreign. Virtually all of the largest banks are international. The majority of the world's wealth is represented outside of our boarders. Cheap, good-quality labor is plentiful in many other countries. Avoid the mistake made by the great majority of U.S. investors, who ignorantly neglect foreign stocks.

Additional Information
Any major brokerage firm or mutual fund company can supply you with additional information on foreign stocks. A listing of two of these companies is shown below. The other companies represent mutual funds or variable annuities that specialize in foreign securities.

Capital Research & Management
333 S. Hope Street, Los Angeles, CA 90071. 800-421-0180.

G.T. Global Financial Services
50 California Street, 27th Floor, San Francisco, CA 94111. 800-824-1580.

Societe General Securities
50 Rockefeller Plaza, 3rd Floor, New York, NY 10020. 800-334-2143.

Templeton Mutual Funds
700 Central Avenue, P.O. Box 33030, St. Petersburg, FL 33733.
800-237-0738.

The Economist
P.O. Box 58524, Boulder, CO 80233. 800-456-6086.

27
Convertible Securities

Stability of principal	✔✔✔
Stability of income	✔✔✔✔
Protection against inflation	✔✔✔✔
Total return	✔✔✔
Tax benefits	✔✔

Definition

As the name implies, a convertible security is something that can be changed into something else. There are two kinds of convertible securities: convertible bonds and convertible preferred stocks. Each can be converted into the issuer's common stock. Once "converted" into the common stock, it cannot be converted back into a bond or preferred stock. After the conversion, the owner has shares of common stock that are no different than the other common stock of the issuing corporation. Until the bond or preferred stock is converted, you receive interest or dividends according to the terms of the convertible security.

How It Works

Let us suppose that the ABC corporation has issued the following securities:

SECURITY	YIELD	PRICE
common stock	3% dividend	$100 per share
preferred stock	5% dividend	$50 per share
bond	8% interest	$1,000 per bond
convertible bond	6% interest	$1,000 per bond

You are trying to decide which of these issues would be best. There is no "right" answer; it depends upon the goals, tax bracket, and risk level of the particular investor. The common stock has the best appreciation potential, but is also the most volatile of the choices. The preferred stock should appreciate if the corporation does well, but not at the same pace as the common stock. The preferred stock is less volatile than the common stock and is therefore less risky; it also provides a higher current income. The bond is attractive for the income-oriented investor, but the interest is fully taxable, and a bondholder does not directly benefit if the corporation's profits rise. The convertible bond does not provide the highest rate of return, but can be converted into common stock (assume nine shares for this example). Obviously, conversion would not make sense while the common stock is trading at less than $110 per share (9 x $110 per share does not equal $1,000). If and when the price of ABC's common stock starts to move up, the convertible bond will look more appealing (and its price will also increase).

As you can see from this example, when you buy a convertible security, there is what is known as a "conversion formula." It shows you how many shares of common stock the convertible bond or convertible preferred stock can be exchanged into. There is never parity. This means that if a convertible preferred were selling for, say, $800, and it could be converted into ten shares of common stock, the common stock would be trading at a price above $80 per share (10 shares x $80 per share = $800). If parity ever did occur, investors would flock to the convertible issue for two good reasons. First, a convertible security normally has a higher yield than the common stock. Second, preferred stock and bonds are safer than common stock. The fact that a security is convertible does not mean that it is not just as safe or safer as a bond or preferred stock that does not include the word "convertible" in its description.

Preferred stocks and corporate bonds normally fluctuate less than common stocks; both issues are also financially safer than common stocks, meaning that if the corporation goes bankrupt, common stockholders are at the end of the line, behind owners of preferred stock, bonds, and convertibles (prior to conversion to common stock), when it comes to dividing up any corporate assets.

So far we have seen that a convertible security has a yield less than that of a similar security that can not be converted; a convertible bond has a lower yield than a regular bond; a convertible preferred stock has a dividend less than that of a preferred stock from the same corporation. We have also seen that people buy convertibles partially in the hope that the common stock of the corporation will also go up. The current income is not bad either.

Advantages

Since a convertible is a hybrid security, part bond or preferred stock and part common stock, it provides several advantages. First, when compared to other investments, it offers an attractive yield, or return. Second, if the common stock goes up in value, the convertible security will also increase in value; if interest rates fall, there will also be price appreciation, since preferred stocks and bonds go up in value when rates drop. Third, these securities are normally highly marketable; if you ever want to buy or sell them, the process is quick and easy. Fourth, they have virtually unlimited upside appreciation potential and limited downside risk. Let us examine this final point in more detail.

Suppose that XYZ Company has the following: a common stock that sells for $10 a share; corporate bonds that are selling at par, $1,000 each, with an interest rate of 9 percent; and a convertible bond that is also selling at $1,000, has a current yield of 6 percent ($60 per year), and can be converted into seventy-five shares of XYZ common stock at any time. Now suppose that the price of the XYZ common stock falls to $4 a share. At this level, conversion becomes even less attractive ($4 a share x 75 shares = $300 — a far cry from $1,000). If this were to happen, the XYZ convertible bond would be worth less, perhaps dropping in value from $1,000 to approximately $800. Is there a chance that the drop would be less? Yes. At $800, the current yield of the convertible would be 7.5 percent ($60 divided by $800); a 7.5 percent yield for a high-quality convertible bond may be too high. Indeed, it would be too high if similar convertible bonds had a yield of only 6 percent. Therefore, the price of the convertible, even though it was "supposed to" fall to $800, might level off at, say, $900 per bond. ($60 divided by $900 = 6.7% — a yield higher than the competition's, but perhaps still fair considering that the conversion into common stock looks less attractive, $4 a share common stock vs. a price at one time of $10 per share.)

Another example of "limited downside risk" would occur if, in the example above, interest rates rose (meaning the value of all bonds and preferred stocks would drop) and the price of the common stock went from $10 to $14 a share. If this were to happen, the convertible bond would "like" to fall in price so that its new price was in line with the then-current yields. (A 1-percent rise in interest rates could translate into a loss of up to 8 percent in value, from, say, $1,000 to $920, for bonds, preferreds, and convertibles alike.) However, this would not happen, since the conversion ratio would mean that a $920 purchase could be transformed into owning seventy-five shares at a price of $14 a share ($14 x 75 = $1,050). As you can see from this second example, a drop in price would not occur, even though interest rates had gone up and other securities had suffered. In fact, the convertible bond would go up in value, now having a price tag in excess of $1,050.

The reason I stated earlier that convertibles have a somewhat unlimited upside potential is that one never knows how high the common stock will go up. A $1,000 convertible preferred stock or bond that can be exchanged for ten shares of a stock selling for $85 a share can double, triple, or quadruple in price if the stock goes up to $170, $255, or $340 in price.

Disadvantages

There are four possible threats to convertible securities: marketability, quality, rising interest rates, and a common stock price that does not go up. Let us examine each of these four points in detail.

Only a few hundred companies issue convertible securities. Most investors do not own any convertibles in any form, and not many mutual funds specialize in them. Only a small percentage of pension plans and money managers deal in these securities. For all of these reasons, convertibles do not trade with nearly the same frequency and narrow bid-and-ask spread as do common stocks, preferred stocks, and corporate bonds. (You want a narrow bid-and-ask spread between the buy and sell price of a security so that the cost of trading is minimized.) This is why the issue of marketability should always be raised before a purchase is made.

Second, there is a question of quality. The reason convertibles are issued is that the corporation is having difficulty raising money by issuing only common stocks, preferred issues, or regular bonds. A convertible is offered as sort of a "sweetener"—a way to increase investor interest without having to give up much. Out of fairness, there are several dozen high-quality convertibles. Nevertheless, always ask your broker the quality rating. Otherwise you may end up with junk, even though you thought that was only possible with poorly rated bonds.

The third and fourth possible disadvantages can be lumped together. Since convertibles are often referred to as a "hybrid security," they benefit, and sometimes suffer, from sharing some of the traits of the common stock and regular bond. All other things being equal, if interest rates rise, a convertible bond and convertible preferred stock will both fall in price, though the drop may only be a fraction of what noncovertible bonds and preferred stocks experience. Similarly, if the common stock drops in price, conversion becomes less attractive and the price of the convertible will also drop. Again the convertible may not fall in price nearly as much as the underlying common stock.

How to Buy and Sell

Convertibles are purchased from the same people and institutions who sell stocks and bonds. You can also participate in this market by owning shares of a mutual fund that owns convertibles (see "Additional Information").

Tracking Performance

If you own a convertible bond or convertible preferred stock, you can find out how it is doing by looking up its value in the newspaper or by being tied into a stock-quote service on your personal computer. The brokerage firm through which you bought the issue can also give you price quotes during the trading day.

The value of mutual funds that include convertibles is tracked the same way you would follow any other fund: via the mutual fund section of your newspaper or by telephoning the fund's toll-free number and asking for customer service or account information.

Historical Performance

Convertibles have been around for over a hundred years. Long-term, their performance has been better than bonds but not as good as common stocks. However, the risk level and price variability of convertibles is much lower than that of their underlying common stocks.

Tax Considerations

The interest or dividends of convertibles are fully taxable. If a conversion takes place, there is no immediate tax consequence. Capital gains or losses result if the purchase price is greater or lower than the selling price, whether or not the security is converted.

Portfolio Fit

Convertibles provide a nice method of reducing overall portfolio risk by adding a new category of investment to your holdings. A convertible security may not end up moving in the same direction as some or all of the other parts of your portfolio. These securities are often overlooked by investment advisors and investors; do not make the same mistake. Convertibles make a lot of sense for most people.

Risks

The biggest risk of convertibles is the risk of default. Since a fair number of convertibles are, or were, issued by corporations with ratings of less than bank quality, the chance of bankruptcy or restructuring should not be overlooked. For this reason, investors are encouraged to stick with those issues that are at the high end of "junk," BB or BBB, or that are rated as "investment grade" (AAA, AA, A or BAA).

A secondary risk of owning convertibles is that the common stock will go down instead of up. When this happens, the convertible loses some of its appeal, unless interest rates have also fallen.

A third has to do with timing. Several convertibles can only be converted within a certain period of time or after a certain date. You should always ask your broker about the details of the issue's convertibility before a purchase is made. If you buy a mutual fund that has convertibles as part of its holdings, you do not have to worry about this feature. The portfolio managers are fully aware of the limitations of every security owned by the fund; this is part of the reason why money managers make so much money.

Unique Features

Convertibles are the only security that allow investors to make a change, going from owning one kind of security (a preferred stock or bond) to another (the common stock). Keep in mind that the conversion is a one-way street. Once you make the conversion, you cannot later change your mind and decide that you want the bond or preferred stock back.

Since we are dealing with something that is sort of like a bond (or preferred stock) and sort of like a common stock, convertibles are often compared to balanced mutual funds, funds that invest in both common stocks and corporate bonds.

Comments

If you do not own any convertibles directly or by way of a mutual fund, then it is time that you seriously consider such an investment. By making a high-quality convertible mutual fund part of your portfolio, or by owning several highly rated individual issues, there is a strong likelihood that your overall risk level will go down and your overall total return will increase. This is because most people have few common stocks, if any, in their portfolios. Common stocks have historically outperformed bonds, CDs, and money market accounts. Convertibles may be more volatile than what you currently own (assuming you are a very conservative investor), but such volatility is something that can be tolerated by most people.

By adding convertibles, you will get away from a portfolio that may otherwise be wholly at the mercy of interest rates, and very likely reduce the price peaks and valleys associated with a pure debt portfolio.

Additional Information

The first source shown below specializes in analyzing individual companies and their stock. The other sources are mutual fund companies that can answer any questions, as well as send you written literature and an application.

Value Line Convertible Survey
711 Third Avenue, 4th Floor, New York, NY 10017. 800-223-0818.

American Capital Asset Management
2800 Post Oak Boulevard, Houston, TX 77056. 800-421-5666.

Calamos Asset Management
2001 Spring Road, Suite 750, Oak Brook, IL 60521. 800-323-9943.

Phoenix Equity Planning Corp.
100 Bright Meadow Boulevard, Enfield, CT 06083. 800-243-1574.

SEI Corp.
680 E. Swedesford Road, Wayne, PA 19087. 800-342-5734.

28
REITs

Stability of principal	✔
Stability of income	✔✔✔
Protection against inflation	✔✔✔✔
Total return	✔✔✔✔
Tax benefits	✔

Definition

A real-estate investment trust (REIT) invests in a pool of mortgages and/or properties. After deducting for expenses and management, income from the real estate and/or mortgages passes directly through to the investors of the REIT. The REIT is run by a board of directors elected by the investors. Each year the investors have the ability to hire or fire one or more of these representatives. Board members are responsible for hiring property managers, accountants, and other staff needed to carry out the REIT's business.

Some REITs are of finite duration, others infinite. A finite REIT means that the REIT organizers intend for all properties (or mortgages) in the REIT to be sold (or for the mortgages to mature) within a set number of years, usually somewhere between eight and twelve. Proceeds from properties or mortgages sold are distributed to the investors; they are not plowed back into the REIT unless a sale occurs during the first few years of the REIT's life.

Most REITs are infinite life. This means that when there is a sale, or when a mortgage matures, the REIT organizers use the proceeds to buy similar kinds of mortgages and/or properties.

How It Works

There are three kinds of REITs: mortgage, equity, and hybrid. *Mortgage* REITs use investors' money to buy mortgages. The REIT does not own any property; it loans its money to a property owner or owners, the loan(s) being secured by the property(s). The property owner makes mortgage payments each month to the REIT. *Equity* REITs use shareholder money to buy real estate. They generally specialize in a certain kind of project or geographic region. Some REITs buy only strip shopping centers, others concentrate on nursing facilities; still others buy commercial or residential property in a specific state or region. Depending upon the kind of real estate you want to include in your portfolio, chances are there will be at least one equity REIT that specializes in that area. *Hybrid* REITs are a combination of a mortgage and equity real estate investment trust. They invest in real estate and also purchase mortgages or make loans.

Advantages

REITs are a form of liquid real estate or mortgages. They offer a way to participate in real estate without having to make a five-to-ten-year commitment, or pay a series of real estate commissions, closing costs, and unexpected maintenance costs, or deal with tenants. More importantly, REITs are an easy and cost-efficient way to diversify your real estate holdings geographically and by type. Imagine how long it would take you to become an expert in, say, commercial real estate in Northern California or a nursing home in upstate New York. Not to mention figuring out who would manage the property and how you would go about keeping tabs on the tenants.

Mortgage REITs provide investors with a safe income stream from a number of mortgages. By owning a small part of several mortgages, instead of buying one or two mortgages or taking back a mortgage on your home, you greatly reduce risk. If one mortgage defaults, you are not wiped out.

People own REIT shares for one of three reasons: current income, growth, or a combination of some growth and some income. Mortgage REITs provide greater current income than equity or hybrid REITs but have no growth potential, unless interest rates decline and the price per share of the REIT goes up. Equity REITs provide some current income, normally about 5 to 10 percent, depending on the kind of REIT, but also serve to offset the future effects of inflation. Approximately half of an equity REIT's total return is from growth; the other half from current distributions.

Most equity REITs have built-in price increases in their income stream. Leasees of the buildings have consumer price index (CPI) clauses or overage clauses (the REIT gets a certain percentage of gross sales) built into the lease or rental agreements. This protects REIT investors against the effects of inflation. Some mortgage-backed REITs have equity-participation clauses (the REIT investors get a certain percentage, usually 10 to 25 percent, of the appreciation of the property that is being used as collateral).

REITs that have a current income normally make distributions quarterly. The checks are either sent directly to the investor or deposited in his or her brokerage firm's money market account. Some REITs will send the checks directly to the mutual fund of your choosing.

Disadvantages

Not all REITs appreciate in value or are able to maintain their income distributions. As everyone who owns real estate or acts as a lender knows, property values do not go up every year; some years prices decline. Nor does every mortgage turn out to be a good one. Sometimes agreements have to be renegotiated so that the borrower does not go bankrupt. The fact that a mortgage REIT starts out with a 9-to-11-percent yield does not mean that it will not decline in the future.

Some REITs are more marketable than others. Just because a REIT is traded OTC or listed on the NYSE or AMEX does not mean that you will be able to sell your shares in minutes. Many REITs are thinly traded, meaning there are comparatively few buyers and sellers. Your order to purchase or sell shares may stay unfilled for several minutes, hours, or days.

Generally, REITs are interest-rate sensitive. When rates fall, mortgage REITs usually appreciate in value, just like long-term bonds. If interest rates fall and public confidence is relatively high, equity REITs usually appreciate too. Conversely, when interest rates are rising, a REIT may decline in value unless its income stream is tied into CPI adjustments.

Another major risk of REITs is that most are leveraged (i.e., their property is generally mortgaged). For example, if a REIT is 80 percent leveraged and the property value declines by 15 percent, then your actual loss would be 75 percent of your investment. This is an extreme example and the risk will be less if the REIT is less leveraged. Some REITs are not leveraged at all.

How to Buy and Sell

When you buy into a REIT, you end up owning shares, much like owning shares of a corporation's stock. As a shareholder you have the right to vote on certain matters that affect your investment. In particular you have the right to vote for the trustees who, in turn, hire management to perform the day-to-day affairs of the REIT. If you no longer like the way the REIT is being run or how it is performing, or if you simply need some money, you can sell your shares. As with stocks and bonds, the price you will receive depends on general market conditions and the kind of REIT you are selling. During certain periods, mortgage-backed REITs outperform equity REITs, and vice-versa. And as with stocks, certain segments or industries are more popular than others during any given time. Thus, an equity REIT made up of nursing homes may or may not be worth as much as an equity REIT that specializes in shopping centers.

Shares of a REIT are bought and sold through brokerage firms. Many REITs trade either on the NYSE, AMEX, or OTC. A commission is charged whenever shares are bought or sold.

Generally, dividends, interest payments, and other forms of distribution cannot automatically be reinvested in additional shares of the REIT. Instead, the shareholder can use the money for whatever purpose he or she likes, including buying more shares of the REIT, if there happens to be any sellers at the time.

Tracking Performance

Since most REITs are traded on the New York Stock Exchange (NYSE), on the American Stock Exchange (AMEX), or over the counter (OTC), you can find out what the share price of any publicly traded REIT is by looking it up in the newspaper. Your broker can also give you a quote over the phone. If you have a computer, modem, and proper software, you can also track the price per share right at home by subscribing to one of the security retrieval services.

Historical Performance

The track record of REITs has been mixed. Historically, equity REITs have done quite well, often outperforming the stock and bond markets. Mortgage REITs have not performed nearly as well. Hybrid REITs fall somewhere in between.

Tax Considerations

Interest payments received by mortgage- or hybrid-REIT owners is fully taxable. Rental or lease payments received by equity owners may be partially sheltered. The amount of sheltered income in an equity REIT ranges from 0 to 25 percent of the distributions.

Any appreciation in the price per share of the REIT is deferred until you sell your shares or when the REIT comes to an end. By being able to decide when a profit, or loss, is to be taken, the investor can better plan his or her taxes to minimize any liability.

Portfolio Fit

Equity REITs are a good addition to many portfolios. The idea of owning a diverse portfolio of real estate, coupled with professional management and expertise, is quite appealing. The fact that you can buy into a REIT that owns a certain *kind* of property or is active in a specific region is merely icing on the cake.

A similar case cannot be made for mortgage REITs. True, their income stream is much greater than that found in an equity or hybrid REIT, but there are better alternatives. When interest rates are low, good-quality high-yield bonds are a better choice—they are more marketable and have a better track record. When interest rates are high, bank CDs, government bonds, and tax-free municipal bonds often make better sense, particularly on a risk-adjusted basis.

Risks

Whenever you own real estate you face two risks. First, if you are a landlord, you want to make sure that your tenants are financially secure and will make their expected payments. Second, you hope that the property appreciates in value most every year. As a lender, the mortgage REIT hopes that the borrower makes payments on time and that the project or property performs as expected. If it does not, the loss may be so great as to force the owner (the borrower) into bankruptcy or into seeking some form of court protection. It is hard to collect on a debt when the borrower has no money.

The other risk associated with REITs is marketability. Before buying shares of a REIT, make sure that there are a good number of ongoing buyers and sellers. What you are looking for is trading activity. You want to make sure that when you decide to sell your shares, there will be a sufficient number of buyers. Strong buyer interest means that you will get a fair market value for your shares. If your REIT is thinly traded, the price you receive will almost certainly be less than fair.

Unique Features

This is the only kind of real estate investment that allows you to buy and sell quickly. Hundreds of thousands of people own income-producing property but cannot sell it quickly. If the market suddenly shifts, as it did in the early 1990s, you may be stuck with that property for several years, unless you are willing to accept fire sale prices.

Few people who own rental property like dealing with tenants. By owning shares of a REIT, you give someone else the job of collecting rents, dealing with pets, and fixing plumbing during the middle of the night.

Even people who love buying and selling real estate or mortgages will agree that there is a real limit to their expertise. Just because you understand commercial property in Los Angeles does not mean you will not be taken advantage of in Houston or some other city. Every business is a business; every piece of real estate has unique characteristics. The market in one city is different from that found in another; residential properties do not have the same characteristics as commercial ones. Most people who own more than one piece of property concentrate in one specific area, usually the same city or county in which they live. This kind of concentration is fine during the good times, but think about what happens during the bad or lean periods.

When an area is hit by high unemployment, most kinds of real estate will suffer at about the same time. People who own properties in that area may see their net worth rapidly erode with a 10-to-25-percent decline in property values. The damage becomes even worse if the properties are leveraged. Large mortgages are a good idea during boom times, but devastating during periods when the incoming rents fail to cover outstanding loan payments. These kinds of problems are less severe with non-leveraged equity REITs. First, diversification minimizes the likelihood of total declines. Second, many have no outstanding debts. These all-cash programs can survive even when vacancy factors double, triple, or quadruple. Finally, the REIT, with its vast holdings, usually has the ability to borrow money during lean times, if necessary. Most individual property owners do not have the net worth to afford such a luxury.

Comments

For the purely income-oriented investor, there are usually better alternatives than REITs. However, for someone who is satisfied with a moderate level of income, coupled with deferred growth potential, this is a good way to go for up to 15 percent of your portfolio. Look for equity REITs that have been around for at least a decade, REITs that have a history of meaningful dividend distributions and price appreciation. As with any other investment, do not expect share price to increase annually. No real estate goes up every single year.

Additional Information

REIT Fact Book
c/o NAREIT, 1129 17th Street, NW, Suite 705, Washington, DC 20036. 202-785-8717.

Review of the REIT Industry
Merrill Lynch & Co., 155 Broadway, New York, NY 10080. 800-637-7455.

29
Variable Life Insurance

Stability of principal	✔✔
Stability of income	✔✔✔
Protection against inflation	✔✔✔
Total return	✔✔✔
Tax benefits	✔✔✔✔✔

Definition

Variable life insurance is a form of whole life insurance. Whole life insurance, in turn, is a combination of term insurance (paying a death benefit—sometimes referred to as "pure protection") and a forced savings plan into which goes the investment portion of each premium payment. "Variable" means that the owner of the policy can direct how the savings part of the account is invested (the part of each premium payment that is not used to pay for the insurance portion of the policy). Investment choices normally range from money market accounts to aggressive-growth stock portfolios.

There are three parties to every life insurance policy: the insured, the owner, and the beneficiary. The insured is the person whose life is being used as a measuring device; the policy stays in effect until the insured dies or the owner cancels the policy. The insured does not benefit in any way. The owner is the person who pays for the policy. He or she decides how the cash portion of each premium payment, which can be monthly, quarterly, semiannually, or annually, is to be invested. The balance of the premium is used to pay the insurer for the risk it is taking. The owner can cancel the policy at any time by declining to pay a renewal premium or by writing the insurer. The beneficiary receives the death benefit when the insured dies. The owner can change beneficiaries at any time prior to the insured's death.

How It Works

Life insurance need not be as complex as it first appears. Just remember that there are only two kinds of life insurance: term and whole life. With term insurance, the beneficiary receives a death benefit if the insured dies while the policy is in force; otherwise, there is no benefit apart from the psychological benefit of knowing that you are providing for someone in the event of your death. In order to get this kind of protection (death benefit), you pay premiums.

In the case of whole life insurance, part of your premium (which is usually paid annually) goes toward paying for the insurance (the death benefit), and part of it goes into an investment. Since you are essentially contributing to a savings plan, from which you can withdraw at any time, the premiums for whole life are greater than those for term. This is only fair, since term insurance has no savings plan that you can take money out of.

With *traditional* whole life insurance, the owner has no investment choices; the money that goes toward the investment portion grows at a set rate. With variable life, the owner (you, the investor), gets to decide in which portfolio the money is to be invested; as with a mutual fund family, you can switch among the different portfolios.

Variable life insurance, just like term and traditional whole life, has a death benefit. The benefit is paid by the insurance company upon the death of the insured, provided the policy is in force, meaning that the premium payments are current.

Advantages

Variable life insurance offers three advantages: financial protection for loved ones, several investment options to choose from, and a number of tax benefits (see "Tax Considerations"). As far as protection is concerned, it is hard to beat insurance. Imagine an "investment" that you pay X for and that is later "worth" 3X or 30X. Well, that is how life insurance works. The only problem is that someone must die before you see that huge return on your investment, that is, on the premiums paid in each year. No matter what you might say about life insurance, it is the cheapest form of protection. How many investment options you have to choose from depends upon the policy you buy; some insurance companies have five or ten different choices, while others have only three or four.

Disadvantages

There are four disadvantages to variable life insurance. First, if the insured does not die while the policy is in force, then part of the premiums have been "wasted" to the extent that they did not provide a final, real, tangible benefit. Second, the cash buildup in the policy (the savings portion) can be withdrawn, but insurance companies often charge the owner interest to borrow *his* own money. The loaned money does not have to be repaid by the owner as long as interest payments are being made. If enough cash remains in the policy, the interest payments can automatically be deducted from the account. Third, there is no guarantee as to how much the savings portion of the policy might grow to before death or liquidation. With variable life, the owner accepts all of the good and bad results of the portfolio's performance (since the owner decides how the money is to be invested). Finally, life insurance has some potentially negative tax aspects (see "Tax Considerations").

How to Buy and Sell

The first thing to determine is whether you need life insurance and if so, how much. There are two groups of people who need life insurance: those whose loved ones are financially dependent on them and those who have an estate that may be subject to estate taxes. (This is a net estate of $600,000 or greater if you are single and $1,200,000 or greater if you are married and plan on someone other than your spouse, such as your children, to inherit more than $1,200,000.) If you do not fit into one of these two categories, chances are that you do not need life insurance.

Do not buy life insurance on your children's lives; it is a "bad bet." On the other hand, just because your spouse does not work does not mean that he or she is not worth a lot. If that homemaker were to die, who would maintain the household and/or take care of you and any children or dependent relatives? Finally, in determining whether life insurance is necessary, try to project ahead. A $200,000 estate, which is at least $400,000 short of being subject to federal estate taxes, can easily be worth close to a million dollars or more fifteen to twenty years from now (when your chances of dying are much greater) just through inflation—the figure could be several million dollars if investments are added during this period.

Like a lot of things in life, the best way to purchase insurance is to shop around. Make sure that you deal with a high-quality insurer; you want to be certain that the insurer is still in business when the time comes to collect on the death benefit or take out a policy loan (withdraw part of the policy's cash value). Rating services like A.M. Best, Moody's, and Standard & Poors are just some of the companies that rate insurance companies as to their present and projected financial solvency. When buying insurance, look for companies that have one of the highest ratings from at least two of these services.

Once the issue of quality has been settled, find out what each of the prospective candidates charges in the way of premiums for the amount of insurance you are looking for. Life insurance is a very competitive product, and some companies charge much more than others for the same coverage (death benefit).

The next consideration is what investment options are being offered and what the performance of these portfolios has been *after all expenses have been deducted.* You are interested in net returns, not some gross figure with no real merit or meaning. Along the same line, you want to find out the mechanics of taking out a loan in case one is ever needed. Find out what percentage of the cash value can be withdrawn and what interest rate is being charged on the borrowed money. (Insurers charge one rate but credit to the account the same or a lesser rate, resulting in an interest-rate charge that may be lower than it first appears.) Also find out any other restrictions or fees that could be charged.

The last thing you need to know is how fast the cash value of the policy builds up. With some policies the upfront expenses are so high that the investor (contract owner) does not see any true accumulation of cash for the first several years. Other policies are priced so that a cash value can be seen during the first year. In the long run the difference may be unimportant, but during the first several years of the policy's life it means a great deal, particularly if the owner intends to take out a loan. You can't borrow out the cash value if there isn't any!

Tracking Performance

Daily returns and performance figures for the portfolios within variable life-insurance contracts (policies) are not quoted in the newspapers as stocks and mutual funds are. To find out how you are doing, you must either wait for a quarterly statement from the insurer or contact your financial advisor (or the insurance company) to get an updated quote.

Some of the portfolios are "clones" of well-known mutual funds. They are called "clones" because the portfolio contains a package of securities similar to that of the parent fund. The track records may be quite comparable, and it is not uncommon to find one of your favorite mutual fund managers running a similar kind of "fund" as part of the variable-life portfolio family.

Historical Performance

The track record of variable-life portfolios is not very extensive, since most of these portfolios have been around only five years or less. Only a small handful of insurers have "funds" that have been around for a decade or longer. The track record of these portfolios can be just as good, or bad, as any mutual fund.

Tax Considerations

The tax benefits of variable life insurance, coupled with the protection it affords your heirs, are what make it so appealing. The investment portion of your account grows and compounds tax-deferred. When death occurs, the beneficiary(s) receives the death benefit (face value of the policy minus any outstanding loans) free of income taxes. When done properly, money loaned out of the policy (borrowed by you) can also be free from income taxes. (Similarly, when you borrow money from a bank, you do not show the loan proceeds as income.) One thing you never want to do, however, is voluntarily cancel a policy. (Death is not considered a voluntary event.) To see how bad things can get, let us go through an extreme example.

Suppose that over an extended period of time, the cash value of your policy grew to $300,000 and you decided to borrow $250,000 from the policy, either all at once or in bits and pieces. The $250,000 is not taxed when withdrawn because it is considered a loan; you are paying the insurance company some nominal rate of interest to have use of this money. A few years—days, weeks, months, or even decades—later, you cancel the policy. You refuse to make any more premium payments, and there is not enough cash build up to pay the premiums internally. During that year, you will have to show $250,000 worth of extra income on your tax return. It does not matter that the money has already been spent or invested elsewhere or that you did not know that cancelation triggered a tax event. You canceled and you have to pay up: in this case, $82,500, if your tax bracket is 33 percent. Be warned.

The tax consequences of taking money out of an insurance policy need not be tragic. If the insured dies while a loan is outstanding, there is no negative tax event. The beneficiary receives the death benefit minus the value of the outstanding loan, plus any interest accrued that has not been paid. The repayment of the loan will also negate any future tax problems.

Portfolio Fit

Variable life insurance should only be purchased by one kind of person: a person who needs life insurance and who fully understands that there are few guarantees as to how the cash portion of the policy will perform. A person, in other words, who needs the coverage and is willing to accept the risks of investing. Traditional whole life insurance provides the owner with a guaranteed rate of return, but one that may end up being much lower, or higher, than what ends up happening in a variable contract.

Do not buy variable life as an investment if you do not need life insurance. When you buy this kind of product, you are paying for insurance, overhead, commissions, and a profit to the insurer. There are better alternatives from a pure investment perspective—even once taxes are factored in.

Risks

The pitfalls of investing in variable life insurance have to do with choosing a subaccount (investment category), lack of information, and quality of the insurer.

As with a mutual fund family, variable life products offer the investor a wide range of choices. You can invest part or all of your money in one or more equity and/or debt-instrument portfolios. The only limitation is the number of subaccounts (or portfolios) the insurance company offers. If you do not like the available choices, choose another insurer.

Before investing in variable life, people need to be aware of one thing: Not all of your premium dollars, that is, your investment, goes toward investing; part of any premium paid covers life insurance. This is how the death benefit is funded. That is why this product is generally not a good idea unless insurance is also needed.

Finally, you must look to the quality of the insurer. Again, make sure that the company you are considering doing business with has a top rating from at least one, preferably two, of the major rating services, such as A.M. Best, Moody's, or Standard & Poors. You want to make sure that your insurance and the investment portion are safe at all times.

Unique Features

What is unique about variable life, what makes it really different from a mutual fund family or variable annuity group (both of which also give you the choice of several different portfolios to choose from) is the tax benefits. Variable life is the only way you can invest in equities in a tax-free manner, through the borrowing process described above. It is also the only way to invest in corporate or government bonds with the same tax advantage.

Comments

Surprisingly, this product can make a lot of sense whether you believe that your life expectancy is just a few days or several decades. The rate of return on this investment becomes astronomical if the insured (you or whoever is listed on the policy) ends up dying within the first several years of purchasing the policy. In this case one would be relying more on the death benefit than on any cash buildup.

The investment portion of the policy can also make this an appealing proposition, depending upon the performance of the subaccounts. These portfolios can end up equaling or exceeding mutual funds and variable annuity accounts that have the same investment objective. Thus, you may not suffer any loss of performance just because this product includes a death benefit.

In determining whether variable life insurance is for you, the real keys are, does someone's life need to be insured (yours, your spouse's, or perhaps one or both of your parents' or in-laws'), and do you have the patience to wait for the value of the account to build up? Variable life does require considerable patience. Generally this asset does not look particularly appealing, short of some kind of stupendous performance in a subaccount, unless it is held for at least ten to fifteen years. Only then have all of the costs been sufficiently amortized, borrowing costs reduced or eliminated, and/or penalties avoided. It is at this point that tax-free withdrawals can begin benefiting you for the rest of your life.

In short, look to this investment if life insurance is needed or if your need for tax-free income will not occur for at least a decade. If you can wait this long, variable life insurance can reap great benefits.

Additional Information

Morningstar Variable Annuity/Life Performance Reports
53 West Jackson Boulevard, Suite 460, Chicago, IL 60604-3608.
312-427-1985.

Part IV

◆　◆　◆

Investments You Should Avoid

30
Investments You Should Avoid

In every area of life there is the good and the bad, and investments present no exception. Many can legitimately fulfill the goals and objectives of most people, depending on where they are in their lives. There are certain investments out there, however, that are patently bad. These are the kinds of things that should be avoided by everyone but gamblers—gamblers and those with delusions about their ability to "predict" market trends and price movements.

Throughout my career as an investment advisor, I have told investors and prospective clients that if we can just avoid the bad stuff, 70 to 80 percent of the battle will have been won. The occasional investment that has an off-year once in a while, or the investment that averages a 7-percent return instead of an 8-percent return; these are not what harm us. Those investments where we are likely to lose everything are what can have a profound and lasting effect on the balance of our holdings and, indeed, our future lifestyle. Before we get to some specifics, let us first describe ways to avoid being a victim.

According to an October, 1992, article in *The Wall Street Journal*, tips from fraud investigators on keeping your money out of the hands of scam artists include:

- Just say "No." Never buy investments from a stranger over the phone, or in person during the initial meeting.

- Get it in writing. Ask for a prospectus or other printed information that describes the risks as well as the potential rewards.

- Investigate any offering that sounds too good. Call the National Fraud Information Center by dialing 1/800-876-7060; a counselor will give you advice and additional leads for more information over the phone.

- Hire professional help. Hire a financial advisor who cannot benefit from the purchase.

- Verify the broker's history. The North American Securities Administrators Association can be reached by telephoning (202) 737-0900; they can tell you how to contact the securities commission in your state. These state regulators, in turn, can tell you whether the person you are dealing with has any past securities violations.

Just as there are bad investments, as we will explore, there are also bad brokers and bad financial advisors. Experts estimate that the number of people who call themselves "financial planners" has grown from a few thousand in the 1960s to over 250,000 today. State and federal regulators estimate that some of these planners cause their clients to lose over $300 million a year. I believe the number approaches several billion dollars a year due to bad advice if you include investment advisors, insurance agents, and stockbrokers. These losses are the result of sloppiness, lack of training, or conflicts of interest.

According to a *Money* magazine survey conducted in 1992 (an interview with thirty-two practitioners listed under "Financial Planners" in the Santa Rosa, California, Yellow Pages), there is indeed cause for alarm. According to the study, "None of the planners answered all twelve knowledge questions correctly. More than half of them got at least one-third of the answers wrong. Nearly one-third could not state within four percentage points the historical long-term return paid by common stocks—a crucial statistic for someone who provides advice on combining various investments to achieve long-term goals. And more than two-thirds said they earned some or all of their income from commissions on the products they sell—an arrangement that creates conflicts of interest."

A former securities commissioner of Maryland has publicly stated that ". . . competence (of financial advisors) issues cost consumers more money than fraud." In fact, in some states, it is claimed, it is easier to qualify as a planner than to get a driver's license!

Stockbrokers and insurance agents like to call themselves financial planners, which they may legally do, because it gives them a certain degree of added credibility in the eyes of existing and prospective clients. According to John Markese, president of the American Association of Individual Investors, "The actual selection of investments is probably planners' weakest area. But I also hear a lot of dissatisfaction when it comes to tax advice, complicated estate-planning questions, and IRA rollovers."

An article in the November, 1992, issue of *Money* offers another piece of alarming information: "Since 1980, the number of financial planning and investment advisor firms registered with the Securities and Exchange Commission (SEC) has more than tripled to 17,500. Unfortunately, the number of government regulators paid to keep an eye on those planners and advisors has increased far more slowly. For example, the ranks of SEC inspectors have risen only 28 percent—from the equivalent of 36 full-time examiners in 1980 to 48 in 1991. The SEC visited only 574 investment advisory firms in 1991—mostly big-money managers, not the small outfits most likely to serve typical investors. At that rate, the average advisory firm could expect to see an SEC inspector once every thirty years."

What does all of this mean to you? Simply, that this is even more evidence of why it is important to arm yourself with the information contained in this book. Take an active role in your future. As you should be coming to realize, investing on your own is not as difficult, or as boring, as you once thought. Let us now move on to the discussion at hand: investments you should avoid.

Always to be Avoided

Investments you should avoid under any circumstances include the following:

- rare coins and stamps

- gemstones, including diamonds

- artwork

- movie or Broadway shows

- penny stocks

- venture capital deals

- anything involving research and development

I know some of these things sound fun, sexy, or exciting. I also know that one of these ventures may someday be presented to you in a way that appeals to your latent greed. Let us take a brief look at each one of these areas before we move on to investments that should be avoided by *most* people. For now, we are just talking about investments that should be avoided by *everyone*.

Rare coins are generally considered anything minted in the U.S. before 1940. These are coins for which the mintage (number produced) was low compared to today's standards. The other important feature of rare coins, from an investor's perspective, is quality or condition. A coin that had very limited mintage, even if it was struck in Roman times, may have little value unless its condition is excellent.

Rare coins became very popular as an investment during the late 1970s and throughout most of the 1980s, first because of high levels of inflation (people were looking for investments that would keep pace with what was then high inflation) and then because of the publicized track record of numismatics (rare coins). These performance figures showed that for several years in a row, rare coins were considered to be the best investment you could go into. Such "investment scorecards" were printed in *Barron's* and other respected publications that had no conflict of interest or axe to grind. The numbers showed that rare coins dominated every other investment for several ten-year periods in a row (1976-1985, 1977-1986, 1978-1987, etc.); the compound annual rates of return were very impressive. The only problem with these figures is that they came from tainted and biased sources.

The rare-coin index used to measure annual rates of return is highly controlled and manipulated. It includes only about two-dozen coins, most of which either never trade hands—they are owned by very wealthy people or museums—or are artificially priced by a small group of dealers. Such an index is highly suspect, indeed, is meaningless, since the average investor does not have the money to buy even a single one of these coins, assuming he or she could find one that was for sale.

The actual track record of rare coins, the kind that most investors have unfortunately purchased, has been less than shining. Cumulative losses of 20 to 60 percent over the 1980s are not uncommon. Such losses are compounded by the fact that a great number of investments doubled, tripled, or quadrupled over the same period of time. The history of rare stamps is even worse.

The story behind investing in numismatics is appealing: very limited supply and a collector base estimated to be anywhere from five to fifteen million in size. It's something like investing in oil: "They ain't makin' the stuff anymore." True, they stopped minting rare coins decades ago; true, dealer, collector, and investor demand has increased, but it is also true that the actual prices of most of these coins have gone down, not up.

It is hard to make money in an investment that routinely begins with a markup ranging from 25 to 200 percent. Buying rare coins is easy; selling them is a different story. Dealers and certain national firms will gladly buy them back from you, but usually at a greatly discounted price.

People like to hold on to hard assets in case of some kind of economic meltdown at home, but such thinking is defeatist and unrealistic. If you need hard assets to flee the U.S. and go somewhere else, where would you go? We consume a third of the world's output; our gross domestic production is almost twice our closest competitor's. If we run into financial difficulty, chances are that every other economy will have been wiped out months or years earlier.

Speaking of hard assets, let's talk a bit about gemstones. Experts widely agree that the safest way to trade or invest in such stones is by buying diamonds. And when you are talking about investment-grade, one carat D-flawless stones, you are talking about a very exciting performer. These diamonds peaked in the very early 1980s at about $60,000 per one-carat stone. By the early 1990s, these same stones were selling in the $15,000 range. Diamonds may be a girl's best friend, but they are certainly not an investor's.

As it turns out, whether you are looking at the last ten, twenty, or thirty years, diamonds used for industrial purposes (you know, the crummy stuff that no one would ever wear) have outperformed the "investment-grade" stuff. The problem with investment-grade stones is that there is a tremendous markup. The grading of these stones has not been standardized, except in the case of diamonds, and even then there are great differences of opinion. A stone that is graded at one level by one expert is often graded differently by another, resulting in a price discrepancy of several thousand dollars.

There is nothing wrong with owning diamonds, investment-grade or otherwise. If you want to buy a diamond, go ahead: just don't justify it as an investment. Buy the stone because you like it or to show your affection to someone.

Artwork is just like diamonds, only more so. Go into any gallery, buy an original piece, lithograph, seriograph, or print, and then try and sell it back to them even a couple of years later. Or try and sell it on the open market. You will be shocked as to what the real market value is.

Most investors are unwilling to spend $10,000 to $50,000 for an original by a well-known artist. So instead they turn to lithographs or seriographs. These are those numbered editions you see all the time. They are signed by the artist and numbered something like "35/800," meaning that you own one (#35) out of a series of "only" eight hundred. Such pieces are sold for anywhere from $1,000 to $15,000. The prospective buyer is told how "hot" the artist is and how quickly his or her other works have risen in price. What these dealers do not tell you is that a seriograph they once sold for $2,000, which is now selling for $5,000 to $10,000 or more, would not be bought back by the gallery for even $1,000. Further, you would have great difficulty getting $1,000 for the piece on the secondary market, a marketplace that includes more sophisticated and realistic buyers and sellers.

Buy art because it makes you feel good. If you want an original, a lithograph, or whatever, first try contacting someone in the secondary marketplace (such as The Art Cellar, at 800-326-2236). This will give you a sobering view as to what you can purchase (or sell) a piece for. If you are a seller, do not be surprised or frustrated if it takes several weeks or months to sell your work of art. The number of buyers and sellers is rather small, compared to the number of people who buy real estate, stocks, bonds, etc.

Speaking of pictures, let's move on to "moving pictures." Few things have the pride of ownership of being able to say to someone, "See that play (or movie)? ... I own part of it." This is fine and nice, and the world certainly needs such patrons and saints to support the arts, but the losses from such ventures are often in the 100-percent range. If you think your accountant is creative when it comes to bookkeeping, go to Hollywood and see some real pros at work. These folks can make a set of books look like something from Alice in Wonderland. (A more appropriate title or analogy might be the title of some movie or play that includes the word "Hell.")

One thing actors have learned that investors have not is the difference between "gross receipts" and "net profits." Well-represented actors who want a piece of a movie or play they star in make sure that they get a part of the gross receipts. Suckers and investors end up buying into deals that talk about all sorts of impressive projections and end up giving away part of the net profits. The words "net profits" in the entertainment business usually mean, "loses forever." Take the television show "The Rockford Files," for example. One of the most popular and talented actors in the history of television is James Garner. Here is a guy who makes acting look natural; Mr. Garner is a real pro, and I have yet to meet anyone who doesn't think he is one of the few greats. "The Rockford Files" was one of the most popular shows ever produced for television. In many parts of the country you can still see *reruns one or more times every day*. Yet according to the studios, this show has never shown a profit. A similar set of facts applies to some of the big box-office movies.

If you like the movies or the theater, by all means, go to them. If you want to support the arts, do so with the understanding that you are making a contribution, not an investment. I don' t think anyone loves movies or the occasional excellent television production more than I do, but I would never invest in such a proposition. As with other investments, don't get involved unless you fully understand what is going on. As Amarillo Slim, a well-known Las Vegas gambler, once said, "If you sit down at a poker table and you don't see a sucker . . . you're it."

If there is one investment that brings out the greed in people, it is penny stocks. Commodities or futures contracts would be a close second. These are stocks that are normally traded on exchanges or in places that you have never heard of; the price per share is quite cheap, often in the range of ten cents to a dollar or two per share. This might make the investment sound harmless; after all, this sounds more like tip money than anything to lose sleep over. The trouble is, most people who buy penny stocks don't just buy a few dollars worth, they buy several thousands of dollars worth.

There are three big problems when it comes to penny stocks. The first is a wide spread between the bid and the ask price (the prices you sell and buy something for). This spread does not benefit you, it does not benefit the broker you go through, it only benefits what is known as the "market maker" or "specialist": the person or company that keeps the stocks in inventory and promotes them to the public. Whenever you see a spread between the bid and the ask price amounting to more than 1 to 5 percent, beware. Chances are this is something to avoid. Second, penny stocks are not as closely regulated as the more traditional securities markets. This lack of attention offers a chance for greater abuse and fraud by the dealers of such low-priced securities. Third, and most important, the track record of penny stocks as a group stinks.

When people buy a cheap stock they are thinking about what it will be like when their $1-a-share stock goes to $2 or $4 a share. Rarely do they think about the day when the stock goes from $1 to 50¢ or even 12¢ a share. For some reason investors never seem to think about an investment going down in price.

Venture capital and research and development deals are both somewhat related to penny stocks. When you invest in one of these deals, you are helping out a company that has some kind of invention, patent, or process that looks promising. Again, the visions are the same. Investors imagine that they are getting in at the ground floor of something that will revolutionize medicine, the automobile, or something else. Occasionally these investments, like penny stocks, do work out, and the returns are wonderful. More often than not there end up being losses or pleas for additional money. Stay away from anything that even sounds like a start-up company. If you doubt what I say, contact any local bank and find out how many new businesses fail (90 percent).

In the three chapters that follow we will examine a series of investments into which billions of dollars have been poured, investments that can by no means be described as "low-risk." As we shall see, the popularity of these investments is no guarantee that they will have a good or even a fair track record. Read on to find out what you should probably avoid and why.

Additional Information

American Numismatic Association
818 North Cascade Avenue, Colorado Springs, CO 80903. 719-632-2646.

Coin Dealer Newsletter
P.O. Box 11099, Torrance, CA 90510. 310-370-5579.

The Gemological Institute of America
1660 Stewart Street, Santa Monica, CA 90404. 800-421-7250.

31
Limited Partnerships

Stability of principal
Stability of income ✔✔
Protection against inflation ✔
Total return
Tax benefits ✔✔✔

Definition

A limited partnership represents a kind of investment between a group of investors, the limited partners, and the organizers of the investment, the general partners. Limited partners have limited liability, meaning that they can lose no more than the amount of their investment. The general partners have unlimited liability, meaning that if someone is injured on partnership property or during the course of partnership business, any award would first come out of existing partnership assets and then directly from the general partners.

A partnership can be formed for almost any kind of business you can think of; the most common kinds of limited partnerships involve real estate, oil and gas, leasing, and cable television.

How It Works

The limited partners have limited authority and power but receive almost all of the proceeds (profits) *after* expenses. The people offering the program are either the general partners or salespeople who represent the program to prospective clients. The general partners make all of the daily decisions, including hiring and firing senior management, determining whom to sell the finished product to, what outside service companies are to be used, etc.

In theory the limited partners have the ultimate power: the ability to replace the general partners. This is rarely done because it is very difficult and often very expensive to organize the investors (the limited partners) into voting as one unit. Depending upon how the partnership agreement is drawn up, any general partnership change could require a *two-thirds or greater* consensus. And, as you have seen in the case of the United States Congress, the chances of getting such a consensus are slim. (President Bush had only one of his vetoes overridden from 1989 to 1992.) More to the point, there have been relatively few successful attempts in throwing out old management (the original general partners) and bringing in new leadership. The organizers, who are either the general partners, their affiliates, or their employees, draw up the partnership agreement (from which the partnership is governed) and include provisions that highly favor their position.

The partnership agreement, more formally known as the partnership prospectus, spells out the business of the partnership, such as to acquire shopping centers and lease them out, to buy existing oil and gas wells for the purpose of operating them and making cash distributions to the investors, to buy and operate cable television systems with the intent of selling them after five to eight years, and so on. The agreement also spells out the backgrounds of the principals (their business experience, education, etc.); any potential conflicts of interest (such as, the general partner is the owner of the maintenance company that will be used for all partnership properties); previous track records (a listing of all of the prior similar programs and what percent of investors' monies have been returned so far); how a general partner can be removed; the compensation of the general partners; and how profits or income are to be distributed.

Concerning the distribution of any incoming money, the split is usually very fair to the investors. It is common to see wording to the effect that the limited partners will receive 95 percent of all payments and the general partners, the remaining 5 percent. When the partnership comes to a close—the real estate is sold, the leased equipment is disposed of, the oil and gas wells run dry, etc.—the limited partners are frequently entitled to a 100-percent return of their original investment, sometimes calculated to include any previous cash distributions, and a 5-to-8-percent annual return on such money before any remaining profits are divided 85/15 (85 percent to the limited partners and 15 percent to the general partners).

Advantages
Partnerships offer several benefits, including professional management, a written plan spelling out its goals and objectives, the potential to make a good or very good return, and a split of net income and profits that highly favors the investors.

The people running the day-to-day operations of the partnership, the management, play a critical role in the success or failure of the program. These people are the ones writing checks, overseeing operations, and hiring independent contractors or employees to perform the partnership's necessary business. An experienced team that knows when to buy partnership assets (real estate, equipment, cable television systems, oil wells, etc.) and how much to pay for such assets can make (or break) the business. The same people must also decide how the properties are to be managed, negotiate leases and sales, and thoroughly understand the markets they are dealing in.

Since the business of the partnership is spelled out in the prospectus, prospective investors can decide before writing any check whether they are attracted to the investment being offered. These clearly defined objectives can help you to determine whether this investment is appropriate for your risk level, time horizon, and tax bracket, and whether it will complement your existing holdings.

The potential returns are also described. The prospectus often spells out what will happen if the occupancy rate is, say 90 percent compared to 80 percent, what the rate of return will be if the equipment is later sold for 50 percent of its original purchase price, how much, if any, of the income stream will be sheltered from income taxes, and what the profit margins will be if oil rises to X dollars per barrel or if the cable system is able to attract Y number of extra subscribers.

Again, the split of any net income and profits is clearly defined. There is no guesswork as to who will get what; the real question is, will there be anything to divide up?

Disadvantages

Limited partnerships also have several potential disadvantages. In fact, this general category includes more potential shortcomings than any investment described previously in this book.

Take first the question of marketability and liquidity. Buying into a partnership is usually easy, but getting out of one is difficult or impossible. Investors may be forced to wait for the partnership's natural termination—which may be fifteen or twenty years after the initial investment. The reason selling partnership units is so difficult is that most partnerships are not traded on any secondary market. This means that you can get rid of your investment only if you or a broker finds someone willing to buy you out. The chance of this occurring is very slim, and even if you do somehow find a buyer, the price offered to you may be ridiculously low, perhaps even insulting. A small percentage of outstanding partnerships are traded on the secondary marketplace; the value of these units ranges from poor to occasionally good.

Second, actual distributions often turn out to be either low or non-existent. In the case of oil and gas programs, the distributions usually start off being fantastic and then become terrible, or non-existent, three to five years into the program. It doesn't matter how good the distribution split looks if there is little or nothing to distribute.

Third, the holding period of the investment tends to be much longer than originally projected. If the prospectus tells you that the general partner intends to buy and hold the properties for seven to ten years, chances are the holding period will be nine to fifteen years. Such language is perfectly legal, and the investors have no real recourse, since the wording includes the words "projected," "hoped-for," "expected," or "anticipated." True, it is difficult to figure out, say, real estate prices and markets several years in advance, but isn't it curious that 95 percent of the time, the projections turn out to have been optimistic?

Fourth, investors are often left in a very frustrating position. The real power, you see, lies with the general partners. The limited partners pretty much have to wait around until the assets are sold or the partnership is terminated. Conditions may change, altering the attractiveness of the program. Changes in the tax laws may transform a good partnership to a bad one. Since these investments cannot be moved in and out of with any kind of speed, if at all, investors find themselves at the mercy of their "elected officials"—the general partners.

How to Buy and Sell

As stated, limited partnerships are easy to buy. Most brokerage firms have several such programs on their approved-product list. A good number of financial planners and advisors also deal in these partnerships. There is often a net worth requirement on behalf of any prospective buyers—for example, the prospectus might say that only people with a net worth of $50,000 and an annual income of at least $40,000 can buy partnership units—but this is usually not a tough requirement to meet. Selling an interest in one of these programs is a different matter, however.

Whenever you buy shares or units of a limited partnership, you should do so in the expectation of owning this investment until its natural termination. Most partnerships last somewhere between ten and twenty years, even though they are often marketed as having a life of only eight to ten years. In the case of an oil and gas income program, the longer the life the better; meaning there is more oil or gas to be sold.

If you decide to sell part or all of your interest in an oil and gas, real estate, cable television, or other program, you may be able to find a secondary marketplace. Most partnerships are not traded, meaning you will have to hold onto your interest until the program goes bust or runs its natural course.

Shares traded on the secondary marketplace are sold at a moderate or severe discount compared to what they are really worth. These dealers know that someone who needs to unload a partnership interest is desperate for cash, frustrated about the program, or, both. Your broker or advisor may tell you that your shares are worth much more than you can realistically get for them on the secondary market.

Fortunately, there are a number of dealers in the secondary market-place. No matter what one of these companies offers, have your advisor get competing quotes from a few other sources. You may be surprised to learn what the discrepancy is from one dealer to another.

Tracking Performance

Accurately tracking the performance of any partnership is difficult at best. These programs are not quoted like stocks or bonds. You can only get a rough idea as to how the program is doing by seeing what units are selling for in the secondary marketplace, but keep in mind that the great majority of these programs are not actively traded (meaning you will never know what they are worth) and that those that are, are, *at the very least*, traded for 15 to 25 percent less than their real value.

The general partners send out periodic reports as to the performance of their programs. These reports are almost always very positive. By the time the reports turn negative, it is usually too late to do anything about it. There is always a host of reasons as to why things did not turn out, but one thing is sure: The partners never blame themselves, their associates, or their sales staff. It is always the economy's fault, or an unexpected drop in prices, or something along those lines.

Historical Performance

The track record of limited partnerships has been poor, and not very likely to show much improvement. At any given point in time energy prices, or cable, or real estate, or equipment, may seem certain to be on the rise, but an unforeseen drop in prices or values could turn a moderately profitable operation into near bankruptcy. These unexpected price changes, coupled with the several layers of fees (overhead), are what have made this investment a disappointment in the past.

The only light on the horizon is that the industry has learned from its mistakes. Fees have come down. It still remains to be seen whether such savings will transform this *conceptually* sound investment into one that actually has total returns that are what they were projected to be.

Tax Considerations

The tax benefits of a limited partnership depend upon the program. In the case of real estate, the quarterly cash distributions are often partially sheltered from taxes; if the program has a 5-to-10-percent cash flow, 25 to 50 percent of this amount may not be taxable because of the depreciation of the buildings and the write-off of daily operating expenses. Furthermore, assuming the properties appreciate, any profits will be deferred until the real estate is sold. A refinancing can give the investors a healthy dose of cash without triggering a taxable event. Certain kinds of real estate programs, such as low income and subsidized housing, also have tremendous tax benefits in the form of tax credits and depreciation. Thus, you may be able to invest $70,000 and get $100,000 of deductions and credits spread out over the next ten to fifteen years.

When it comes to oil and gas programs, investors can write off part or all of their investment, as well as shelter income from the program using what is known as the depletion allowance. The tax benefits with oil and gas can be high, because it is a risky business and Congress wants to encourage the country to be energy self-dependent. There are also what are known as oil and gas income programs. In these partnerships the general partners buy existing wells and/or fields that have been producing (proving themselves) for at least a couple of years. The amount of oil and/or gas is known with a high degree of certainty; what is not known is what energy prices will be one, five, or ten years from now. Since oil and gas *income* programs do not subject the investor to any drilling risk (the partnership is buying proven fields), only a portion of the income is sheltered.

Leasing programs also come in more than one form. "High-tech" leases involve the leasing of equipment (computers, peripherals, medical devices, etc.) that may become obsolete within a three-to-five-year period of time. For this reason the lease payments (income stream to the investors) are usually in the 20-to-35-percent range annually. "Low tech" leases, such as cargo containers and railroad cars, have a much longer expected life (ten to fifteen years) and therefore throw off much less income on an annual basis. Since equipment is being fully depreciated no matter what kind of equipment is involved, it is not uncommon for investors to have 75 to 100 percent of the income stream sheltered for the first four to six years of the program.

In the case of cable television, operating equipment and the actual cable is being depreciated; you cannot depreciate labor or land. For this reason, approximately 25 to 60 percent of the income from these programs is sheltered from taxes for the first several years. Additionally, if the cable system is later sold for a profit, such gains are deferred until the actual sale.

Portfolio Fit

If you believe you cannot get enough diversification with some of the more traditional investments described throughout this book, you may find this investment appealing. After all, owning fuel, equipment, real estate, cable TV operating systems, and so on makes a lot of sense, at least on paper. Yet chances are that you will do much better by owning the common or preferred stock of a large domestic or international oil (or real estate or entertainment) company. Shares of stock can be easily traded, the income stream is almost always much more reliable, and you will have no trouble finding out what the investment is worth. If energy (real estate, cable TV, etc.) prices go up radically, your investment will also increase quite a bit.

Risks

The greatest risk of owning a limited partnership is that you will lose part or all of your investment. Losses in stocks, bonds, and mutual funds, when they occur, are usually small or modest. In the case of most partnerships, the losses are frequently moderate or extreme. For those who do make some ·money or at least break even, real returns are still pretty poor when you consider the time value of money. The $10,000 investment you get back ten years from now will have much less purchasing power, to say nothing of lost opportunities (you could have gone into other investments).

Once again, there is always the chance that the rules of the game will suddenly change. You might enter into one of these investments expecting great tax benefits, only to find Congress taking them away in a couple of years, as happened to real estate in 1986. Such adverse tax changes are not very likely, however, and should not be your primary consideration.

Then there is the liquidity or marketability risk. If you want to get out of a partnership before it runs its natural course, you are about 90 percent certain to be flat out of luck. If you happen to be in a program that trades on the secondary market, the price you will receive will probably be something well under true market value. Traders take advantage of your anxiety to sell on the limited marketplace by offering prices 10 to 50 percent less than what the units would sell for if they were as marketable as a well-known stock or bond.

Finally, there is the risk that you may have unknowingly signed a letter of intent or obtained a letter of credit. A "letter of intent" means that you guarantee to invest X amount more money into the program, either as a staged pay-in over a year or more or in the event that the general partners need more operating capital. A "letter of credit" is a similar guarantee, but it is made by the bank on your behalf. Either way, you have to sign something. Investors often sign such documents without really understanding the additional liability they are incurring. If you fail to fulfill any signed agreement, the partnership will sue you, and rightly: contract ignorance is no excuse. In the case of a letter of credit, your bank will gladly pay off on its guarantee, but will then turn to you for reimbursement, either liquidating your collateral or taking you to court. Letters of credit and letters of intent are not widely used today, and apply only to limited partnerships, but you should still be cautious about anything you sign.

Unique Features

Limited partnerships are the only investment described in this book that do not give you the freedom to come and go (buy and/or sell whenever you like). Their marketability ranges between poor and non-existent.

On a more positive note, some limited partnerships provide tax benefits that you cannot find with other traditional investments. Tax credits, deductions, and, to a lesser degree, sheltered income, are not easy to come by.

Comments

It is recommended that you stay away from all partnerships, with the possible exception of certain all-cash (non-leveraged), low-tech leasing programs. Although there have been, and continue to be, a small number of limited partnerships (also referred to as "direct investments") that will perform well, such investments are few and far between. Why try and find the one in ten that may do well when you can pick almost any other investment described previously in this book and be almost guaranteed to do better? Besides, the chance of your having the knowledge or patience to pick that one-in-ten winner is quite remote. Don't think your tax attorney or accountant will fare any better than you.

What it all comes down to is the hype, or printed word, versus reality, the actual track record of these investments. Projections, figures, charts, stories—they may sound great, but get a reality check. Find out how programs like the one you are considering have fared in the past. In almost all cases it is the broker and general partners who do well. They are the ones, remember, who get their money or compensation first. They operate on *gross* profits, while sharing agreements with the limited partners are based on *net* profits.

Additional Information

If you do decide to invest in limited partnerships, two of the better programs are Brauven (a real estate income program) and IEA (a cargo-container leasing company). These companies may be contacted by telephoning or writing to:

Brauvin Real Estate Funds
333 West Wacker Drive, Suite 1020, Chicago, IL 60610. 800-272-8846.

IEA
444 Market Street, 15th Floor, San Francisco, CA 94111. 415-677-8990.

32
Options

Stability of principal
Stability of income   ✔✔
Protection against inflation   ✔✔
Total return   ✔
Tax benefits

Definition

An option provides its owner with the right to buy or sell a specific number of shares of a specific stock for a specified price within a certain period of time. The person who buys the option is referred to as the "option buyer"; the person who sells is known as the "option writer" or "option seller."

How It Works

Options, like stocks, are traded on an organized exchange; as with stocks, you cannot buy an option unless someone is willing to sell it to you. If you think a certain stock, or the market in general, is going to go down, you would buy what is known as a *put* option. If you think a certain stock or the market is going to go up, you would buy a *call* option. You can buy as many put and call options as you like. Over 1,000 stocks are optionable—from blue-chip issues to high-growth equities. "Optionable" means you can buy or sell puts or calls on them. There are also a number of market indices you can bet on in trying to guess whether the overall market, or the segment that represents the index you are dealing with, is going to go up or down. When you buy or sell options, you are dealing in what are known as "contracts." A contract represents a hundred shares. Thus, if you told someone you had just purchased six contracts, you would be talking about six hundred shares.

A put option allows you to put stock to someone; to make them buy shares of the stock from you at a set price. A call option allows you to call stock away from someone; to make someone sell you a specific number of shares at a set price. Let us go through two examples so you can better understand the process.

First, let us suppose that you thought IBM stock was going to drop by several points over the course of the next few months. You could make money on this event, should you prove correct, by buying a put option. Suppose IBM were currently selling at $70 a share and you thought it was going to go to $60, or less. You could buy some IBM puts, three contracts, let us say (thereby "controlling" three hundred shares). Suppose further that you paid $2 (two dollars times three hundred shares equals a total purchase price of $600, plus brokerage commission) for a striking price of $70. This means that you can force someone to buy up to three hundred shares of IBM stock from you for $70 a share, even if IBM were trading for only $68, $59, $40, or whatever amount per share. Finally let us suppose you purchased January contracts. This means that your ability to make someone buy these three hundred shares expires at the end of the third week in January. If the option is not exercised between now and then, it becomes worthless.

To make the example positive (but negative for IBM), suppose that IBM stock went up a little, down a little, and then down a lot. (Pick any variation you want, but just imagine that the price is much less than $70 a share and that there is still some time, days, weeks, or months, before the third Friday in January.) Since IBM is now quite a bit below $70 a share, the option you paid $2 per share for is now worth, say, $8 a share. Why? Because if you can buy IBM for, say, $62 a share on the market and sell it to the person who sold you the option for $70 a share, the agreed-upon price, you have a built-in profit of $8 a share—perhaps more, if IBM continues to fall. That's the good news. The bad news is that the actual price of the IBM option, which can range from 0 to $5 to $10 or more dollars per option, can and will fluctuate. The price depends upon how much "life," that is, time, is in the contract (the more time, the more valuable the contract) and what the price of IBM stock is. If IBM goes up instead of down and is now trading at, say, $83 a share, the option becomes worthless. There is no way you are going to go out and buy IBM at $83 a share and make someone buy it from you at only $70 a share.

Let us now turn to an example involving call options. Change the facts or circumstances completely. Let us now imagine that you think Apple stock is headed for a large price rise over the next nine months. (The time period with options can range from one day to up to a year; you, the purchaser, make the decision.) Apple is currently trading at $47 a share and you think it is going to go to $60 within nine months. You decide to buy seven contracts at $4 a share (seven hundred shares times $4 a share equals $2,800). For a fee of $2,800, plus any commission charge, you are now betting on what will happen to Apple stock, or at least seven hundred shares of it. Imagine that you are lucky and Apple stock starts to increase in value the very day after you bought the options—which still have nine months of life to them. If Apple were to climb, say, $8 over the next couple of weeks or months, the value of your options would increase from $4 to $12, probably due in large part to the momentum that appeared to be created.

You can sell your options at any time before they expire. When you sell part or all of your contracts to someone else, they then have the right either to buy shares of a specific stock (a call option) or to make someone buy a specific number of shares of stock (a put option). When you sell out your options, you are out of the picture (or investment), for better or worse. Like stocks, options can go up and down unexpectedly.

Advantages

The biggest advantage of options is that you can "control" a modest or large number of stocks with a relatively small amount of cash. Notice that in the IBM example I talked about buying a contract for only $2 a share, even though IBM was trading at $70 a share. That's quite a bit of leverage: for every $2 put up, you control $70 (one share) worth of IBM stock.

It is this leverage or control that makes options so exciting, or so depressing. In the IBM example, if IBM moves by $4 a share, that represents only about a 5-percent move in value for someone who owns the stock outright ($4/$70). Yet a $4 move for someone with a $2 option can represent a 200-percent (or more) gain.

The other advantage with options is that they can be used to increase one's current income. This strategy I am about to cover is the only way to deal conservatively in options. If followed, this strategy would make the scorecard (the total number of check marks) at the beginning of the chapter much more appealing.

Let us now suppose that you own a thousand shares of the XYZ Utility company, a stock that normally fluctuates between $16 and $19 a share during the year. The stock currently trades at $18 a share. You like the stock, particularly the quarterly dividend it pays. In fact, you would rather not sell the stock. Nevertheless, you would like more income, so you decide to sell a call option on all one thousand shares—ten contracts, in other words. Your broker tells you that August contracts, with a striking price of $20, are selling for 50¢ each. This means that you can pick up an extra $500 (50¢ times 1,000 shares equals $500) by allowing someone to call away (let them buy it from you) your XYZ stock for $20. You think this is a good bet because the stock is only trading at $18 a share and has traditionally not gone above $19 a share. You decide to sell the ten contracts.

By selling options, you get money right away. In return, you are on the hook for a certain period of time. Specifically, your liability does not end until the contract expires, August, in our example. If the option is not exercised before the market closes on the third Friday of August, you are off the hook. If the contract is exercised (the stock is called away from you), you must sell it for the agreed-upon price, $20, even if it is then selling for $22, $23, $25, or $30 a share.

Disadvantages

When you buy an option, time is always working against you. The less time you buy (that is, the less time remaining until the contract expires), the less likelihood there is that the desired event will occur. Moreover, when you buy an option, you are hoping that the price of the stock will go up a lot (if you are buying calls) or that the price will plummet (if you are buying puts).

Thus, the disadvantage to buying options is simple: You could lose part or all of your investment. You are free to sell your options at any time before they expire at the then-current market price, but this price may be similar, higher, or lower than what you paid. This is the risk you take or the reward you gain.

When you sell an option, you are hoping that the stock will not move very much, that the option will not be exercised. If it is, you are going to have to sell stock you probably don't want to sell, or worse, buy shares of a stock at a price higher than what it is trading for on an exchange.

The person who sells the option gets to keep and spend the money as soon as the purchase takes place. The option seller does not have to wait and see whether the contract expires worthless or is exercised.

How to Buy and Sell

Options are bought and sold just like stocks, through a brokerage firm. You can choose pretty much any firm you like. Normally it takes less than two minutes to buy these contracts and not much longer to sell them. The options marketplace is very active, and there are always lots of buyers and sellers.

Tracking Performance

Options are quoted every day in the newspaper. Since the value of an option can fluctuate wildly during the day, however, you may wish to be in regular contact with your brokerage firm. It is not uncommon to see an option appreciate 50 percent one day and drop over 50 percent the next. It is also not uncommon for an option to move very little in price, up or down, on any given day. Price movements depend upon how the underlying stock is performing, or the overall stock market, if you are dealing with market index options.

Historical Performance

The track record of people who deal in options has been terrible. It is usually only a matter of time before the investor loses all of his or her option money.

Sometimes the investor gets lucky and makes a big killing on the first couple of trades. At this point the person begins to think she knows what the market (or stock) is going to do next; she has a "gut reaction" or "vision." Then it's only a matter of time before the almost-inevitable occurs—a total loss.

The only kind of investor who has consistently made money in options is the person who sells call options on stocks already owned. This is the person I referred to earlier, the one who was just trying to increase his current income. Unfortunately, the track record even for this kind of option seller (when you sell options on stocks you already own you are called a "covered call writer") is not very impressive. This is because whatever extra income is made from selling options is usually offset by eventually having to sell someone else stock that has appreciated and that may continue to go up in price. Picking up a couple of bucks per share is nice, but it doesn't mean much if the price of the stock rises several dollars a share and you only get to see a little of that appreciation because you had to sell it to someone else along the way.

Tax Considerations

There are no tax benefits to buying and selling options. The person who sells the options must report any income received for the year. The person who buys the option must report any profits or losses from the transaction. If the option buyer pays $2.25 for an option and later sells it for $1, there is a $1.25 capital loss, multiplied by the number of shares involved.

Portfolio Fit

Do not deal in any kind of option play or "investment," except perhaps as a covered call writer (selling options on stocks you already own). And even this strategy is questionable for any extended period of time.

The chance of making a lot of money in a short period of time is always appealing, but do not get caught up in "lotto fever"—you'll catch pneumonia and die. Almost everyone who gets hooked on options thinks he has the special touch or that the market is different this time. If some of the smartest, and richest, people in the country have fallen flat on their face with this investment, which is really more like gambling, don't for a minute think that you are better or different. Stay away!

Risks

When you buy an option, there is a good chance you will lose some or all of your money. When you sell an option on your own stock, the worst thing that can happen is that your stock will be called away, that you will have to sell it for a profit or a small loss. However, if you sell options on a stock you do not own, what is known as a "naked writer," the losses can be downright nasty. Look at IBM stock in 1991-1992 as an example. When IBM was at $120, if you sold a hundred put contracts (ten thousand shares) at a striking price of $115, meaning that you never thought IBM would drop below $115 a share, you would have been in deep trouble by the end of October, 1992. At that date, assuming the contract was still alive, IBM was trading at $68 a share. With a striking price of $115 and a then-current price of $68—a difference of $47 a share—the loss would be a staggering $470,000 (10,000 shares times $47 a share). Think about it: When you sold the puts, your potential profit was fixed at $20,000, assuming you sold each option for $2, yet your potential loss was virtually unlimited ($470,000 in this real-life example).

Unique Features

What is unique about options is that they have a limited life and are, in most cases, extremely volatile. Unlike stocks, which never expire, or bonds, for which the date of maturity really doesn't matter, options have a short life. They are naturally volatile (unless you sell covered call options) because of the leveraging factor described above.

Comments

Options are included in this book because it is a favored trading tool for some brokers. Year in and year out I hear numerous stories of investors who get into these things not really knowing how bad things can (and usually do) get.

The brokerage community is attracted to options because they can generate tremendous trading commissions over time. Obviously, any kind of commission is going to cut into your potential profit. The commissions on a per-trade basis are fair and reasonable, but when you are trading in and out of these things on a daily, weekly, or monthly basis, the costs really pile up. It would be nice to say that these fat commissions are your biggest concern, but they are not. It is a fact that time is always working against you (unless you sell covered calls) and that sooner or later you will hit a bad streak and suffer tremendous loses in your options trading account.

Additional Information

The most popular exchange for options is the American Stock Exchange (AMEX). The AMEX publishes a number of informative brochures on options, including the buying or selling of puts and calls. For more information, write to the following address:

AMEX
86 Trinity Place, New York, NY 10006. 212-306-1000.

Chicago Board Options Exchange, Inc.
400 South LaSalle Street, Chicago, IL 60605. 312-786-7442.

The Options Clearing Corporation
440 S. Lasalle Street, 9th Floor, Chicago, IL 60605. 800-938-8665.

33
Commodities

Stability of principal	
Stability of income	✔✔
Protection against inflation	✔✔
Total return	✔
Tax benefits	

Definition

A commodity is anything that comes from the ground, grows on the ground, or feeds on the ground. Examples of commodities include all metals (gold, silver, copper, etc.), all grains, fruits, and vegetables (wheat, corn, oranges, coffee, soy beans, etc.), and all livestock (pigs, chickens, cows, etc.).

Commodities are actively traded on certain boards, such as the Chicago Board of Trade. What makes commodities so exciting is the use of *futures contracts*. A futures contract gives the owner the right to buy or sell a certain amount of a certain commodity, such as a hundred thousand pounds of sugar, at a specific price, such as 11¢ a pound, at a specific date—the day the contract expires. It is called a *futures* contract because you are entering into a contract today for an event that will take place in the future.

How It Works

Most people who deal in futures contracts do so because they believe that a certain commodity will go up or down in price by some date in the future. Through the use of "leverage," putting up a comparatively small amount in order to control a large amount of the commodity, profits or losses can be quite high. Let us go through an example to see how this works.

Suppose you believe that gold, currently at $340 an ounce, was due for a rally. You feel almost certain that between now and the end of the year it will get up to at least $400 an ounce. You have $20,000 to invest in gold, which will get you just under fifty-nine ounces ($20,000 divided by $340 an ounce). If gold does go up to $400 an ounce, your gross profit would be $3,540 ($60 an ounce profit multiplied by fifty-nine ounces). This doesn't seem like enough to you, so you phone your broker to see whether there is a way to make more money. The broker tells you that there is: there is something called gold futures contracts, and you can make a killing.

You are told that by putting up $20,000 you can control $400,000 worth of gold, 1,176 ounces. This means that if gold does go up by $60 an ounce, your profit will be $70,560. Not bad when you consider that you only invested $20,000, and all of this profit was made in just a few months. This sounds so good, you decide to buy some gold contracts.

Unfortunately, instead of going up, gold ends up going down. You have the ability to sell your gold contracts at any time, but you decide that the losses you have been incurring will soon stop and that gold will start to go up in price. It does not. As the price of gold drops further, you start receiving calls from the brokerage firm, asking you for more money to "cover your position"—meaning your original collateral of $20,000 is now virtually worthless, and so the brokerage firm needs more cash or securities to protect itself. You have to send in more money because that is what you agreed to when you signed a bunch of papers you did not quite fully read or understand.

The tragedy of this story can go on and on, but as you can begin to see, what began as an exciting idea quickly turned into a nightmare. Little did you realize, when you went into this investment, that you might have to feed it continually until the day of doom, or sell somewhere along the way, thereby limiting your losses.

On the delivery date, when the contract expires, you are expected to pay for the 1,176 ounces of gold you had previously put a "deposit" on. If gold is selling for, say, $300 an ounce, and you contracted to buy it at $340 an ounce (hoping that it would climb to some figure above $340 an ounce), you will be out of pocket a total of ($40-an-ounce loss times 1,176 ounces) $47,040 (this assumes that you hold onto the contracts to the end). The good news is that you have already paid $20,000, plus any "margin calls" along the way—meaning requests for additional money to increase the collateral. The bad news is that you are still going to be out an additional $27,040. If you do not have this extra money, no problem. Your brokerage firm will either sue you or liquidate the necessary amount of securities in your account, which you pledged as collateral when you first went into this investment.

Advantages

The advantage of futures contracts is that you can make a lot of money in a short period of time. It is not uncommon for someone to make 50-, 100-, 400-, or even a 1,000-percent return on his or her investment within a few weeks or months. This means you can legally gamble right from your own home by using your phone and setting up an account at a brokerage firm. You don't need to travel to Las Vegas or Atlantic City.

Out of fairness to futures contracts, the other advantage they offer is that you can limit your losses, usually within a narrow range. Thus, if you see your, say, $10,000 investment drop by several hundred dollars, you can sell your futures contract(s) at that same moment. Similarly, you can set a goal that if your investment rises by, say, 20 or 40 percent, you will also sell out. You never have to wait until the due date (referred to as the "delivery date") of the contract.

Disadvantages

Futures contracts, along with certain kinds of option trading, are about the only way an investor can lose more than his investment (by getting what is known as a "margin call").

How to Buy and Sell

You buy and sell futures contracts through your broker. He or she will ask you what commodity you want to trade in (gold, silver, wheat, cattle, etc.); what period of time you are looking for (do you want a contract that is less expensive because it is expiring in a few days or weeks, or one that is more costly but gives you several months of breathing room?); how many contracts you want to buy or sell (e.g., one contract of silver is a thousand ounces); and what price you are looking for. (If silver is trading at $3.80 an ounce, the futures market might charge you the equivalent of $4 an ounce because the marketplace feels that the price will go up between now and the expiration date.)

Before you can buy or sell futures contracts, the brokerage firm you deal with will want to make sure they have certain forms signed by you on file. These forms show that you understand all of the risks involved, that you can lose more than your initial investment, that securities or cash in your account may have to be raised on short notice in order to meet a possible margin call, etc. Finally, and most importantly, the firm you deal with will make sure they have enough of your cash or collateral (securities) to hold onto in case the unthinkable happens (you lose more than your entire investment).

Tracking Performance

Since futures contracts can react violently during any given five- or ten-minute period (or values may shift very little for several days or weeks), the day's closing values in the nightly newspaper may not satisfy your needs. You may wish to phone your broker several times a day, if necessary, to see how much money you have lost or gained.

Historical Performance

The historical prices of commodities has generally been up. The price of gold today is higher than it was thirty years ago. A barrel of oil costs more than it did twenty-five years ago, timber is more expensive now than it was five years ago, etc. Unfortunately, such long upward trends have nothing to do with how you will fare, since futures contracts last only about a year or less. (You decide the time period, within certain parameters). As we have already seen, something that is in great demand and has a finite supply, such as oil, can go up and down quite a bit in price over a several-day period of time.

What is more to the point is what happens to people who trade in futures contracts over any extended period of time. The news here is pretty grim. I have yet to meet anyone, whatever may be claimed in newsletters or in the occasional newspaper article, who has made money in commodities over any extended period of time. Yes, I know what you're thinking. You are thinking that things will be different for you. That you are only going to make a couple of trades, double or triple your money, and then get out. Believe me, if this were as easy as it sounds, everyone would be doing it.

The reality is that it takes several thousand dollars to trade in futures contracts and much more than that as collateral to back your trades. Furthermore, there is only a fifty-fifty chance that the commodity you are dealing in will go up. What happens if you lose a few thousand dollars on the first trade? Will you double up on the next trade? What happens if you lose on this trade? Will you quit (and regain your sanity), or will you continue to gamble (you can hardly call this investing)?

Tax Considerations

Trading in futures contracts results in capital gains or losses. These events result in taxable events at the end of each year. There is no way to shelter or avoid taxes when trading in commodities contracts.

The only good thing you can say about any trading losses is that you can use them to offset gains elsewhere in your portfolio or to reduce your earned income, or carry them forward to next year. The good thing about losses is that you never lose them, at least not until death. If you can't use them now, you can keep moving them forward to future years.

Portfolio Fit

A few respected studies show that *managed* futures contracts ("managed" meaning that you invest in a professionally managed pool of contracts that provides you with diversification and somewhat less risk) can actually reduce a stock-and-bond portfolio's risk. The studies point out that this can happen because commodity prices often move in a direction contrary to security prices.

Conceptually I believe these studies, but the track record of professionally managed pools of commodities (vaguely similar to mutual funds) is less than appealing, simply because the costs associated with these managed accounts are extremely high. Once everyone gets paid, there is often little left over for you. True, some accounts have fared well over certain periods of time, but the chances of your being able to get into them (most of them have $50,000 to $500,000 investment requirements) at the right time (their long-term record may be good, but you may not have enough cash in reserve to ride out the bad times) is highly unlikely.

If you like this kind of gambling, you would be much better off investing in an aggressive-growth stock, something you can buy at $4 a share and hope that it goes up to $20 a share. Such an alternative is almost as ridiculous and foolish, but at least you have a small chance of making a profit. In the case of futures contracts, whether you invest on your own, with the help of a broker, or as part of a pooled account, the deck is stacked against you.

Risks

When you deal in futures contracts there is a strong possibility that you will lose more than 100 percent of your initial investment. The commodity you are betting on may indeed go up or down in price, just as you thought, but this may happen the day, week, month, or year after you have sold your contract(s). When it comes to futures contracts, you must choose the right commodity and the right time. Without both of these in your favor, you will lose money.

If you could call ignorance a risk, then this would be a second risk associated with futures contracts. The ramifications (loss potential) of this kind of investing are not fully understood or appreciated by the casual or novice trader. Investors have a tendency to imagine how much money they *could* make. Few sit down, take out a pencil, and start calculating how much they could *lose* if the price of the commodity started to move against them.

Unique Features

Few investments allow you the ability to leverage yourself so much as to make or lose a great deal of money in a short period of time. This is the only way most investors can deal in wheat, orange juice, cattle, and hogs besides at the grocery store or at the breakfast table. Such investing (and it really should be called gambling) has a certain "ruralness" about it. Instead of being on a farm planting seeds or slopping hogs, you are on the phone trading this stuff. Kind of makes you feel like a farmer.

Comments

Stay away from this investment. I don't care how convincing an article or broker might be, this game is strictly for losers and fools. There is no trading technique, strategy, or secret that can help you trade successfully in futures contracts. Do you think for a moment that someone would teach you such "secrets," even for a million dollars? Why would someone part with information that would truly be worth tens of millions, or even billions, of dollars? They wouldn't, of course. The people who trade in greed make all of their money by selling you books, tapes, or courses. Believe me, no matter what they claim, they aren't stupid enough to actually follow their own advice.

Additional Information
You can learn more about futures contracts and commodities by contacting a brokerage firm or The Chicago Board of Trade. But to get the real lowdown on this investment you are probably better off going to a Gamblers Anonymous meeting.

National Futures Association
200 West Madison Street, Suite 1600, Chicago, IL 60606. 312-781-1300.

Osters Communications, Inc.
219 Parkade, Cedar Falls, IA 50613. 319-277-6341.

34
Second Mortgage Loans

Stability of principal	✔
Stability of income	✔✔
Protection against inflation	✔✔
Total return	✔✔
Tax benefits	

Definition

A second mortgage loan, referred to as a "second trust deed" in the West, is a *junior* obligation collateralized by a piece of real estate. In return for lending someone money, the property owner promises to pay the lender a set rate of return for a specified period of time. In the case of an *interest-only* loan, the borrower is paid back his or her principal upon maturity of the loan. If the loan is *amortized*, the borrower receives interest and a portion of principal back with each payment. Normally, payments are made monthly. The term of the loan may be for as little as a few months or as many as forty years. The terms and particulars of the second mortgage loan are fully spelled out at the time of the loan.

How It Works

Suppose you sell your home for $200,000. The buyer has $20,000 for a down payment but cannot qualify for a $180,000 loan. You may decide to "take back a second" for $30,000. The bank or savings and loan association is now willing to make a $150,000 loan for something that is worth $200,000. They make the loan to the buyer, securing a first mortgage. If the borrower does not make payments, the lender can force the sale of the home and recover the balance of the loan, plus any costs and expenses incurred. If any money is left over, the owner of the second mortgage loan, you in this example, can collect part or all of the remaining balance on the junior loan.

Second mortgage loans (second trust deeds) are called "junior" loans or "liens" because they stand in line behind the first mortgage. If the holder of the first does not collect 100 percent of what is due, the second will not get anything. In no case is the owner of a second mortgage loan entitled to more than the outstanding loan plus any costs, fees, or penalties that were agreed to at the time the mortgage was created. Any such excesses belong to the property owner.

The owner of the second mortgage loan has the right to bring a cause of action against the property owner according to the terms of the loan agreement. You do not have to wait until the first mortgage loan owner brings suit.

Second mortgage loans are accepted as a way of selling a home. By your willingness to "take back paper," your house becomes more appealing to a wider range of prospective buyers. The owner may want an all-cash deal, but this kind of sale can only be accomplished if the buyer can make a significant down payment and qualify for a loan without help ("help" meaning need to obtain a secondary loan).

There are other ways of owning second mortgage loans. You may have a friend, relative, or acquaintance who needs money to buy a piece of property. The person may not have enough funds to buy the property outright or obtain a conventional first mortgage. The person turns to you and offers you a deal: "Loan me X dollars for a period of Y and I will pay you Z rate of interest on your money." The property could be residential, commercial, or industrial. It could be raw land or contain several units. The decision to loan this person money is yours. Your decision will depend upon how much you trust this person, the value of the land, and whether you would someday consider owning the property. (In the case of default, the first and/or second mortgage loan holder may end up being the new owner in lieu of getting part or all of the money due.)

Another way of owning second mortgage loans is by going to a company that specializes in these instruments. There are dozens of mortgage companies in major cities. Virtually all of them would like to borrow your money in exchange for giving you a set rate of return. Mortgage companies make their profit by charging the borrower an interest rate of $X + Y$, plus fees and points, and paying you X rate. Investors' money should be secured by one or more mortgages.

Finally, there are limited partnerships that specialize in mortgages. These entities package a number of mortgages; investors, known as "limited partners," give their money to the partnership and, in return, receive monthly or quarterly income. The partnership scrutinizes the mortgages before purchase and administers and oversees operations, collections, and payments. Investors in limited partnerships must normally wait until the partnership ends before they can get out of the investment. This does not mean that limited partnerships are bad; it just means that the great majority of them lack marketability.

Advantages

Second mortgage loans have two advantages. First, the rate of return is normally much higher than what you can get from most other investments. If T-bills are paying 5 percent and junk bonds are paying 11 percent, a second mortgage loan may be offering 12 to 15 percent. The real rate of return may be even higher; if you originate the loan, you may end up charging the borrower *points*. One point represents 1 percent of the purchase price. Points are costs associated with the loan and are paid upfront. An example as to how this works may be helpful.

Let us suppose that someone wants to borrow money from you to buy an apartment building, duplex, or home. They want to borrow $20,000 and promise to pay you 12 percent annually ($2,400 a year in interest). The length of the interest-only loan is to be five years. At the end of five years you will receive back your entire $20,000 in one payment. You accept all of the conditions of the loan, but counter by adding, "And I want three points up front." Since each point represents 1 percent of the loan, this translates into an upfront fee of $600 ($20,000 x 3 percent). Your *real* rate of return is greater than 12 percent a year because, in essence, you are only lending $19,400 ($20,000 - $600 in points). If you take $2,400 (the 12-percent interest rate) and divide it by $19,400, the actual yield is 12.37 percent.

The second advantage of owning a second mortgage loan is that you may be able to call the shots. If you are lending someone money directly, the agreement can contain penalty provisions and language as to how disputes will be resolved, whether the loan is to be amortized or interest-only, and whether the mortgage is assignable (allowing you and/or the borrower to sell or transfer it to someone else).

If you invest through a mortgage company, then the second possible advantage is that you may end up with a more secure investment backed by a pool of mortgages. The company will also handle all of the management and administrative chores associated with money lending.

If you invest through a limited partnership, you may end up with the same advantages as going through a mortgage company, plus possibly a *participation provision*. A "participation" clause means that the partnership is entitled to a certain percentage of the profits if and when the borrower sells or refinances the property. Such a sharing arrangement may be beneficial to both the borrower and the partnership. The borrower may be able to negotiate better terms by giving up "some of the action." The lenders, you and the other limited partners, have a chance of owning something that pays interest and has some appreciation potential. This can act as a hedge against inflation—assuming the property goes up in value and a sale or refinance occurs while the partnership still owns the paper.

Disadvantages

Second mortgage loans (second trust deeds) have two big disadvantages: default and marketability. Tens of thousands of investors have lost part, usually all, of their investment because of borrower default. The money you lend is only as good as the property backing it. True, the value of the property may be $1,000,000 and the outstanding loans may total $700,000, leaving you a $300,000 cushion. You may ask how such a situation could be dangerous. The answer is, "easy." First, the appraisal may have been unrealistic (exaggerated). At the time you made the loan, the property may only have been worth $600,000. Two, the appraisal may have been legitimate, but real estate can drop just as fast as your once-favorite stock. A $1,000,000 property last year could be worth $500,000 in less than a few years.

If the value of your collateral drops, the borrower may have little incentive to continue making payments to you, the mortgage company, or the limited partnership. What is more likely is that the borrower simply does not have the money or the tenants in the building are refusing to pay or have vacated the premises.

Unfortunately, the losses in second mortgage loans are not usually minor. Unlike a bond, which may "only" drop by 10 to 20 percent in value, when a loss occurs in the second mortgage loan market, it often spells disaster. The lender is left with a worthless note or a piece of real estate that is not even worth the value of the *first* mortgage.

The other problems with second mortgage loans are marketability and liquidity. Unlike stocks, bonds, and a few limited partnerships, there is no secondary marketplace to sell your second mortgage loan if you are in need of ready cash. You may be able to sell your second mortgage loan to someone you know, but the chances of this are not very great. When was the last time a friend or relative offered to buy your shares of IBM stock or General Motors bonds directly from you so that a brokerage commission or fee could be avoided? And IBM and GM are well-known companies. What are the odds that someone will offer to buy a second mortgage loan secured by a strange piece of property by someone unknown? This then raises the issue of resale value. If you are somehow able to find a buyer for your second mortgage loan, how much will you have to discount it in order to unload it? After all, anyone thinking about buying a seasoned second mortgage loan must wonder how secure it is. Phrased another way, "If this is such a good deal, why are you selling it?"

How to Buy and Sell

Second mortgage loans can be purchased by going to a mortgage company or by purchasing units of a limited partnership that specializes in these investments. You can structure your own second mortgage loan by taking back a mortgage on your home or by directly lending money to someone who is trying to acquire or refinance a piece of property.

There is no readily available source to buy your seasoned second mortgage loan. If you have lent someone money directly, you may be able to structure a deal so that the loan is paid back early. Otherwise, your only option is to advertise in a local newspaper or contact your friends or business associates.

Tracking Performance

There is no practical way to "see how you are doing." As long as the borrower is making payments on a timely basis, you may have no concern as to his or her net worth or the property's current value. If payments cease or are late for several months in a row, you may feel more secure by getting a current appraisal of the property and/or an updated financial statement from the person you lent the money to.

Historical Performance

Second mortgage loans have been around for as long as people have been borrowing money to finance the purchase of real estate. Their historical rate of return pretty much tracks that of conventional mortgages, once you add on a few percentage points. In general, as interest rates rise, so do the rates offered by new second mortgage loans; as rates fall, new second mortgage loans also fall in yield. However, since second mortgage loans are not bonds, one cannot say that when interest rates fall by, say, 2 percent, second mortgage loan rates also fall by the same amount. The only completely true statement you can make about second mortgage loans is that the lender is able to get what the market will bear.

There is no way of knowing what percentage of first, second, or third mortgage loans have defaulted. No real estate industry source has ever compiled hard statistics or currently tracks such figures. However, once you factor in what are estimated to be industry-wide losses, the return is not particularly appealing. In fact, on a risk-adjusted basis, the true returns are probably quite poor.

Tax Considerations

The interest portion of any mortgage loan payment is fully taxable. You must declare this income in the calendar year in which it is received, not paid. If you end up selling a mortgage loan for less than you paid for it, a capital loss may be declared unless it was your personal residence or vacation home. If the second mortgage loan is sold for more than its original price, a capital gain results. If the loan is amortized, any return of principal must be subtracted from the original loan amount before a capital loss or gain is computed.

You are only taxed on the interest payments received. Though payments may be due each month, if the lender defaults on one or more payments, such defaults are not declared for tax purposes until they are repaid. If there is a permanent default and the property or properties are sold or taken back by the mortgagor (that is, the lender or lenders), the capital loss is determined by subtracting the purchase price of the second mortgage loan from the sales price. As previously mentioned, such a resulting loss can be minor or quite high.

Portfolio Fit

Typically, second mortgage loans are short-term loans, lasting five years or less. They are best suited for the investor willing to take a somewhat unconventional risk; a risk that is normally classified as at least "moderate" unless the mortgage is part of a pool or within a limited partnership portfolio (the risk level may then drop to "low" or "conservative").

Since the interest from these assets is fully taxable, they are best suited for self-directed retirement plans (pension or profit-sharing plans where you are able to choose the investments) or for people in low tax brackets. This investment should never be purchased by a conservative investor unless this is the only way the person's own property can be sold.

Risks

The greatest risk of owning a second mortgage loan is the risk of default or continual delays in payment. Other than foreclosing on the borrower or taking him or her to court, you have no real redress. Due to normally limited maturity, interest-rate risk is rarely an issue with second mortgage loans.

This is one of a handful of investments that is risky for another reason: the general public perceives this type of investment as being safe, when in fact it may well be quite dangerous. Thus, one could say that "perceived safety," a false sense of security, is another risk of second mortgage loans.

Unique Features

What is special about second mortgage loans is that they are an investment that you can tailor to your own needs, provided the other party agrees. No other investment described in this book can be fully structured by the investor. The higher-than-normal rate of return is not necessarily unique, but it is out of the ordinary.

Comments

Most people would be wise to avoid second mortgage loans unless (a) the loan involves property you own and (b) there are no other reasonable alternate ways to structure a sale. To think, "Well, if I have to end up taking back the property, it won't be so bad, I'll just resell it" is short-sighted and naive.

In a bad real estate market, your eventual loss from such a set of circumstances can be quite high. And do you really want to go through the trouble of managing (or selling) a property that may be located hundreds or thousands of miles from your new residence? A "defaulted" property becomes somewhat tainted in the real estate brokerage industry, and this often results in negative word of mouth. ("Oh, just make an offer.... The owner is desperate.... The former owners have moved away and just want to put this behind them....")

In the past, second mortgage loans have created a false sense of security by their owners. Lenders feel that everything is fine and safe since real estate "can't drop *that* much"—and even if it does, there is probably recourse against the other assets of the borrower. The reality is that neither of these forms of security may exist.

Many, many mortgage companies have gone under. The people who run these firms are supposed to be "experts." If they cannot always tell a good deal, what chance do you have? More importantly, think about this investment conceptually. You are dealing with a borrower who is unable to acquire traditional financing. This person must, instead, resort to paying what are often outrageous rates of return, not to mention the substantial up-front points and fees that are usually involved. Do you really want to be in the position of lending money to someone who is desperate? And are you really prepared for the possibility that you may someday own and/or manage this piece of real estate?

A much better alternative would be to invest in a high-quality, high-yield bond fund, or even one or two individual corporate bonds that are rated B or BB. Your current yield will be almost as high, they are much easier to sell if cash is ever needed, and if there is a loss it is usually quite small. You may be surprised to learn that the losses in the junk bond market have been much less than those experienced in second mortgage loans. In fact, over the past couple of years, the losses in the *first* mortgage loan market have been four to eight times greater than those in the high-yield bond market. And, if one sticks to those types of high-yield bond funds recommended earlier in this book, the gap becomes much greater.

Additional Information

Contact your local bank or mortgage broker to learn more about how second mortgage loans work and the different ways they can be tailored to fit your needs. If you want to learn more about second mortgage loans as part of a real estate investment trust (REIT) or limited partnership, here is a sample of companies you can contact:

NAREIT
1129 20th Street NW, Suite 705, Washington, DC 20036. 202-785-8717.

Washington Real Estate Investment Trust
4936 Fairmont Avenue, Bethesda, MD 20814. 301-652-4300.

Federal Realty Investment Trust
4000 Hampton Lane, Suite 500, Bethesda, MD 20814. 301-652-3360.

Part V

◆ ◆ ◆

Specific Considerations

35
Individual Bonds, Bond Funds, or Unit Trusts?

The material presented in this chapter has largely been covered elsewhere in the book. The intention here is to allow the reader an easy basis for comparison in selecting among individual bonds, bond funds, and unit trusts.

Definition
An individual bond represents an obligation by a corporation, municipality, or agency, or by the federal government to the owner of that certificate (the investor). The owner, or investor, has lent his or her money to a specific entity and expects interest and eventually principal repayment from that public or private enterprise. A bond fund and unit trust represent a portfolio of several dozen different bonds. The investor owns a very small fraction of each bond in the portfolio but expects payment from a certain source—the unit trust organizer or mutual fund group. When you invest in a mutual fund, you own shares of that particular fund. When you buy into a unit trust, you are purchasing units, sometimes referred to as shares, of a very specific portfolio.

How It Works
As you know by now, there are three different ways to buy or own bonds: individually, in a unit trust, or as part of a mutual fund. When interest rates go up, all three forms of ownership will decrease in value. Bond funds will usually decrease a little less than unit trusts or individual issues. Conversely, when interest rates drop, all three forms of bond ownership will also be enhanced, with unit trusts and individual bonds increasing a little more in value than similar mutual funds.

The reason mutual funds do not experience quite the same drop or gain in value when there is a movement in interest rates is that a mutual fund is not a fixed portfolio. Money is being added to a mutual fund all of the time, either through existing investors' reinvesting interest payments or by new purchases from existing and brand-new investors. A unit trust is a fixed port-folio. It is never added to; if you want to own more of the same kinds of bonds, you have to go out and buy into another unit trust or look for individual bonds. In short, a unit trust cannot create more units or shares, as a mutual fund can.

If bonds are dropping in value because of a rise in rates, the new money that is entering the fund will now be buying new, higher-yielding securities. These new purchases will help beef up the yield of the portfolio ever so slightly. The slight increase in yield translates into less of a loss, since prices of existing bonds will not have to drop as much to offer other purchasers a competitive yield. The reverse is also true. When rates are falling, you do not want new money invested in a mutual fund because it will have a tendency to dilute the portfolio's yield slightly downward. This is because, if rates have fallen, any new money is invested in now lower-yielding instruments. These instruments go right into the portfolio, affecting new and old investors alike.

In the case of a unit trust, no new money is ever added. The unit trust may initially raise, say $10,000,000. Once the entire $10,000,000 has been bought by investors at $100 or $1,000 a share, there can be no new or additional purchases. The portfolio remains fixed. The only time a bond will now leave the portfolio is if the underlying corporation (the issuer) becomes financially troubled and the unit trust managers fear that it may harm their unit-trust shareholders (the investors). If a bond is sold, or called away by the issuer, then unit trust owners receive a larger-than-normal check to reflect this "return of principal."

In the case of individual bonds, the security cannot become diluted. You are the owner of the five, ten, twenty, etc. bonds. No one else owns these particular bonds.

Advantages

One cannot say that one form of ownership is better than another. The decision as to how you should participate in the bond market depends upon your circumstances and your perceptions of the future. There are specific advantages to each form of ownership.

Individual, or separate, bonds provide the investor with a known creditor, rate of return, quality, and repayment schedule. Assuming the issuing corporation or municipality does not run into financial troubles, there are really no surprises. When you buy individual bonds, you know exactly when your principal matures, and this may be important if the money is earmarked for the purchase of a car, to pay for tuition, or for the down payment on a house.

Unit trusts offer a limited amount of professional management but a tremendous amount of diversity. Instead of owning an individual bond, obliging you to rely on the future success or stability of a particular corporation, a unit trust allows you to spread your risk around. By owning a small part of several different bonds, you greatly reduce your chances of sustaining a medium or large loss brought about by a bankruptcy, reorganization, etc. Unit trusts can also be chosen to pay income on a monthly, quarterly, semiannual, or annual basis. When you buy an individual bond you have no choice—it always pays semiannually. Like individual bonds, unit trusts can be easily sold in the secondary marketplace. The price per bond or unit depends upon the general level of interest rates and the remaining maturity of the security you are trying to sell. A unit trust is a way to get professional management and modest investor benefits without having to pay much for overhead.

Bond funds offer professional management much more active than that of unit trusts. This is why the management fee of a fund is higher than the fee charged by a unit trust. In addition to active management, a fund allows you to make exchanges within the same fund family for only $5. You get no such "family of funds" when you buy a unit trust. Mutual funds also offer other advantages: systematic withdrawal plans that provide you with monthly income, and check-o-matic programs that allow your bank to send one or more mutual funds a specific dollar amount to be automatically invested each month.

Disadvantages

There are also disadvantages to each form of ownership. Individual securities are riskier, since your fortune is tied to one corporation or municipality. If a highly rated company decides to acquire another, has disappointing profits, or incurs large losses (or the revenue from a public facility is less than expected), the underlying bonds may also suffer. If you want to sell an individual bond, you will pay a fee (this "commission" is built into the price of the bond) to get rid of the bonds and probably another fee or commission to buy something else. It is also more difficult to get information on a particular security.

Mutual funds provide a certain degree of uncertainty in that your portfolio has no maturity date, except in the case of a small handful of funds. As something in the portfolio matures or is sold, it is replaced by something else. This disadvantage is more psychological than real. Second, you have no control as to what goes into the portfolio. You have to rely on management.

In the case of unit trusts you also have no control as to what is in the portfolio, but you know before you purchase shares (or units) exactly what the portfolio is composed of (the number of bonds, the range of maturities, the average coupon rate, or yield, and what percentage of the portfolio is rated AAA, AA, A, etc.). Unit trusts do not offer any exchange privileges. If you want to get out, you can easily sell your shares, but you may end up paying something to get into another investment. Finally, unlike mutual funds and individual issues, unit trusts are not tracked in the newspaper. Getting a current price requires a phone call.

How to Buy and Sell

Individual bonds and unit trusts are bought through a brokerage firm, either full-service or a discount company, or by going through your financial planner or investment advisor, who, in turn, goes through a brokerage house. Mutual funds can be purchased through the mail, at a large number of banks and savings and loan associations, by telephone if you have a broker, or by using your investment counselor.

Individual bonds, unit trusts, and mutual funds are sold exactly the same way they are purchased. There is no commission charge for shares of a mutual fund, unit trust, or individual security. However, you should be aware of certain things. In the case of mutual funds, some may have a back-end penalty or contingent-deferred sales charge. Be sure to check into this. When it comes to unit trusts, an upfront fee was paid, in a somewhat disguised form since it was built into the price per unit, but there is never a fee for a sale or redemption. Remember, a brokerage firm does not handle trades for free. The charge is not called a "commission," but the effects are the same. Before buying or selling an individual bond, whether a government obligation, municipal issue, or corporate variety, ask the broker what the "mark-up" or "mark-down" will be.

Tracking Performance

Thousands of individual bonds are quoted in the newspaper each day. If the security is being held by a brokerage firm, in what is known as "street name," the firm's statements will give you a rough figure as to the bond's value. If you have a computer, you can follow performance during the day by subscribing to an on-line (modem) service that is transmitted either by radio frequency or by telephone line. Virtually any brokerage firm can also give you a quote over the phone.

Unit trusts are not covered in newspapers. To check how you are doing, you will have to rely on a brokerage firm statement or a telephone call to the unit trust group or to the broker of record.

Almost all mutual funds are covered in the paper. The majority of funds listed will show two prices: the "ask" and the "bid," sometimes referred to as the "NAV" (net asset value). The bid price is the value of your shares if you were to sell them at this time. The asking price is how much it would cost you if you were to purchase shares. The difference between the bid and the ask price is the maximum amount of commission being charged by the mutual fund. Your actual purchase price is lower if your purchase equals or exceeds a certain dollar amount. For example, if there were a 4.5-percent spread between the bid and the ask price, that tells you that it will cost you a 4.5-percent commission to buy shares of this fund. This commission charge drops to 4 percent if $50,000 or more of the fund, or any other fund within the same fund family, is purchased within the next thirteen months. The commission drops further if the purchase is $100,000, and still further if investments total $250,000 or more.

Historical Performance

The performance of unit trusts, individual bonds, and bond funds are very similar. During bad bond markets, such as 1975-1981, all bonds suffered. The greater the maturity, the greater the suffering. The fact that a bond is part of a unit trust's or mutual fund's portfolio does not shelter it from the loss. During bond bull markets, such as 1982-1987, virtually all bonds saw tremendous appreciation.

Since the composition of a bond fund is constantly changing, the track record of this kind of ownership is somewhat different than that found with a unit trust (which is only passively managed) and an individual issue. A good bond manager, by a combination of skill and luck, can sometimes avoid large losses or post gains during periods of uncertainty. The better-performing bond funds have out-performed the best unit trusts and individual issues.

Tax Considerations

When it comes to taxes, individual bonds really outshine the competition. As the owner of the bond, you decide if and when a sale will occur prior to maturity. The only thing you cannot control is whether the bond includes a "call feature," and whether such a provision will be exercised by the issuing corporation or municipality.

Unit trusts are almost as good as individual issues, except that the sheer magnitude of the portfolio may make it difficult for the investor to determine when, and how much, of the portfolio can be "called away" by the issuer during any given year. Apart from a bond's being prematurely redeemed by a corporation or municipality, or a fund's being sold because the issuer is now financially troubled, little capital gain or loss activity takes place in a unit trust.

Bond funds, on the other hand, are often the kings of activity. The turnover rate of a bond fund (how frequently bonds are bought and sold) can be modest or seemingly excessive. A great deal of activity is not necessarily bad, providing the net result is a taxable gain. After all, paying a capital gains tax is not so bad—it means you have made a profit. In fact, a tax loss may not be so bad either. You can use it to offset gains somewhere else, or there may well be an offsetting net gain in the bond fund next year. Regardless of whether there is a gain or loss, the point is that this is something you have no control over. You roll with the punches and hope that the net result benefits your particular situation.

Portfolio Fit

For almost all investors, unit trusts and/or bond funds are the preferable form of ownership. If you buy an individual bond, you will always have to worry about the financial status of the issuing company, whether the bond is being called away, or whether some other news will affect its quality. More to the point, it is doubtful that you are going to monitor its performance or price by reading annual reports or plotting the bond's price each day.

Unit trusts and bond funds are both professionally managed. If something starts to go wrong, management steps in and prevents the problem or tries to limit any losses. In the case of the more actively managed fund, management can also seize on special buying opportunities, adding bonds at a good price and passing on the value or profits to the investors.

Risks

The risks associated with unit trusts and bond funds depend upon what kinds of securities are owned by the particular group. When unit trusts and bond funds have most or all of their assets in bonds that mature in five years or less (known as short-term portfolios), neither one has much of an interest-rate risk. Intermediate-term unit trusts and bond funds (average maturities of six to fifteen years) have a moderate amount of interest-rate risk, while the more traditional funds and trusts, with maturities averaging twenty years or more, may have greater current yields and appreciation potential, but their loss potential is greater as well, when interest rates begin to rise.

As you may recall, a bond with a maturity of fifteen to thirty years will drop approximately 4 percent in value if interest rates rise half a point. Such a drop may only be temporary (if rates then fall half a point, most, if not all, of the 4-percent drop will be erased), or it may be the beginning of an upward trend in interest rates. As an example, if the cumulative upward movement in interest rates were in the 3-percent range, a long-term corporate or government bond would drop about 25 percent in value.

This drop would only be on paper; as the bond gets closer to its maturity date, or rates begin to fall again, its value would increase. Upon maturity, all bonds are worth their face value, normally $1,000 per bond. The same thing is true with unit trusts. As the bonds in their respective portfolios mature and there remain only a few years until the portfolio is dissolved, any gains or losses due to interest rate changes will begin to fade away. Thus, bonds in the trust that were bought for $1,000 each, dropped to $800, then rose to $1,300, would still be worth exactly $1,000 when they mature.

This process is less severe, for better or worse, with bond funds. Since funds normally have an inflow of capital, which unit trusts do not, securities are being purchased and sold all of the time. Such an influx has a somewhat dampening effect on the appreciation or loss in bond values. The volatility can still be rather high, however.

In addition to any interest-rate risk (which, you now see, can be controlled or minimized depending upon the maturity of the bonds in the fund or unit trust), there is also the issue of default risk. In the case of U.S. government-backed bonds, such a risk does not exist; in the case of municipal bonds, the chances of any of the bonds within a unit trust or bond fund defaulting are extremely remote—in about the 1-in-300 range. Corporate bonds are something different. Unit trusts and mutual funds can greatly reduce default risk by sticking to corporate bonds that are highly rated (single A or higher) and by diversification.

Some bond funds and unit trusts have moderate or large positions in high-yield securities, often referred to as "junk bonds." Even these portfolios are not nearly as risky as you might suspect, if they are well managed and, more importantly, are mostly made up of bonds rated single B or higher. Bonds rated B or BB have a small default risk, something that can be quite acceptable in a diversified portfolio. For example, if a high-yield unit trust or bond fund has a current yield of 11 percent and a default rate of 1 percent each year, the net return of 10 percent is still much better than the yields offered by higher-quality issues.

Finally, some funds and unit trusts include foreign securities. As discussed in chapters 19 and 26, this raises the issue of currency risk. Such a risk can be beneficial when the U.S. dollar weakens (foreign bonds rise in value) or harmful when the dollar strengthens (foreign securities decline in value). You can normally tell whether the unit trust or fund you are considering has international issues as part of its portfolio by its name (the XYZ Global Bond Fund, the ABC Aussie Unit Trust, etc.).

Unique Features

Unit trusts are somewhat special because their management is often passive. This means that the portfolio is only semi-actively managed. Less management and staff mean lower operating costs, which should translate into higher returns for the investors, but it can also mean greater losses, at least on paper, during bond-market declines.

Bond funds, on the other hand, have very active management. The number of bonds bought and sold during a single year can be almost staggering. Through luck and skill, some bond fund managers have been very effective in reducing risk. (Thus, when it looks as if rates might begin to rise, a manager may start to sell off the long-term securities and replace them with ones whose maturities are in the five-to-eight-year range).

Comments

If you want diversification, funds or unit trusts are for you. You should have no difficulty finding one or more portfolios that fulfill your criteria—short-term, global, high-yield, tax-free, etc. If you think interest rates will remain level or drop, unit trusts can have a slight edge over their mutual-fund counterparts. If you believe rates may increase, or if you want the flexibility of moving money within a family, funds are the clear choice. There is no expense in getting out of a unit trust, but there is a built-in fee to buy into one.

All in all, there is no clear-cut winner here. Many investors are disgruntled with what appears to be a continuous eroding in certain bond funds' price per share, even when rates are stable or declining. Such erosion does not occur in a unit trust when rates are level or dropping. On the other hand, there are several points in favor of the fund approach, like being able to move money at little or no cost, check-writing privileges in certain cases, active management, the addition of new investors' monies to help stabilize values, and so on.

The emphasis of your decision should be on the *character* or content of the portfolio, not on whether it is a fund or unit trust. The way the product is packaged is not a big concern.

Additional Information

John Nuveen & Co.
333 W. Wacker Drive, Chicago, IL 60606. 800-351-4100.

Van Kampen Merritt
1 Parkview Plaza, Oakbrook Terrace, IL 60181. 800-225-2222.

36
Individual Securities or Mutual Funds?

The material presented in this chapter has largely been covered elsewhere in the book. The intention here is to allow the reader an easy basis for comparison in deciding between individual securities and mutual funds.

Definition
When you buy shares of a specific stock or bond, you own individual securities. When you own shares of a mutual fund (or unit trust), you own a very small percentage of a pool of securities (stocks and/or bonds). When you own shares of just one mutual fund, you own part of a portfolio that may be made up of fifty to a hundred or more individual securities. Both kinds of investments are securities and regulated by state as well as federal agencies.

How It Works
When you buy individual shares, you are betting on the fortunes of a specific company. If the company increases its profits or earnings, the stock often responds positively. If it becomes financially stronger, the rating of the company's bonds may also go up, driving the price of its bonds upward. Conversely, if something goes wrong, the price of the corporation's securities may drop.

When you own shares of a mutual fund, you are not betting on how one, two, or even three companies will fare. Instead, you are placing your trust in a portfolio manager who has selected dozens and dozens of companies. The stocks or bonds in the portfolio may represent a specific industry but are more likely to represent several different segments of the economy.

At the time of purchase, or later, you can request that the certificate remain at the brokerage firm (this is known as being "held in street name"), sent to you, or, in the case of mutual funds and unit trusts, held by the issuing fund or unit trust group. In most cases it is best to have the certificate held by the brokerage firm or fund (unit trust) group. This makes a subsequent sale much easier. If certificates are held by the brokerage firm or mutual fund, dividends, capital gains, or interest payments can be automatically re-invested into additional shares of the fund. In the case of individual securities and unit trusts, any income or gain generated can go directly into a money market fund.

Advantages

When you invest in individual securities, there are two kinds of risk: systematic and unsystematic. *Systematic* risk refers to risk that cannot be diversified away in the stock or bond market. It represents market risk. Phrased another way, when the stock market takes a beating, a large number of stocks drop in value, even though their profits, market share, quality of management, or research has not changed. Systematic risk represents 30 percent of the risk of investing in the stock market.

Unsystematic risk represents the risk that is unique (for better or worse) to a particular corporation. These special features include management's style, market share, name recognition, market niche, the quality of research and development, or the use of a special formula, product, or service. This kind of risk represents the other 70 percent of the "risk pie." It can be completely eliminated by diversification: owning shares of just one mutual fund or owning shares of twenty to thirty individual stocks. Thus, you can eliminate the majority of the risk associated with stocks by owning shares of just one diversified mutual fund.

What is surprising about the elimination of unsystematic risk is that it does not substantially decrease your return potential. This is one of the few examples in the world of investing where risk is not commensurate with return. In fact, some studies show that there is no decrease in return potential with a diversified portfolio compared to a one-, two-, or three-stock (or bond) portfolio.

Mutual funds offer other advantages besides that of eliminating most of the risk of investing in securities. Funds provide professional, full-time management. They also allow you the ability to switch from one portfolio to another for only a $5 fee. If you owned several different stocks or bonds, the cost of exchanging them for different issues would be several hundred dollars, even if a discount brokerage firm were used. With a mutual fund you can go from, say, a growth fund to a government securities fund simply by making a telephone call.

Mutual funds can be structured so that they pay you a monthly income, no matter what kind of funds you invest in; a securities account at a brokerage firm cannot be set up this way. According to this arrangement, known as a systematic withdrawal plan (SWP), mutual fund investors can instruct the fund to send them X dollars per month. Once the account is set up for a SWP, you never have to make the request again, but if you decide to terminate, suspend, increase, or decrease the service, it can be done at any time without cost or fee. This feature allows investors a steady and predictable stream of monthly income, no matter what the stock or bond market is doing.

Owning an individual security does have its advantages, however. First, you can concentrate your investment in one company. With some luck, the stock can go up quite a bit. Or, if the bond is not highly rated, the company's turnaround can beef up its rating, causing the bond to move up in value by several percentage points. Some investors also like studying annual reports and research papers on a specific corporation. Occasional newspaper stories can make the experience of owning an individual security even more personalized.

Disadvantages

No matter how bright the future looks for a company, things change. Management quits, dies, or is replaced. Market share changes as a result of a competitor's new product or innovative advertising campaign. Earnings reports are disappointing, causing the price of the stock to begin to slide. The fact that you have bought the stock or bond at its "fifty-two-week low" does not mean that it will not hit a new low tomorrow, next week, next month, or next year. Annual reports tend to be very optimistic. Not being able to read between the lines could give an investor a false sense of security.

One of the most difficult parts about owning a specific stock or bond is deciding when to sell it or buy more. Owning investments can often be an emotional experience. People own investments out of fear (the safety of bank CDs and money market accounts), hope (save enough to buy a house, pay for a college education, or retire), or greed (this thing is going to double in a couple of months). It is perhaps for some of these reasons that most people buy at market highs and sell at market lows. Everyone likes to buy clothes and cars on sale, but no one seems to like to buy stocks or bonds when they are "on sale."

A mutual fund manager removes most of this anxiety. A disciplined fund manager can look at the situation more objectively; he or she was not the one to recommend you go into it in the first place.

How to Buy and Sell

Individual securities can be traded in almost all of the ways you would buy or sell shares of a mutual fund and unit trust. Mutual funds offer more options since you can send a check and application directly to the fund company. Many banks and insurance agencies now provide mutual fund desks where their clients can come in for counsel or to make a trade.

If you have an account at a securities firm, you can simply telephone in a buy or a sell (for individual securities, funds, or unit trusts). Depending upon how well the broker knows you, purchases can be made even when there is no money in the account. Then you have up to five business days to pay for the transaction. "Business days" do not include the weekend or holidays, so if you placed a buy order on Tuesday, you would have until next Tuesday to settle (pay for) the trade. This is true whether you are buying stocks, bonds, or shares of a unit trust or mutual fund. You can also sell the same securities just as easily, even when you have physical possession of the certificate; just bring it in or send in the certificate within five business days.

If the five-day rule is not met, the brokerage firm may give you an extension of a few more days. If the trade is not settled by that time, meaning you have not come up with the cash or delivered the securities, the firm will be forced to "sell you out" (reverse the trade) and bill you for any losses, fees, or commissions.

When you own shares of a stock or mutual fund, you decide when to sell them. When you own an individual bond, the bond issuer (the XYZ Corporation or the ABC Municipality) may be able to call away your security—force you to sell it back to them at a prespecified price. Bonds in a unit trust and mutual fund are not immune from such an event, but in the case of a fund you do not have to do anything about it—the fund manager receives the prepayment and invests the money into something else. In the case of unit trusts, each investor is sent an additional sum, representing his or her pro-rata share in the redeemed bond. You, the investor, are free to do whatever you want with this partial return of principal.

Tracking Performance

Mutual funds and stocks are quoted daily in the newspaper. So are several thousand bonds. Municipal bonds and all unit trusts do not appear in the paper. Instead, owners must contact their broker for a current quote. Unit trust owners can also telephone the trust administrators to find out what their shares are worth on any given day.

Historical Performance

When taken as a whole, the track record of mutual funds and unit trusts has been much better than that of individual securities. At first this may strike you as an odd statement; after all, unit trusts and mutual funds are made up of stocks and bonds. But there are lots of instances of corporations going bankrupt and investors losing everything. There is not one example of a fund going out of business and shareholders losing their money.

As you can see, the price swings of owning individual securities can be much more extreme than those of owning a mutual fund. In fact, you can control your risk in a fund or unit trust, depending upon the kind of fund or trust you buy into and the management style.

Tax Considerations

Income and sale proceeds are the two tax considerations for every invest-ment. Income can come from stock dividends or interest from bonds, CDs, or money market accounts. All income is taxable in the year in which it is received or credited to your account *except* earnings that have accumulated in a qualified retirement plan; interest and/or dividends in an annuity, to the extent they are not distributed; and interest from tax-free bonds.

Net sale proceeds, defined as the selling price minus any fees or com-missions, are taxable to the extent that they exceed the original purchase price, the price you paid for the asset plus any fees or commissions. This is known as a "capital gain." All capital gains are taxed in the year in which the proceeds are received or credited to your account. If the net proceeds are *less* than the purchase price, there is a capital loss. A capital loss can be used to offset, dollar for dollar, any capital gain, not necessarily one in the same year.

When you purchase individual securities, the only potential taxable event you control is the timing of the purchase or sale of that asset. No one can "force" you to sell a stock, bond, or any other investment for a profit or loss, except when a security, such as a bond or certain kinds of preferred stocks, matures or when a bond is called away (the issuer forces you to sell the bond back to the municipality or corporation).

Paper profits are not taxable. If you buy an individual security for X and it is now worth X + Y, the profit, "Y," is a "paper profit": although it is real, the asset has not yet been sold. If an asset is sold for the same price for which it was purchased, there is neither a gain nor a loss.

Upon your death, your beneficiaries inherit your asset(s) based on their fair market value on the date of death. A subsequent sale by them will result in a taxable gain (to the beneficiary) to the extent that the net sale proceeds are greater than the value of the asset on the date of your death. If this figure is less than the fair market value at death, the "new" owner can declare a capital loss, even though the net proceeds may be much higher than the price you paid for the asset. There is no required holding period during which the beneficiary must own the investment before he or she can sell it for a profit or loss.

All of this applies equally to mutual funds and individual securities, in-cluding municipal bonds. However, in the case of mutual funds (and unit trusts), the investor must be aware that he or she cannot control or dictate when a security in the portfolio is sold. If a fund or unit trust decides to sell some of its stocks or bonds, the net result will almost certainly be a taxable gain or loss. All of the realized gains and losses for the calendar year are net-ted out. ("Realized" means the security was actually sold, unlike a "paper profit," which means you have a gain but the fund manager or unit trust still holds the appreciated asset.)

At the beginning of the next year you are sent a "Substitute 1099," which indicates a single-dollar figure representing either a capital gain or a capital loss. The form, which is sent by the mutual fund or unit trust group, will also indicate any dividends and/or taxable interest paid by the fund. These items must be reported and taxes must be paid. You cannot escape taxation simply because you have opted to have such gains, dividends, and/or interest reinvested in the fund or sent to your son or daughter.

Portfolio Fit

The individual securities best suited for most portfolios are highly rated municipal or government bonds. Otherwise you are probably better off owning different kinds of mutual funds to fulfill your desired level of diversification. A mutual fund or unit trust can watch over your portfolio full time with an objectivity most individuals do not possess. Equally important, the people running these portfolios often have a tremendous amount of experience and access to information that would not be financially practical for most individuals to acquire.

Risks

In the case of individual securities, the biggest risk is neglect or indecision—knowing when to sell or buy more. The other risk of owning individual stocks and bonds is that they are often based on a story. The broker or advisor tells the client she should buy X because the company is about to come out with a miracle cure or product. The decision then becomes somewhat emotional, with the client not understanding that there is often little relationship between the "sizzle" (the story) and the "steak" (the reality). Stocks and bonds can go down in value even if the product or breakthrough is successful.

When it comes to mutual funds, the biggest risk is chasing last year's winner. The fact that an aggressive-growth or bio-tech fund was up 68 percent last year does not mean that it cannot drop by 20 to 50 percent next year. There is virtually no relationship between a stock, bond, mutual fund, or unit trust's performance from one year to the next. In fact, there is a fifty-fifty chance that a top-performing fund will be in the bottom half next year, or the year after that.

The other risk of investing in mutual funds is not being properly diversified. Almost all investors are either too conservative (concentrating on bond funds, CDs, and money market accounts) or too aggressive (going heavily into speciality or aggressive-growth funds). The key to successful investing is to strive for very good returns by finding the middle ground.

Unique Features

When you own individual stocks, you receive annual reports from each company you "partially own." Bondholders do not receive these reports. All mutual fund owners are sent annual reports from the fund group; this report summarizes the fund's holdings as of a certain date. Annual reports are almost always optimistic about the future. It does not matter how good or bad last year was, the people writing the report think the future will be just fine.

Comments

You should now be convinced that the majority of individual securities are not for most people. If you do not buy any of the arguments made in favor of mutual funds (professional management, switching privileges, objectivity, someone to watch over your holdings, etc.), the elimination of unsystematic risk alone should convince you (doing away with 70 percent of the risk).

If you own individual securities right now and have decided they should be repositioned into mutual funds or unit trusts, discipline yourself. Decide at what price you will sell what you already own. Pick two prices: One that reflects a certain percentage gain, and one that reflects a percentage drop from the current price. When either of these points is reached, sell. Again, the only individual securities most individuals should own are investment-grade municipal bonds and government securities.

Additional Information

American Funds Service Co.
135 South State College Boulevard, Brea, CA 92621. 800-421-0180.

National Association of Securities Dealers
33 Whitehall Street, New York, NY 10004. 212-858-4000.

SoGen International Fund
50 Rockefeller Plaza, New York, NY 10020. 800-334-2143.

37
Bond Swaps

Definition

Bond swaps involve the sale of one or more bonds and the subsequent purchase of another bond or bonds. Swaps can be done with individual securities, mutual funds, and unit investment trusts. These "exchanges" are done for one or more of the following reasons: (1) to increase or decrease the quality of a bond portfolio, (2) to shorten or lengthen the maturity of one's bonds, (3) to increase or decrease the face value of the holdings, (4) to beef up or cut down current income, and/or (5) to lock in a profit or trigger a tax loss.

A bond swap is not an investment per se. It is a financial planning strategy that can help you accomplish certain goals.

How It Works

The best way to effectuate a bond swap is by contacting your broker and telling him what you are trying to accomplish (see points 1-5, above). The advisor can then get a price quote on your current bonds and begin looking at what is available to replace your existing holdings. The best way to see how a bond swap works is by illustration.

Assume that you own $50,000 worth of corporate bonds rated BAA. These bonds have a maturity date of 2020 and a coupon rate of 10 percent. You are concerned with current economic conditions and believe there will be a severe recession in the near future. You do not want to own bonds rated BAA because you feel that the underlying corporation could go bankrupt in bad times, so you contact your broker and say, "I want to get out of these bonds and buy something safer (rated higher). I do not want to end up with fewer than fifty bonds worth $50,000 (face value). See what you can do." Given these instructions, the broker does her homework and telephones you back within an hour with the following information: "I can get you face value for your bonds and we can then buy fifty bonds rated AA with a coupon rate of 8.5 percent and a maturity date of 2021. What do you think?"

Your first reaction is one of slight disappointment. Your income stream will drop from $5,000 a year to $4,250 (8.5 percent of $50,000). However, the quality of your bond portfolio has gone up by two grades (from BAA to A to AA). The odds of your losing any or all of your principal have been decreased radically. The price being paid will be the loss of $750 of annual interest; less, once you figure in the *after-tax* difference. Virtually nothing else has changed. Maturity has been extended by only one year, from 2020 to 2021. Face value is unchanged (you will still get $50,000 at maturity).

Another reason you might want to do a bond swap is that your bonds have dropped in value. Suppose you bought $100,000 worth of BBB-rated municipal bonds in 1976. These hundred bonds had a maturity date of 2005 and a coupon rate of 5 percent. It is now, say, 1993 and you notice that BBB-rated tax-free bonds with a maturity of thirteen years have a current yield of 7 percent. The bonds you bought in 1976 have a remaining maturity of thirteen years and a current market value of $84,000 (remember: when interest rates go up, the value of bonds go down). You decide to sell your bonds for a loss and simultaneously purchase similar bonds that also have a 5-percent coupon rate, are worth 84¢ on the dollar, and have a remaining maturity of thirteen years. In other words, you have bought something virtually identical to what you have just sold. You do this because your advisor tells you it is a good idea, but your first reaction is, "This guy is nuts. Nothing has changed." You are wrong.

By selling bonds for $84,000 that had originally cost you $100,000, you have a $16,000 loss. This loss can be used to offset capital gains, dollar for dollar. If you do not have enough capital gains during the year, the loss can also be used to offset ordinary income, dollar for dollar, up to $3,000 per year. (There is no $3,000 annual limit when it comes to offsetting capital gains.) Any remaining loss not used to offset capital gains or ordinary income can be carried forward to future years. The loss is carried forward until it is completely used up. You never lose your losses. There is no limit to the number of years the loss can be carried forward.

As you can see by this second example, the bond swap this time was done for tax purposes. The income stream remained the same: you bought another hundred bonds for $84,000 and these "new" one hundred bonds throw off the same $5,000 of tax-free income each year. The maturity date and quality of the portfolio was also unchanged. Uncle Sam wants to share in your gains. Let him also share in your losses!

Advantages

As you can see from these two examples, there are several advantages to a bond swap. Triggering a tax loss or beefing up the quality of one's holdings are just two of the reasons why savvy investors like bond swaps. Again, other reasons include increasing your current income, increasing the face value (your principal at maturity), and lengthening or shortening the remaining maturity of the bond portfolio. As you might have guessed, these benefits come at a cost: If you gain one thing, you lose something else. If you want to increase current income, for instance, you will probably have to decrease the quality of the holdings since lower-rated bonds pay more income. If you shorten the maturity of your portfolio, there is a good chance that the current income will go down or that the quality will decline. Occasionally, you can kill two birds with one stone. If you lengthen a bond portfolio's maturity, there is a good chance that your income stream will also go up.

Disadvantages

There is no disadvantage of a bond swap per se. What you are after (increased income, better quality, etc.) may be accomplished by giving up something that is not important to you. For example, if you are looking strictly for current income, an increased yield at the price of a lengthened maturity date is of no concern. The bondholder had no plans ever to get rid of the bonds, whether they went up in value or fell. Other times the trade or exchange may require you to make a small sacrifice, a trade-off such as more income but a drop in quality by one or two levels.

There are ways to counter these disadvantages. If you are not willing to give up some quality for more income, then perhaps you would be willing to add five or ten years to the maturity. Or maybe you want to lock in a capital gain (your bonds have gone up in value by $8,000) and decrease future interest-rate risk by accepting new bonds with a shorter maturity, and you are thus willing to accept less future upside potential. Short-term bonds do not fluctuate up or *down* as much as longer-maturing securities.

The real point to focus on here is that there are several ways to go when it comes to a swap. If the new bonds offered to you tomorrow do not fit your objectives, pass and wait for another day.

How to Buy and Sell

Bond swaps are transacted the same way you buy a stock or bond, by contacting your broker and telling him what you are trying to accomplish. The two sides of the swap do not have to occur at the same time or even during the same week, month, or year. For example, a tax loss is created as soon as you sell a bond for less than you paid for it; the same thing is true with a gain you want to preserve. After your bonds are sold, the proceeds from the sale will stay in your account—usually, but not always, earning money market rates of return. When your broker has a "good deal" for you, the sale proceeds can be used for the next purchase (the other side to the swap). Alternatively, you may decide that you no longer want to own government or corporate bonds. You may conclude that because of your now-higher tax bracket, municipal bonds make more sense than government obligations. Or that you have had enough experience with bonds and want to use the money to buy some real estate or a growth mutual fund. Any of these things can be done. They may not qualify as a "swap," but the tax consequences or other results will still be similar to a swap.

Tracking Performance

To figure out how you have done, simply calculate what you began with, the amount received upon sale, and what the proceeds were used for. The exchange may be painless, beneficial, or slightly costly. The consequences are something you decide upon before the swap takes place. There are no surprises if you are given all of the facts prior to any sale.

Historical Performance

Bond swaps have been a favored trading technique for dozens of years. This kind of activity frequently occurs at year's end as taxpayers try to control their taxes as much as possible. Swaps are also commonly seen when the economy moves from one phase to another. As things get better, people are willing to invest in lower-rated bonds that get a higher yield. When economic conditions worsen, investors like to flee to safety, giving up some current income or extending current maturities.

Tax Considerations

There is a definite tax consequence whenever a swap occurs. After all, you are selling something. The chances that the sale proceeds will exactly equal the purchase price are not very high. Therefore there is almost always at least a minimal capital gain or loss. Sometimes these profits or capital losses can be substantial, depending upon the value of one's bond portfolio and how many of the bonds are actually sold. Remember, a gain or loss is recognized even if new bonds or other investments are not purchased after the sale.

There are two ways to avoid a taxable event. First, make an exchange within a variable annuity's "family of funds." Unlike a switch within a mutual fund, variable annuity exchanges remain tax-deferred. The only other way to ensure that a gain or loss is not recorded is to do the swap or sale within a qualified retirement plan. Gains or losses in an IRA, Keogh, pension plan, 403(b) plan, etc., are not recognized while money remains in the account.

Portfolio Fit

There is no question that a bond swap is the perfect "fit" or means to accomplish certain desired goals. If you want to do something else, you have to get the money from some other source to do it. Moreover, you call the shots whenever a sale or swap takes place. You decide how much is to be sold, what is to be bought with the proceeds, and when the event is to take place.

Risks

There is no risk to a bond swap if both sides of the transaction, the sale and subsequent purchase of new securities, take place simultaneously. This is something your stockbroker can coordinate with little involvement on your part. If, instead, you order the sale and then wait to do the other half of the swap, the delay may either benefit or hurt you. A delay can be helpful if the price of bonds goes down after your sale and before the next purchase. The delay can be a little costly if bond prices move up, instead. In this case, you could always delay the purchase further, hoping that bond prices will drop back down.

Unique Features

What is special about a bond swap is that the IRS will share part of any loss with you. Most people think that the government only takes, but this is not always true. If your bonds have lost value, Uncle Sam will give you a tax break.

The other unique feature of a swap is the number of options or objectives that can be accomplished—more income, better quality, consolidation, etc. It is nice to know that just because you bought a five-, ten- or thirty-year bond does not mean you are stuck with it until it matures or you die. Losses, profits, and income streams can be cut or structured so that they may even increase.

Comments

Not many people know about bond swaps. This is a strategy you should explore with your broker, even if you never plan on owning a bond. Many of the same concepts and benefits work if you own stocks, mutual funds, unit trusts, real estate, or silver bars.

When people first learn about bond swaps, they are reluctant to go through with the idea if there is to be a loss. They reason that the $20,000 bond portfolio now worth $17,000 has not really suffered a $3,000 loss as long as the bonds are still owned. There is only a loss if a sale takes place. This line of reasoning is completely wrong. Your net worth is based on the value of all of your holdings (minus liabilities) at any given point in time. If your home dropped in value from $300,000 to $240,000, you would not be fooling anyone, much less yourself, by saying it was still worth $300,000. Likewise, when a stock goes from $10 to $13 a share, I doubt many people think of this as a "non-event." On the contrary, they are very happy to see how much money they have made—even though the gain is still on paper. Losses must be viewed in the same light. Whether on paper or realized, a loss is a loss.

The fact that your stock, real estate, gold, or bond portfolio has suffered a loss does not mean that *all* is lost. In such a case the loss should, quite possibly, be realized and the proceeds put into an alternative investment, perhaps one that will appreciate faster than your existing bonds, or whatever you are selling. Many investors mistakenly believe that when something drops in value, it will magically go up in value just as quickly. The same people look at this loss in isolation, believing that a bond that drops from $1,000 to $800 will have a better chance of going from $800 back to $1,000 than a different bond, stock, or mutual fund has of appreciating $200 in value.

Additional Information

There is no book or pamphlet that details all aspects of a bond swap. A book about income taxes can detail how a loss or gain is created and when and how it can be used to offset a gain or loss. If you still need help in this area, you may be better off talking to your accountant. If you want to gain more knowledge about income taxes and some general strategies, consider one of the following sources:

Tax Facts
c/o National Underwriter Co., 505 Gest Street, Cincinnati, OH 45203. 800-543-0874.

CCH Estate Planning Guide
c/o Commerce Clearing House, Inc., Chicago, IL 60646. 312-583-8500.

Gabriele, Hueglin, and Cashman, Inc.
44 Wall Street, New York, NY 10005. 800-422-7435.

38
Global Diversification

The material presented in this chapter has largely been covered elsewhere in the book. The intention is to clarify some of the issues involved in deciding whether to diversify into global securities.

Definition
A global portfolio is one that invests in securities from several different countries, including the U.S. The securities can be stocks and/or bonds and may be issued by a specific country or by a corporation domiciled there. A foreign portfolio invests exclusively outside of the United States International funds, unit trusts, and portfolios are synonymous with "foreign." A "domestic" portfolio is made up solely of U.S. securities and assets.

How It Works
You can take a domestic (U.S.-only) portfolio and make it global very easily. Simply reposition (sell) some of your U.S. securities and buy similar foreign securities. If you owned a government securities fund, for example, you could exchange half of it for a foreign bond fund. If you have a growth fund, you could sell 30 to 50 percent of it and buy into a foreign equity fund. Alternatively, you could sell all of your individual stocks or bonds (or mutual funds and unit trusts) and use the money to buy a *global* stock and/or bond fund.

Advantages
There are only two advantages to having a global portfolio: less risk and better returns. Sometimes a pure-U.S. portfolio will have less risk than a foreign or global portfolio of similar securities, but this is the exception, not the rule. Similarly, there are years when domestic securities outperform their foreign counterparts. In fact, over the past twenty-five years, U.S. stocks have outperformed foreign stocks eight times. But, as you can see, this is more the exception than the rule.

Disadvantages

Going global has both psychological and currency disadvantages. Psychological because most investors are afraid to own foreign stocks or bonds; they feel they do not know enough about such investments and so must be taking a greater risk. The reality, however, is something different. If you own shares of a growth fund or an individual stock or bond, say IBM or GM, take out a piece of paper and pencil. Write down everything you know about that security. If you can write more than a small paragraph, congratulations, because most people (and brokers) do not have even that much information.

The "currency risk" is the other potential disadvantage. I say "potential" because the value of the currencies representing the securities of the different countries you have invested in can just as easily end up being an attribute as a detriment. When you own foreign stocks or bonds, you hope the U.S. dollar declines against the currency(s) of the issuing corporation. For example, if you own German bonds or stocks, you hope that the deutschemark appreciates against the dollar while you own these bonds. If, instead, the currency declines in value against the U.S. dollar, your profits can be eroded. If the security has also dropped in value, the actual loss would equal the drop in value plus the drop in the currency's value.

Suppose that it took two Swiss francs to equal a dollar and that your favorite Swiss stock (or bond) was selling for two francs. You would take your dollar, have the broker convert it into two francs, and buy one share of the Swiss stock. If the stock went up in value to three francs, and the exchange rate was still two to one, your Swiss francs would be converted into $1.50, representing a 50-percent gain. Change the facts slightly and see what happens. Let us suppose instead that the stock appreciated from a value of two to three francs but that the dollar was now stronger and it took three francs (formerly only two) to equal one dollar. In this second example, your 50-percent profit has been completely wiped out by a 50-percent decline in the franc's value, making the net profit zero.

How to Buy and Sell

As U.S. consumers, we buy and sell investments and other assets in U.S. dollars. Before a foreign security can be purchased, your dollars must be converted to one or more different currencies. You need not concern yourself with the mechanics of this conversion; the brokerage firm, unit trust, or mutual fund does it for you automatically.

A far more important decision is whether your global portfolio will include foreign bonds, stocks, and/or money market instruments. Ideally the global portfolio should include parts of all three of these securities for purposes of maximum risk reduction. When interest rates are falling in one country, they may be rising or stabilizing in another. When rates fall, bonds appreciate in value, but yields on money market accounts fall. Conversely, when rates are going up, bonds drop in value, but returns on money market instruments rise. When rates fall, stocks often appreciate. However, there have been extended periods when rates and stocks both dropped. Finally, when stocks are doing well in one country, they may or may not be doing well in another.

So there is often very little relation or correlation between the stock and bond markets around the world. Yet surprisingly, virtually all of the major markets around the world have experienced very good returns in their stocks *and* bonds over the past five, ten, fifteen, and twenty years.

The best way to go global is through unit trusts and mutual funds. These institutions keep close tabs on the direction of interest rates, current economic policies, and the political concerns of several nations. They have a good sense as to where money should be invested. A number of funds and unit trusts specialize in global bonds, stocks, and/or money market instruments.

Tracking Performance

One of the advantages of using a mutual fund or unit trust is that tracking performance becomes easy. You do not need to get quotes from several different stock and bond markets. You simply contact the fund or trust and ask about the price per share or unit of the particular investment you own.

Historical Performance

One of the major attractions of a global portfolio is its performance. The track record of both global stock and global bond funds has been excellent over the years. While U.S. securities are lying flat or going down, their foreign counterparts may be doing quite well. Over the past twenty-five years there have only been seven years when U.S. stocks were down. During each of these seven years, foreign stocks were either down less or showed a positive return. Similarly, there have only been a few years when long-term U.S. government or corporate bonds showed a loss on a total return basis; during these same years, bonds in other countries were posting positive returns.

Tax Considerations

One of the greatest concerns of U.S. investors is the taxation of foreign securities. Americans are afraid that they will have to pay some foreign government taxes on interest, dividends, and/or capital gains and then turn around and pay a similar amount in taxes to Uncle Sam. Fortunately, because of reciprocal tax treaties, this is rarely the case.

With the exception of Mexico and one or two other countries, the U.S. has signed reciprocal tax treaties with its trading partners. This means that whatever you pay in foreign taxes on your foreign investments will be credited to you dollar for dollar on your U.S. tax return. Thus, owning foreign securities does not mean that you are going to pay any more, or less, in U.S. taxes. The only ramification of such ownership is that some of your tax dollars are going to another government instead of Uncle Sam.

Portfolio Fit
No portfolio should be without global securities. Ultra-conservative investors may want to add only foreign short-term government bonds and money market funds to their current U.S. holdings. Conservative investors should also consider some long-term foreign bonds and perhaps a risk-conscious international stock fund. Conservative-to-moderate investors should be more equally balanced among U.S. and foreign stocks, bonds, and money market accounts.

Risks
The biggest risk of going global is including the "wrong" countries in your portfolio. The wrong choices are often those nations whose stock markets have soared over the past few months or couple of years. Returns of 75 to 225 percent look very enticing; after all, who wouldn't want to double his or her money in just a few months? This is the same type of thinking that somehow fails to realize that these same markets may decline by 20 to 80 percent during the next year. A good example of this has been Mexico.

During the early 1990s, the Mexican stock market soared. If your timing was just right, you made a killing. If it was wrong, you were almost wiped out. More to the point, the average annual return of the Mexican stock market over the past ten and fifteen years has been quite poor—something financial writers rarely write about. Newspapers and periodicals like to write exciting stories; it helps sell copy. The next time you hear about how great the Brazilian, Spanish, Taiwanese, or some other small market has been doing, see if the author shows you average annual returns for long periods of time. Chances are he won't; the article would lose much of its edge if the whole story was told.

By avoiding the "exciting" stock and bond markets, places where yields and returns are way out of line with the rest of the world, you greatly minimize the risks of global investing. A good rule of thumb is to stay clear of what are referred to as "emerging markets"—stock markets that are not very old or have only done well recently but poorly for the last ten years. These are the kinds of markets that would be described as "erratic"—places like Mexico, South America, Taiwan, and a few other countries.

Unique Features
There are very few examples in the world of investing where one gets a greater return with *less* risk. A global portfolio is one of these exceptions.

When your portfolio is spread out across several developed nations, only a small portion of your holdings will suffer if the U.S., Japanese, or some other market collapses.

A global portfolio also gives you the opportunity to be in places that appear more favorable than the United States. If a mutual fund manager sees that economic activity is picking up or interest rates are declining in one country, he or she can increase the fund's exposure to that particular market. Conversely, if it appears that a government is trying to choke off inflation or is doing something to depress business growth, security positions can be sold off and the proceeds used elsewhere. With a purely domestic portfolio, you do not have that kind of flexibility.

Comments

If one wanted to boil down the information in this book into just a handful of suggestions or rules, increasing investors' exposure to foreign securities would be one such strong suggestion. A global portfolio will increase your returns and increase the overall safety of your portfolio. And, when it gets right down to it, isn't that what we all want?

Additional Information

Institute of Certified Fund Specialists
7911 Herschel Avenue, Suite 201, LaJolla, CA 92037. 800-848-2029.

The Dearborn Investment Companion
by Gordon K. Williamson, c/o Dearborn Financial Publishing, Inc., 520 North Dearborn Street, Chicago, IL 60610. 800-621-9621.

39
Qualified Retirement Plans

Definition
A qualified retirement plan allows people with *earned* income (money received as a salary, tip, bonus, or commission) to shelter part of their earnings from current taxation. The most common plans include IRAs, Keoghs, pension plans, 401(k)s, 403(b) plans, and profit-sharing plans. The amount you can contribute, and write off, depends upon what kind of plan you have and any limitations put on it by the employer. These plans are called "qualified" because they meet IRS requirements; adherence to these guidelines is what makes the contributions (investments) tax-deductible and the growth and/or income tax-deferred.

How It Works
How a qualified retirement works depends upon the kind of plan(s) you have. The only things all such plans have in common is that:

- You must be working in order to make a contribution. You can be retired and still have a plan, but you can no longer make contributions.

- Contributions made by you, or on your behalf, are usually tax-deductible.

- Earnings and appreciation grow tax-deferred.

- No taxes are due until money is taken out of the account.

- Money can be transferred from one account (or employer) to another without triggering a tax event.

- Money taken out before a certain age, normally $59\frac{1}{2}$, is subject to an IRS penalty and/or income taxes.

- You can have multiple accounts, but the aggregate contributions must not exceed the prescribed limits described below.

- The contributions can be invested in almost anything but collectibles (U.S. minted gold and silver coins are currently the only exception), most options, and direct ownership of real estate (or anything else that is considered self-dealing); the only other limitations may be those imposed by the plan itself.

Individual Retirement Accounts (IRAs) are for anyone who is under $70\frac{1}{2}$. You can contribute up to $2,000 per calendar year (up to $2,000 per spouse if both spouses are working; $2,250 if your spouse is not working). Everyone who is currently working and under $70\frac{1}{2}$ can make such a contribution, which will grow tax-deferred; the question is whether the *contribution* is tax deductible.

Keoghs are for people who are self-employed or who work for someone who is not incorporated. There are two kinds of Keogh plans: profit-sharing and defined-contribution. Profit-sharing plans allow you to contribute and deduct anywhere from 0 to 15 percent of your net earned income (income after business expenses); the percent can be altered each year. Defined contribution plans allow contributions up to 25 percent of net earned income (the formula is complex but works out to a maximum of about 21 percent for the boss or owner); once a percentage figure is chosen (1 to 25 percent) it cannot be changed later unless the plan is terminated. Hybrid plans are also allowed (part profit-sharing for the flexibility and part defined-contribution to take advantage of the higher maximum contribution).

Pension and profit-sharing plans, also referred to as corporate plans, work the same way as the two kinds of Keogh plans just described. The percentage figure is determined by the employer; investment choices are determined by the corporation. Under some corporate plans, the employees are able to choose one or more investments from a list; other plans do not give employees any options.

TSAs, also known as 403(b) plans, are for teachers, school administrators and staff, hospital personnel, and anyone who works for a non-profit organization. As with a corporate plan, you cannot contribute to a 403(b) plan unless it has been set up by the employer. In short, you cannot force your boss to start any kind of retirement plan. People eligible for TSAs may contribute up to 25 percent (or $9,500, whichever is less) of their salary each year.

401(k) plans are a kind of corporate retirement plan. Unlike pension or profit-sharing plans, which require contributions only from the employer, 401(k) plans allow both the employee *and* the employer to make contributions. This kind of "matching plan" lessens the employer's burden.

Advantages

Qualified retirement plans offer three advantages: deductibility, deferred growth, and investment options. A deduction lowers your taxable income, which in turn lowers your income taxes. Deductible contributions lower your taxable income dollar for dollar. Once the investment is made, it grows and compounds tax-deferred. Taxation is postponed until withdrawals are made. Finally, you have a wide range of investment choices, essentially limited only by the employer (or yourself if you have an IRA), ranging from CDs to stocks and bonds.

Disadvantages

The first disadvantage of a retirement plan is that the investments may not grow at the rate you expect. A 7-percent compound growth rate compared to 12 percent over twenty to thirty years can mean that you end up with tens or hundreds of thousands of dollars less than you expected. The second disadvantage is that contributions to certain kinds of retirement plans may not be fully or even partially deductible. It all depends on the kind of plan(s) you have and your level of income (and that of your spouse). Third, the investment choices offered by your employer may not suit your particular risk level. Finally, money taken out prematurely can be subject to an IRS penalty and income taxes.

How to Buy and Sell

One of the common misconceptions about retirement plans is that they have a set rate of return. The yield or return within a qualified retirement plan depends upon *how* the money is invested. Usually, the employee (you) decides how and where the money goes.

Trading within your retirement plan is pretty much the same as it is with a regular account. Apart from the issue of taxes, the only difference is that self-dealings (direct ownership of real estate, an interest in a business you control or partially own, etc.) and most forms of collectibles (rare coins, stamps, baseball cards, gold bullion, paintings, etc.) do not qualify for these plans. In addition, your company's plan may try to simplify administrative costs and time by limiting investment choices.

In the case of retirement plans you directly control, such as IRAs, trades are often handled directly between you and your broker. There are no special procedures or forms to fill out.

Tracking Performance

You track the performance of a retirement account the same way you do any other investment. If one or more of the assets you have chosen are not publicly traded, contact your employee benefits coordinator or the investment company. One or both of these people or entities will be able to get you current prices.

Historical Performance

The track record of retirement accounts depends on the investment(s) chosen. For the most part, Americans have selected very conservative investments for their future well-being; bank CDs, fixed-rate annuities, and government securities. The track records of such investments do not change just because they are part of a retirement program.

Tax Considerations

Again, contributions to most kinds of retirement plans are fully deductible. In the case of IRA accounts, it depends on whether you or your spouse is covered by another kind of plan and how much income you make each year. For married couples, where one or both spouses are covered by another qualified plan, IRA contributions are not deductible if the couple's combined net earned income is over $50,000 ($35,000 for individuals or couples who file separate returns). The IRA contribution is fully deductible if the covered couple has income of less than $40,000 ($25,000 for singles). Finally, IRA contributions are fully deductible if the individual or couple is not covered by another plan, no matter how great their income. Following the aforementioned restrictions, deductibility is the lesser of 100 percent of net earned income or $2,000.

Profit-sharing-plan contributions, whether part of a corporate plan or Keogh, are deductible for up to 15 percent of net earned income, or $30,000, whichever is less. In the case of defined-benefit plans, the formula is the lesser of up to 25 percent of net earned income or $30,000. In the case of 401(k) plans, the limit is $8,728 (normally up to 15 percent of one's salary). TSAs (403b plans) have a cap of $9,500 annually.

You can have more than one retirement plan, but the contribution limits are not increased. It may be desirable to have more than one plan, depending upon how much one plan allows you to sock away and/or the investment choices it offers.

In the case of most plans, withdrawals made prior to age $59\frac{1}{2}$ are subject to a 10-percent IRS penalty. This penalty can be avoided if you are disabled, or in the event of your death (your heirs would avoid any penalty). Furthermore, the IRS considers any such withdrawals ordinary income, similar to getting a bonus at work, for the calendar year in which the money is received.

Portfolio Fit

This is one of those areas universally recommended for anyone who qualifies. There is nothing quite like an investment you get to deduct as if it were a business expense or the interest portion of a mortgage payment, watch as it grows tax-deferred, and then later withdraw from pretty much at your own pace.

Risks

There are only two risks to retirement accounts: early withdrawals and poor investment choices. Early withdrawals (pre $59\frac{1}{2}$) can be subject to penalties and taxes. Thus, in an emergency, the benefits of tax-deferred growth can be offset by the 10-percent IRS penalty and the resulting current income taxes. Let us go through an example to see how the benefits of deferred growth can (or appear to) be wiped out by a penalty.

Suppose there were two investors, X and Y; both had $10,000 to invest and each expected a compound annual return of 12 percent. Investor X decided to set up a qualified retirement plan and was able to invest the entire $10,000 in a profit-sharing plan. Over the next five years, the portfolio grew at 12 percent a year, tax-deferred. At the end of five years an emergency arose and he was forced to liquidate the entire account. Prior to liquidation the account was worth $17,623 ($10,000 growing 12 percent for five years). After the account was closed down, the figures look like this: $17,623 - $1,762 (the 10-percent IRS penalty) - $4,934 (assuming a 28-percent tax bracket, the taxes due on $17,623) = $10,926. In short, over a five-year period, because of the penalty and taxes, the original $10,000 had a net growth of $926.

Investor Y decided to invest her $10,000 in the same investment, but not as part of a qualified retirement plan. A 12-percent growth rate for someone in a 28-percent tax bracket nets out to a 8.64-percent return on an after-tax basis. Over a five-year period, $10,000 growing at 8.64 percent compounded equals $15,134 (after taxes). At this point, it looks as if Investor Y, the one who did not use a tax-sheltered retirement account, beat Investor X, the person who set up a qualified retirement plan, by $4,208 ($15,134 - $10,926). However, this is not the case.

Investor X was able to deduct his contributions; Y could not. A $10,000 deduction for someone in the 28-percent tax bracket equals a $2,800 federal income tax savings. By taking $2,800 (the tax savings) and investing it in something that has an after-tax return of 8.64 percent, the money grows to $4,237 at the end of five years. Since $4,237 is a greater number than $4,208 (what was thought to be the advantage of Investor Y who used after-tax dollars but did not later face a 10-percent penalty or income taxes all at once), setting up a qualified retirement plan still makes sense, assuming the money is not touched *for at least five years.* (Investor Y gains the edge if the account is disturbed within four years and/or a pre-tax rate of less than 12 percent is used.)

A much greater concern, assuming retirement money is not touched for at least a few years, is *how* the money is invested. Qualified retirement plans are not immune from bad results. The only difference is that you cannot write off losses in a retirement account. (Of course, gains are not currently taxed either.)

Unique Features

What is special about qualified retirement plans is their tax benefits. There is virtually no other investment that you can initially write off, then watch it grow without having to pay any current income taxes. To fully appreciate the benefits of tax-deferred growth (or income), imagine $10,000 compounding over a twenty-four-year period at 12 percent (assume a 33-percent state and federal tax bracket throughout the example).

At the end of twenty-four years, a $10,000 tax-deferred investment is worth $160,000; after paying taxes (canceling out the initial benefit of writing off the investment), the investment is worth $110,000. The same $10,000, growing at the same 12-percent rate but being taxed at a 33-percent state and federal income tax rate each year, is worth $80,000 at the end of twenty-four years. This $30,000 difference ($110,000 - $80,000) is due to one thing and one thing only: tax deferral. Both investments are taxed, but one is taxed each year and the other is taxed at the end.

Comments

Using qualified retirement plans whenever possible is a strongly recommended strategy for investors at all ages and at all risk levels. The greater the rate of return you assume (which presumably translates into a higher risk level), the greater the benefit of tax deferral. But you can be as conservative as you want with the invested money. Younger investors may wish to set aside less each year than an older individual or couple who has a more stable job (salary) and has already bought a house, furnishings, automobiles, etc. One of the beauties of most kinds of retirement plans is that you decide how much to invest each year (subject to ranges, except in the case of a defined contribution plan, which is fixed once it is set) and where the money is going to be invested (subject to the plan's investment options).

Additional Information

IRA and Keogh: New Opportunities for Retirement Income
Federal Reserve Bank, Philadelphia, Public Information Department, P.O. Box 66, Philadelphia, PA 19105. 215-574-6115.

Pershing
Division of Donaldson, Jufkin & Jenrette
777 South Figueroa Street, Suite 1310, Los Angeles, CA 90017.
800-421-5847.

40
How to Set up Your Accounts

Definition

Whenever you open an account at a financial institution or purchase a piece of property, including your personal residence, you are asked how you want to take title. The way in which the name appears on a deed, mortgage, checking account, or account form at a brokerage firm has legal as well as practical ramifications. Most people give little thought as to how title will be held because they think it is not important. As you will see, it is very important.

Why It Is Important

From a legal perspective, title is important in the event of death, divorce, separation, or if a minor or incompetent person is involved. From a practical perspective, there are limits or constraints as far as trading or withdrawals are concerned. In both cases it comes down to two points: taxes (income as well as estate) and ownership. A mistake could cost you hundreds or thousands of dollars; worst yet, it could cost you the value of the entire account, even if it has a value of hundreds of thousands of dollars.

The most common forms of ownership are separate, joint tenancy with rights of survivorship, community property, living trust, and custodian. Each of these forms of ownership, as well as the resulting ramifications, will be discussed.

Different Forms of Ownership

An account titled as separate, listing just one name, can only receive instructions from that person. Even though this person may be married, only he or she can make withdrawals or place buy and sell orders. A bank or brokerage firm that allows someone other than the person listed on the account title to take money out, liquidate position(s), or place any kind of order will be liable for any resulting losses. The only exception to this rule is if the account records indicate that this "separate" person gave someone else trading authority (similar to a power of attorney). Any tax liability, such as reporting dividends, interest, or capital gains, is the responsibility of the person whose social security number appears on the account form.

People title accounts with friends, lovers, spouses, children, and relatives for a variety of reasons. They may do it for convenience ("If you ever need a little money and I'm not available, here is an account you can get at"), security ("If I become incompetent, I want you to pay my bills"), affection and loyalty ("Now that we are living together/married, let's have joint accounts"), or for estate-planning purposes ("When I die, I want you to have this account . . . and I want to avoid probate"). Whatever the reason, few understand what this *really* means.

Joint tenancy with rights of survivorship, often abbreviated as "jtwros," represents an account owned by two or more people or entities. The co-owners do not have to be related or live at the same address. In the case of any form of joint ownership, such as jtwros or community property, any of the parties can liquidate part or all of the account. The financial institution is not required to get permission or give notification to the other parties. However, changes in the account, such as changing the address where statements or checks are to be sent, the inclusion or elimination of one or more of the joint owners, or changing the social security number listed on the account, requires the written approval of all parties listed. To investigate the ramifications of joint ownership, let us go through an example.

Helen Nicoll is sixty-five years old. She has a daughter whom she wants to inherit everything upon her death. Helen decides to open up a $50,000 savings account at a bank and have her $300,000 securities account at a brokerage firm retitled. In both cases, the accounts will read, "Helen Nicoll and Marcy Nicoll, jtwros." What the bank and brokerage firm almost surely failed to do was to tell Helen what could happen. They did not tell her that even though everyone at the bank knows that it is really Helen's money, her daughter could phone up tomorrow and say, "Close out the entire account, I'll be by in a few minutes to pick up a $50,000 check." (The check, by the way, could end up reading Helen Nicoll and/or Marcy Nicoll—meaning that Helen's signature would not be required to cash the check.) Nor did the brokerage firm tell Helen that Marcy could phone up tomorrow and say, "Sell all of my mom's tax-free bonds and use the proceeds to buy shares of some wild and speculative penny stock."

Besides these practical considerations, let us look at the legal consequences of this joint account. Let us suppose that a few days, weeks, months, or years later, Marcy gets sued (she is found negligent in an auto accident or is named in a lawsuit at work for discriminating against men). If she is found liable and has either no insurance or insufficient coverage, both the bank and brokerage account could be attached and sold to settle the suit.

Now remember, this is money that Helen had planned on using during her retirement, money she cannot replace. Marcy's salary is such that it would take her twenty to thirty years or more to pay back her mom.

So far we have been picking on Marcy. Let us suppose that Marcy is a model citizen but is married to someone who is not. Her husband pressures her into liquidating part of the joint accounts for a "sure-fire business opportunity," or one of Marcy's kids needs an expensive operation not fully covered by insurance; the number of possibilities grows almost exponentially when more players are added.

Community property, sometimes abbreviated as "c/p" has the same practical and legal ramifications as jtwros, but with a couple of different twists. First, "c/p" accounts are only allowed for a married couple. Second, either spouse can will his or her share of the "community" to whomever they like—the other spouse, a secret boyfriend or girlfriend, or a child from a previous marriage. With jtwros, upon the death of any party, the decedent's share of the account is evenly divided among the remaining co-tenants (usually just one person remains). This is true regardless of what the joint tenants intended or what the decedent's will or trust says.

Accounts titled under a trust allow the named trustees, usually a husband and wife or a parent, to conduct transactions, including liquidations, without the permission or knowledge of the other party(s). The trust can be worded so that both trustees must agree, or so that any transactions be in writing and signed by both parties, but this is more the exception than the rule. In the case of a living trust, the social security number of one of the trust creators (a single person or one of the spouses) is used.

Custodian accounts are most commonly used for minor children, although they can be used for the assets of incompetent adults. Under a custodial account, only the custodian has authority; there cannot be two custodians listed on the account, even if the account is for a minor child and both parents are alive and well. The person for whom the account is intended, the minor child or incompetent adult, is listed, along with his or her social security number. Common wording for such an account would be, "Pete R. Ward, custodian for the benefit of Jill Hollingsworth." Pete would remain the custodian of the account until Jill became an adult (age eighteen in most states, up to age twenty-one in some states, age twenty-five in California) or, if she were an adult, until she became legally competent.

The person for whom the account is set up ("fbo"—for the benefit of) cannot direct what is bought or sold in the account; this minor or incompetent has no control over the account. The custodian has complete control, limited only by the rule that the money, securities, etc. in the account must be used for the benefit of the child (or incompetent).

Advantages

The way in which an account is titled can have advantages when it comes to flexibility, estate planning, and income taxes. The more people you have listed on the account, the easier it is for monies to be liquidated and sent out in case of an emergency (while you are ill, on vacation, incapacitated, etc.). When one of the owners dies, accounts can also pass directly to the remaining co-owners without being subject to the delays and costs of probate. Income taxes can be saved, since accounts only require the use of one social security number. The recipient of any income, reinvested monies, or capital gains could be someone who is in a lower tax bracket than you.

Disadvantages

Some of these same advantages can also turn ugly. You wouldn't care much about estate planning and possible tax savings if a jointly owned account, mostly or fully funded by you, was being raided without your knowledge. Yet this is perfectly legal. On a similar note, an account wherein the owners are titled as "co-tenants" (compared to "joint tenants") may mean that on the death of one owner, the replacement (the decedent's heir) will not be to your liking. Or, there is always the possibility that an existing owner or "new" co-owner wants the account liquidated at a time when the market is suffering (a panic sale, perhaps). These are things you cannot really control when there are multiple owners.

Buying and Selling

Anyone listed on the account can buy or sell any or all assets in the portfolio. Multiple signatures or telephone conference calls are not required. In fact, the brokerage firm involved is under no duty to contact any of the other owners when one wants to make an addition or withdrawal. This leads us to the issue of notice.

When you open an account that lists more than one owner (the person or people who do the actual funding are not given any priority), an address is given. If it is not your address, you may want to make sure that duplicate confirmations of any trades and copies of all monthly (or quarterly) statements are also sent to you. This way, you will at least know what is going on in the account, even if it is after the fact.

Tax Considerations

When any kind of joint account is opened, only one of the owner's social security numbers is used. This means that it is the responsibility of anyone else receiving income, dividends, or sale proceeds to report his or her share to the IRS. In the case of single accounts, the name on the account must correspond to the social security number listed.

Comments

How you title an account can have far greater ramifications than the performance of the assets in the portfolio. If you are thinking about opening an account with another person, even a spouse, make sure that you fully understand the laws of your state. These are the laws that determine what will happen to the account in the event of death, a minor becoming an adult, a divorce, or the liquidation of assets.

Additional Information

Books or articles on estate planning, joint tenancy, or community property (only nine states follow c/p laws) can provide you with tips, strategies, and additional warnings. If you are thinking about setting up a living trust or are concerned about the disposition of your estate, consider the following sources:

College for Financial Planning
4695 South Monaco Street, Denver, CO 80237-3403. 800-553-5343.

Your Living Trust
by Gordon K. Williamson, published by Putnam Books, 200 Madison Avenue, New York, NY 10016. 212-951-8400.

American College
270 Bryn Mawr Avenue, Bryn Mawr, PA 19010. 215-526-1478.

41
Constructing Your Own Portfolio

Step One: What Kind of Investor Are You?

As you have seen, there are lots of good investments out there. The key is to determine which ones are best for you. No investment is good if it brings you sleepless nights. Similarly, an asset is not right for you if its rate of return or growth is not high enough to meet your goals and objectives.

If you're not sure just how much risk you feel comfortable undertaking, then this quiz is for you. It is part of a brochure called *Investment Planning Made Simple* from Oppenheimer Fund Management, Inc. (800-525-7048). The quiz is reprinted by permission of Oppenheimer Fund Management, Inc. Copyright © 1992, Oppenheimer Fund Management, Inc. All rights reserved.

Simply answer the following questions as honestly as possible, choosing the answers that most closely match your attitudes toward investing. The evaluation at the end of the quiz will help you identify what kind of investor you are.

1. An investment loses 15 percent of its value in a market correction a month after you buy it. Assuming none of the fundamentals have changed, you:
   (a) Sit tight and wait for it to journey back up.
   (b) Sell it and rid yourself of further sleepless nights if it continues to decline.
   (c) Buy more—if it looked good at the original price, it looks even better now!

2. A month after you purchase it, the value of your investment suddenly skyrockets by 40 percent. Assuming you can't find any further information, what do you do?
   (a) Sell it.
   (b) Hold it on the expectation of further gain.
   (c) Buy more—it will probably go higher.

3. Which would make you the happiest?
   (a) You win $100,000 in a Publisher's Sweepstakes contest.
   (b) You inherit $100,000 from a rich relative.
   (c) You earn $100,000 by risking $2,000 in the options market.
   (d) Any of the above—you're happy with the $100,000, no matter how it ended up in your wallet.

4. You inherit your uncle's $100,000 house, free of any mortgage. Although the house is in a fashionable neighborhood and can be expected to appreciate at a rate faster than inflation, it has deteriorated badly. It would net $1,000 monthly if rented as is, or $1,500 per month if renovated. The renovations could be financed by a mortgage on the property. You would:
   (a) Sell the house.
   (b) Rent it as is.
   (c) Make the necessary renovations, and then rent it.

5. You work for a small but thriving privately held electronics company. The company is raising money by selling stock to its employees. Management plans to take the company public, but not for four or more years. If you buy stock, you will not be allowed to sell until the shares are traded publicly. In the meantime, the stock will pay no dividends. But when the company goes public, the shares could trade for ten to twenty times what you paid. How much of an investment would you make?
   (a) None at all.
   (b) One month's salary.
   (c) Three months' salary.
   (d) Six months' salary.

6. Your long-time neighbor is an experienced petroleum geologist and is assembling a group of investors (of which he is one) to fund an exploratory oil well. The well could pay back fifty to a hundred times the investment. But if it is dry, the entire investment is worthless. Your friend estimates the chance of success at only 20 percent. What would you invest?
   (a) Nothing at all.
   (b) One month's salary.
   (c) Three months' salary.
   (d) Six months' salary.

7. You learn that several commercial building developers are seriously looking at underdeveloped land in a certain location. You are offered an option to buy a choice parcel of land. The cost is about two months' salary, and you calculate the gain to be ten months' salary. You:
   (a) Purchase the option.
   (b) Let it slide—it's not for you.

8. You are on a TV game show and can choose one of the following. Which one would you take?
   (a) $1,000 in cash.
   (b) A 50-percent chance at $4,000.
   (c) A 20-percent chance at $10,000.
   (d) A 5-percent chance at $100,000.

9. It's 1994, and inflation is returning. Hard assets such as precious metals, collectibles, and real estate are expected to keep pace with inflation. Your assets are now all in long-term bonds. What would you do?
   (a) Hold the bonds.
   (b) Sell the bonds and put half the proceeds into money funds and the other half into hard assets.
   (c) Sell the bonds and put the total proceeds into hard assets.
   (d) Sell the bonds, put the total proceeds into hard assets, and borrow additional money to buy more.

10. You've lost $500 at the blackjack table in Atlantic City. How much more are you prepared to lose to win the $500 back?
    (a) Nothing. You quit now.
    (b) $100.
    (c) $250.
    (d) $500.
    (e) More than $500.

Calculating The Results
You now have the information you need to choose the proper path(s). To determine your investor profile, total your score on the quiz using the point system below. Then follow the investor profile that most closely matches your personal needs and risk tolerance level.

Risk Tolerance Scoring
Total your score using the point system below for each answer that you gave.

QUESTION	RESPONSE				
1.	(a) 3	(b) 1	(c) 4		
2.	(a) 1	(b) 3	(c) 4		
3.	(a) 2	(b) 1	(c) 4	(d) 1	
4.	(a) 1	(b) 2	(c) 3		
5.	(a) 1	(b) 2	(c) 4	(d) 6	
6.	(a) 1	(b) 3	(c) 6	(d) 9	
7.	(a) 3	(b) 1			
8.	(a) 1	(b) 3	(c) 5	(d) 9	
9.	(a) 1	(b) 2	(c) 3	(d) 4	
10.	(a) 1	(b) 2	(c) 4	(d) 6	(e) 8

If your score is 32 and over: You're an adventuresome, assertive investor. The choices available to you promise dynamic opportunities. Remember, though, that the search for more return carries an extra measure of risk.

If your score is 19 to 31: You are an active investor who's willing to take calculated prudent risks to achieve greater financial gain. Your investment universe is more diverse.

If your score is below 19: You are an income-oriented investor who's averse to high risk. Stick with less volatile investments until you develop the confidence or desire to take on more risk.

Some Sample Portfolios

There is no single test, or even series of questionnaires, that can exactly reflect the kind of investor you are. Results will vary depending upon current events, the mood you are in when the test is taken, and the wording of the questions. Keeping this very important point in mind, let us look at some examples of what your low-risk portfolio might look like based on a range of scores from the test above.

ultra-conservative investor (a score of 10 to 15 points)

category	weighting
money market funds	15%
U.S. Treasury notes	15%
municipal/government bonds	15%
foreign bonds	15%
short-term global bond funds	10%
utility stocks	10%
convertible securities	10%
balanced funds	10%

conservative investor (a score of 16 to 19 points)

category	weighting
money market funds	10%
U.S. Treasury notes	10%
municipal/government bonds	15%
foreign bonds	15%
short-term global bond funds	10%
convertible securities	10%
utility stocks	10%
balanced funds	10%
high-yield bond funds	10%

conservative-to-somewhat-moderate investor (a score of 20 to 25 points)

category	weighting
money market funds	5%
U.S. Treasury notes	5%
municipal/government bonds	10%
foreign bonds	15%
common stocks	10%
foreign stocks	10%
convertible securities	10%
utility stocks	5%
balanced funds	20%
high-yield bond funds	10%

moderate investor (a score of 26 to 32 points)

category	weighting
foreign bonds	15%
short-term global bond funds	5%
common stocks	15%
foreign stocks	20%
convertible securities	10%
balanced funds	20%
high-yield bond funds	15%

moderate-to-slightly aggressive investor (a score of 33 to 40 points)

category	weighting
foreign bonds	15%
common stocks	25%
foreign stocks	25%
balanced funds	20%
high-yield bond funds	15%

While reviewing these portfolios, keep in mind the following points:

- When "municipal/government bonds" are recommended, you should go into municipal bonds if you are in a federal income tax bracket of 28 percent or higher.

- If your point score is less than 26, it would not be a mistake to double or triple the municipal or government bond positions and cut back on some of the other categories.

- Balanced funds are made up of both common stocks and corporate bonds. The weighting for the bond portion normally ranges from 30 to 70 percent, depending upon the fund manager's perception of interest rates, the overall economy, and the stock market.

- Return figures and yields are not given because they will change from the time this book is published and the time you finish reading it. There is also the concern that you may try to be more aggressive (not being true to yourself) to capture those extra percentage points of return.

Modern Portfolio Theory

The five portfolios just shown are based on getting you some of the best risk-adjusted returns possible. They have been constructed using three things: standard deviations, correlation coefficients, and historical returns. The concept and practice of modern portfolio theory (the idea of getting the same return with less risk or getting a higher rate of return with the same amount of risk) is a subject that could take up an entire book. The founders of MPT (modern portfolio theory) were recently awarded the Nobel Prize in Economics for their work in this area over the last thirty-five to forty years. The essentials of MPT are the three points just described. Let us briefly see what each one means.

The range of returns of an investment from its norm is called the *standard deviation*—to what degree a specific investment's returns differ from its average annual rate of return. The broader or wider this dispersion of returns (imagine a scatter graph with a line representing the average annual rate of return and a bunch of dots above and below this line), the greater its volatility. High volatility often means greater risk. Thus, all things being equal, we want the most predictable returns possible (a small dispersion of points on that scatter graph).

Correlation coefficients show how one investment relates to another. You and I know that some investments have a tendency to move up together at about the same time and at about the same degree. (If long-term government bonds appreciate by 2 percent in one month, chances are that high-quality corporate bonds will do about the same thing over the same month.) This means that these investments would be *positively correlated*. Two investments that move in a random fashion (such as U.S. stocks and Japanese stocks) have a *random correlation*. This means that when one moves up, the other may move up, but at a different time and/or amount; and in fact the other investment may not move at all, and may actually drop. A *negative correlation* coefficient means that when one investment moves up, the other investment will most likely move down in value or yield. A good example of this would be bonds and money market funds. When interest rates go up, bonds drop in value, but the yields on money market funds increase. (The price per share of a money market fund always remains a constant $1.)

Historical returns indicate how the investment has performed in the past. Although there is little relationship among the performances of a stock, bond, piece of real estate, or other asset from one year to the next, a good case can be made for some general trends over extended periods of time. The "historical returns" aspect of constructing a portfolio, using MPT or any other program, is a weak link, but we have countered that by using several different investment categories. This means that in hindsight we will discover that a few of the selected investments did as expected, some did better than expected, and some did worse than expected. The "bad" should cancel out the "good" surprises, leaving you with the most precise means available to gauge future returns for a complete portfolio.

Some Final Thoughts

Guess what? Even though you may not feel completely confident at this particular moment in time, you are ready to go. Before you actually make any moves (trades, purchases, or sales), first review the introductory pages, which talk about risk, reward, equities, and debt instruments. If you are married, sit down with your spouse and talk about your game plan. Your spouse may think of ideas that you had never considered. After you have a sense of what you are trying to do with your money (send both kids to college in seven years, retire by age sixty, buy a new car in three years, purchase a more expensive home in four years, etc.), you are ready to proceed to the next step: gathering *specific* information.

The final information you will need is track records, brochures, and/or prospectuses from the investments you are thinking about going into. As mentioned before, make sure your money is divided up among several categories; realize that last year's (or last decade's) winner may be this year's disappointment. You will only protect yourself through diversification.

Finally, act on your beliefs. Do not wait until some expected rise or decline in the stock, bond, or real estate markets occurs. This kind of thinking implies that you know something that professional traders don't. If interest rates were expected to go down over the next month, or the stock market was expected to crash, why are professionals buying stocks, bonds, and so on every day—are they stupid?

You will probably not know anything more about investing a few months from now than you do today, assuming you have followed the steps suggested in this book. Remember what I said at the outset: Your money is doing something right now. To think that your money or assets are somehow protected simply because they are in a passbook savings account or money market fund is foolish; even now they are being subjected to the effects of inflation and income taxes. Get used to the fact that *every* investment carries with it certain risks. You now know what risks are acceptable and what you can do to minimize them. I don't need to end by wishing you luck; you don't need luck if you follow this book. Instead, I wish you well.

Additional Information

An Insider's Guide to the Wall Street Journal
Wall Street Journal, 200 Liberty Street, World Financial Center, New York, NY 10281. 212-416-2000.

Money
Time and Life Building, Rockefeller Center, New York, NY 10020. 212-841-4881.

Kiplinger's Personal Finance Magazine
P.O. Box 8884, Boulder, CO 80328. 800-544-0155.

International Society of Pre-retirement Planners
2400 South Downing Avenue, Westchester, IL 60153. 312-531-9140.

Index

About the Author

Gordon K. Williamson, JD, MBA, MS, CFP, CLU, ChFC, RP, is one of the most highly trained investment counselors in the United States. Dr. Williamson, a former tax attorney, is a Certified Financial Planner and branch manager of a national brokerage firm. He has been admitted to The Registry of Financial Planning Practitioners, the highest honor one can attain as a financial planner. He holds the two highest designations in the life insurance industry: Chartered Life Underwriter and Chartered Financial Consultant. He is also a real estate broker.

Gordon Williamson is the author of several books, including: *Your Living Trust, All About Annuities, Sooner Than You Think, The Dearborn Investment Companion, Investment Strategies Under Clinton and Gore,* and *The 100 Best Mutual Funds* (which is updated annually). He has been the financial editor of various magazines and newspapers, and a stock market consultant for a television station.

If you have any questions concerning investments in this book, feel free to contact Gordon Williamson directly by telephoning 800-748-5552. Mr. Williamson is also available for seminars and workshops.